Body Politics
in Development

About the author

Wendy Harcourt is a feminist researcher and activist working at the Society for International Development in Rome as senior advisor and chief editor of the quarterly journal *Development*. Since 1988 she has built up the journal, now recognized as one of the most honest and critical quarterly publications on development. Born in Australia, she lives in Italy and is actively engaged in global feminist politics through her work with Women in Development Europe, European Feminist Forum and the Feminist Dialogues. Her work and commitment to global gender justice have taken her around the world, teaming up with UN policy makers, research institutes, women's groups and social justice movements. She has written extensively on globalization and development from a gender perspective. *Body Politics in Development* is her first full-length book.

Wendy Harcourt

Body Politics
in Development

Critical Debates in Gender and Development

Zed Books
LONDON AND NEW YORK

Body Politics in Development: Critical Debates in Gender and Development was first published in 2009
by Zed Books Ltd, 7 Cynthia Street, London N1 9JF, UK
and Room 400, 175 Fifth Avenue, New York, NY 10010, USA

www.zedbooks.co.uk

Designed and typeset by Long House Publishing Services
Cover designed by Rogue Four Design
Index by Mike Kirkwood
Printed and bound in the UK by the MPG Books Group

Distributed in the USA exclusively by Palgrave Macmillan, a division of St Martin's Press, LLC,
175 Fifth Avenue, New York, NY 10010, USA

A catalogue record for this book is available from the British Library
Library of Congress Cataloging in Publication Data available

ISBN 978-1-84277-934-7 hb
ISBN 978-1-84277-935-4 pb

Contents

Acknowledgements

Twenty years is a long time in the making of a book, and it would be impossible to name all the people individually who have helped and inspired me to write. I would like to acknowledge all those people I have met in different faraway places, whether in classrooms, workshops, conferences, clinics, offices, universities, fields, homes or planes, who shared with me their stories and insights on body politics. I would also like to thank the many people who have worked with me on projects, be they journal issues, advocacy campaigns, workshops or publishing ventures – and in particular my colleagues on the editorial board of the journal *Development*, my friends and mentors in the Women and Politics of Place and the SID South Asia Network collectives, my feminist collaborators in FEMSEM, Women in Development Europe, the European Feminist Forum and the Feminist Dialogues. Then there are the people who have nurtured the writing of this book in the last months; friends and family who listened to all my plans as the book unfolded. I would like to thank in particular my friends at Clare Hall, Cambridge, and colleagues at the Society for International Development International Secretariat in Rome, for good conversations and lots of understanding. Very importantly, I need to thank the people who took the time to read and comment as I wrote. My parents, Joan and Geoff Harcourt, were, as ever, long-suffering readers of every chapter. Their kindness and encouragement helped me throughout. Di Owen also deserves a special thank you for reading each chapter with an eye to keeping me laughing and writing especially if my voice faltered. I also received welcome advice from people who read specific chapters. Their insights have greatly improved the book. Thank you to Vinca Bigo, Niclas Hällström, Veronique Mottier, Khawar Mumtaz, Marjan Radjavi and Gill Wu. Thank you to the anonymous reader from Zed Books and Kitt Bohn-Willeberg for their keen-sighted observations that helped me to complete the manuscript. Last, but not least, are the three people who have lived most closely with me and the book, with my absences and frustrations, and who just by being there made sure I went the distance. Thank you to Claudio, Caterina and Emma Claire to whom this book is dedicated.

Introduction

Invisible Bodies

In 1988 I was invited to address an international audience of nearly 1,000 people in Delhi, India on women and culture. Aged 28, I was the hastily booked replacement speaker for an opening day plenary of the nineteenth triennial World Conference of the Society for International Development. Having just completed my PhD on 'medical discourse related to the female body', for this entirely new venture into development I decided to compare nineteenth-century European gynaecological practices for curing female maladies with twentieth-century African practices of female genital mutilation (FGM). My argument was, to me, quite straightforward. If we now dismiss the nineteenth-century medical practices of removing ovaries, propping up lapsed wombs and incising the clitoris as dangerous and misinformed, why could we not, learning from history, speak about and end similarly dangerous practices today?

I could tell something was wrong as I began to speak. A hushed silence fell. And when I proceeded to elaborate in great detail, as enthused PhD scholars are wont to do, on the intricacies of nineteenth-century European gynaecological practices compared to current practices in Africa, frantic notes were sent to me by the chairperson to stop. Not quite sure what was going on, in good student activist manner I continued – if speaking by now a little faster, which did not help matters. I managed to reach my conclusion: that we had to break the silence around female genital mutilation and see it not as a tabooed topic to be upheld as cultural tradition but as a human rights issue that needs to end in the same way that gynaecological practices 100 years earlier were curtailed (Harcourt 1987). Then I sat down to muted applause. At question time, hands shot up. The first question was, 'Who is that woman, who gave her the right to speak?' The rest of the questions remain a blur: it seemed that the talk had made an impact, but not quite in the way I had intended. Finally, I stood up with a huge sense of relief to move from the stage – only to see a line of European and African women striding towards me with determined, angry looks on their faces. I made a sharp right turn and ran into a cupboard at the side of the stage where I stayed for what seemed hours until some Indian friends not connected to the event came to my rescue and smuggled me out of the hall.

During the rest of the conference I managed to grasp to some extent why my talk was so sharply at odds with what was considered appropriate for international women and development panels on culture. The first issue was my speaking at all. As a young, white Australian woman, I did not have the authority to speak and in doing so I was not respecting other cultures, in this case African culture and tradition. Second, I was 'bringing in' European history, which, I was told, was not relevant to development today. Third, I was questioning medical science, not something one questions in development, which is about bringing modern knowledge to other cultures. Fourth, I was not a development expert and so I did not understand that this topic was highly sensitive and not to be broached publicly – certainly not from a feminist perspective. Fifth, I should have been talking about women and culture. I should not have focused on embodiment, with so much detail on what was done to the body: this belongs to anthropology, perhaps; it is not what development is about. And last, I gathered it was better just to write about these issues, in appropriate places, presumably specialized journals, as several people told me they would not have been so upset if they had read my paper first. Indeed it was published as part of the proceedings and evoked no response at all. Evidently, before a mixed audience of men and women from North and South, speaking of such matters was distasteful and a little shocking.

Fourteen years later, having undertaken many 'gender and development' projects, written books, and engaged in meetings and debates at the United Nations, research institutes, and non-governmental organizations, I was invited to participate in a meeting on female genital mutilation in the Italian Parliament. The meeting had been called by a very prominent Italian politician, Emma Bonino, and the leading gender and development organization in Italy, AIDOS. It was held in one of the plush and luxurious rooms reserved for the Senate, which required the audience to pass through several security points in order to enter. When I arrived the room, holding several hundred people, was full. At the front were the invited ambassadors and politicians; at the back were rows of excited high school children who had been bussed in for the occasion. The presentations were to be divided into two parts, the charismatic Bonino acting as mistress of ceremonies. There was an air of excitement as television cameras clustered expectantly, waiting for the Prime Minister of Italy to arrive. The first speakers were medical doctors, some Italian, some from African countries. They all, one by one, with the aid of slides projected on a large screen, proceeded to show in graphic detail examples of mutilated genitals, women suffering in childbirth, close-ups of screaming and fearful little girls, old women holding dirty and unhygienic knives outside huts, blood, pus-filled scars and stitching. Interspersed were statistics of deaths and details of legal steps and charters drawn up to stop this abominable practice. The ambassadors looked decidedly uncomfortable in their plush chairs. The horror-stricken silence of the school girls who had been chattering happily on their arrival was palpable. Two of them were hurried, pale and ill, from the room. The smiling politician smoothly continued to introduce each medical expert, emphasizing for the cameras and journalists just how dreadful the practice is and how the Italian public must meet a responsibility to end it.

The second round of panelists were then brought on, moved up from the front row where they had been afforded a close-up viewing of the slides. They looked a little shaken and somewhat thrown by the setting, the cameras and the chat-style format. Bonino, speaking into the cameras, now proceeded to tell of her own personal journey through African lands, meeting with different women who were determined to stop this appalling practice. She had also started to learn Arabic and had travelled far, visiting the rural projects of AIDOS which for many years had been doing projects in Somalia, a former Italian colony, and other places to stop female genital mutilation. She explained to us that some of the courageous women she had met in Somalia, Egypt, Tanzania, The Gambia and Ethiopia had now been invited here to Italy on the first step of their tour to share their own experiences with European audiences. Smilingly, she encouraged each woman to speak, explaining to the audience in some detail where she had met them. Some in tears, some defiantly, some in whispers spoke for a few minutes of their meeting with the politician and then of their shame at being mutilated and of how much they wanted to stop this dreadful practice for their daughters' sakes. Some spoke of the projects funded by AIDOS which were ensuring the practice would end. Just as the last woman from Tanzania was to speak, an excited ripple among the journalists and organizers of the meeting indicated that, even if a little late, the Prime Minister himself had arrived. He strode into the room, and was greeted by the now beaming Bonino. He graciously conceded to listen to the last speaker. Unlike the others this speaker, a human rights activist and journalist, stood up and went to the speaker's podium. She turned to the audience and, having first directly welcomed the Prime Minister, she told us that she did not want us to think that all Africans hated the clitoris. Nor that all African women were mutilated in the horrifying ways we had witnessed today. Indeed, she herself had not been subject to such mutilations and in her country there were poems written to the clitoris. She then proceeded in her own language, Kiswahili, to share with us such a poem.

Silence greeted such unorthodoxy; the somewhat baffled Bonino quickly thanked her and immediately turned to ask the Prime Minister to address us and the cameras. On cue, he duly presented the head of AIDOS with a large cheque to start the European Campaign, congratulated Bonino on her hard work, wished them luck and apologized that he had to leave for another very urgent appointment. With that he exited, and with his departure the meeting closed.

That afternoon I spent some time with the African women witnesses. They were staying in a small hotel near my office and had been given daily allowances and a free afternoon to sightsee before the next stop. They were somewhat uncomfortable about the session, but pleased that the Prime Minister came. They stated to me that these public sessions telling personal stories and the shock tactics of showing graphic illustrations were 'how you do things in Europe'. They appreciated my concern about the objectification of black women and their bodies, perhaps even agreed it was condoning the popular image of the dark continent of Africa, full of dangerous practices and the need for Europeans to give money to end them. During my 14 years of working in gender and development (and more since) I had seen how images of women's bodies from 'other places' fed into racist stereotypes of women in 'developing' countries needing to be rescued from dire poverty, unhealthy lifestyles and prejudicial cultures. Their voices and experiences were dismissed in imaginaries that objectified them as ignorant, at best different, and in both cases needing to be rescued. The response of the African women was, yes, this imagery was unfortunate, but it was the best way to raise money. Besides, they were very grateful to AIDOS for organizing the trip and the funding raised would support their work at home. Even the last speaker from Tanzania said it was a good media event. They agreed that talking about their own bodies and the experience of mutilation was something they would not do publicly at home, but in Italy as guests, somewhat anonymous, part of a large and important European campaign, being looked after so graciously, it was fine.

What was going on? Why were the main protagonists of this event finding it all perfectly okay? They might be sympathetic to my worries, but it transpired they were indeed *my* worries; they were happy to move on to the next event, keen to see more of Europe, raise more money. Why did I feel so uneasy? Here was the bold-faced speaking out about female genital mutilation that I had urged development workers to do years ago in Delhi. So why did I feel so suspicious of this campaign, of the theatre and performance? Of submerged assumed sexualities that bubbled out? Of images of black bodies, of pain smoothed away in medical description? Who was the authoritative voice here? Not the women who told their experience, faltering and in tears, surely. How could a politician smile at the tears of another woman in front of the cameras and call it strategic, call it fund raising, call it development? Why, once again as a white feminist trying to work in solidarity and in honesty in the field of gender and development, was I just so out of my depth? What were the power plays that seemed so suspiciously like those of colonial times? What was a young Tanzanian woman doing defending in her own language the pleasure of the clitoris to an Italian prime minister? And why was that situation happening in the Italian Parliament in front of schoolgirls?

This book is something of an answer to those questions as I try to unravel the deep contradictions in body politics that are pushed up to the surface in such gender and development events.

It is not a simple topic. There are layers of meanings and understandings that very often those involved in the day-to-day practice of social and economic justice work do not take time to think about. I aim to dig down into those contradictions and feelings of unease that the subject of embodiment raises. Talk about the actual experience of pain, pleasure, strain, sexuality, birth, health and disease is rare in development policies. These issues are side issues to 'macro' discussions on trade, finance and economic growth, yet embodied experience of women and men is at the core of what it means to live through what 'development' imposes on people. In order to understand how to think about those experiences I have found it useful to look at the work of those who have had the time to think through the concepts of the body and embodiment. I have been lucky enough to take some time to read about the body, during a short sabbatical in Clare Hall, Cambridge, twenty years after I completed my PhD, and after spending those years working as a feminist activist and researcher on gender and development in various guises. I found, somewhat to my surprise, that the body has moved to centre stage to feminist philosophy, sociology, anthropology and geography. Scholarship has moved on from the male-defined universal texts on the body with titles like *A History of the Body* (Turner 1984), *A History of Women's Bodies* (Shorter 1982), *The History of Sexuality* (Foucault 1976), accompanied by defiantly woman-centred books like *Body/Politics:Women and the Discourses of Science* (Jacobus *et al.* 1990), *The Reproduction of Mothering: Psychoanalysis and the Sociology of Gender* (Chodorow 1999), *Of Woman Born: Motherhood as Experience and Institution* (Rich 1979) and *The Dialectics of Sex: the Case for Feminist Revolution* (Firestone 1979). Just two decades on there now exists a hugely complex and fascinating array of work that has gone way beyond the earlier work in the 1980s, new work that historically and conceptually prise apart assumptions of the body inside and out. Examples include Judith Butler (1993) on sexualities, Liz Grosz (1994) on corporeal feminism, Anne Fausto-Sterling (2000) on sexing the body, Donna Haraway (1997a) on technoscience, Margrit Shildrick (1997) on embodiment, Chandra Talpade Mohanty (2003) on post-colonial writings on global feminism and racism, and many feminist readings of the Foucauldian concept of bio-power (a topic I engaged with in my own thesis).

Once I started reading I itched to go back to rethink my own engagement in gender and development and understand the importance of the body. Just the very fact that speaking about practices like female genital mutilation caused so many contradictory and uncomfortable reactions suggests there is something to be uncovered and explored. At the same time, I wondered why these analytical insights were not at the heart of gender and development discourse and practice. Or were they? Had I just missed them because I was so bound up in other more 'obvious' subjects of gender and development?

The challenge in writing this book was therefore both to go deeper into my history and to use those experiences to translate the very densely written texts on gender, the body and embodiment. I wanted to see if those insights could be understood and used by people like me, who were bound up in the everyday practices of gender and development, feminism and social justice work. I wanted to see if I could tease out the contradictions, understand the gaps, look again at the obvious to uncover the details in the practices that might help explain the difficulties body politics raises for gender and development. At the same time I wanted to write a book that would engage in conversations with those writing theory. I loved the idea that I could respond to all the metaphor and simile, the poetic hints of feminist texts. I wanted to debate with them about how useful their work was, and to encourage much more interaction and discussion to go below all the density and sometimes impenetrability of their wordplays. Hence I needed to work out how to cross the borders among academic feminists and practitioners in gender and development as well as feminist activists around the world working on body politics and gender. But as I attempted to do so I found myself facing a deeper challenge.

As the two opening stories suggest, I needed to find my own authoritative voice. The best strategy, I felt, in reading the texts, and thinking back over my hardly straightforward engagement in development, was to speak openly and unashamedly of my own experiences as a way to illustrate some of the complexities of body politics in gender and development. Such a project, however, struck a chord of dread in me that is familiar to many women writers. How could I assume that my experiences – my 'I slots' as Margrit Shildrick engagingly calls them – are valid? On the 'male stream side', I am not holding any particular place of authority. I edit a small journal, I belong to several women's networks, I attend workshops and conferences, I write a few pieces when invited to do so. On the feminist activist side, I am situated as a white, educated, employed woman in her forties holding two Western nationalities, married with two children and an ambiguous sexual history. I live in Europe, so I am a traveller to 'other places' but with no authentic 'Global South' experience, be it 'development project' training or living for long stretches in some second home in the 'Global South'.[1]

Yet in crossing such borders along the margins of development practice, I have been part of the 'colourful' array of women coming together from around the world, celebrating the differences in their lives and deploying those differences to change injustice. My engagement, knowledge and power can be found in the in-between conversations. I have learnt a lot from the shared stories that spoke of diverse identities and different cultures, other languages and sexualities. I have learnt strategy and method together with women in the corridors of the United Nations, during the meals in kitchens and other places where schemes were hatched. I have been supported in the moments of breastfeeding my daughters in workshops, holding the hands of others' children in hotels I will never see again, bringing people to my home. My knowledge comes from the midnight intimacy of emails, in the shared hugs, tears, smiles, winks and laughter. I can speak with some confidence of the embodied reality of development, in my lived experience and engagement with other bodies, with our differences and struggles for gender social justice to be heard, recognized and respected in our planned but also fun and impromptu moments together. This book takes me and I hope the reader deeper into embodied lived experience and why that matters in gender and development.

Having started boldly with two autobiographical slices of my life I shall diverge from, without abandoning, that narrative mode. I explore in as open a way as possible some of the facets of body politics in development by revisiting some of the key debates in gender and development in the last two decades. I hope the pace is easy and enjoyable, more of a chat than a lecture. Indeed, I think the decision to write this book was clinched in a conversation held on an Atlantic flight bound to New York for a Commission on the Status of Women meeting at the United Nations. As I sat poised to revise my notes for the meeting, a chatty New Yorker, living not one hundred metres from the UN, challenged me to tell him what difference I and the thousands of other women going to the UN would make, beyond forcing him to reroute his dog's walks on those days.

So, as with the gentleman on the plane, I need first to define what body politics is. The first chapter explains body politics and gender in development discourses conceptually and historically, with reference to some of the key feminist texts on embodiment and gender. It does so by setting out some major moments for body politics in recent development discourse. I also revisit some of the work I did as part of a collective project on women and the politics of place.[2] Here I explain why I take gender and female embodiment as the major foci of the book.

In the rest of the book I discuss, with inevitable leakages, some of the types of bodies assumed in gender and development discourse, and the critiques of those assumptions by feminist theory and practice. This is a huge area to cover in a short book, and therefore my discussions centre on selected contributions to the debates on body politics – those that I see as central to gender and development discourse and the engagement of women's movements in transnational development processes.

In Chapter 2 I revisit the concept of the reproductive body with discussions on population control, maternal mortality, abortion and contraception, as well as examining the strategies to break the silence around the male reproductive body in development. In the third chapter I explore the embodied experiences of paid and unpaid productive work, in and outside the home, in factories, fields, bars, kitchens, hospitals and offices. I take up the metaphor of the markings on the body as I look at the gendered strategies used to organize work, family and the often forgotten right to rest. I try to make the apparently obvious distinction between reproductive and productive work a little less easy by exploring the overlapping productive and reproductive roles of women, particularly in the gender and development discourse around the 'care economy'.

In the fourth chapter I look at one of the central topics of gender and development: sexual and gender-based violence, fundamentalism and militarism. I am particularly interested to understand how rape is no longer a silenced, tabooed issue. I trace examples of women's struggles against rape, domestic violence, rape in war and fundamentalism as practised on rejected and abused bodies, and diverse strategies to combat it at different levels in different places. Given recent post-9/11 times, and the many conversations on terrorism and abuse in prisons, I also raise issues around men's bodies in relation to militarism, and touch on the critique of development as violence in itself. Within this chapter I also take up a discussion of sexualized bodies.

In Chapter 5 I look at the recent feminist explorations of sexualities and at how those conversations are entering (or not) into the contested and usually marginal debates around sexualities in development discourse. I am particularly interested in the impact of the HIV and AIDS epidemic and the consequent acknowledgement of men who have sex with men, and the ambivalence around the issue of pleasure in development discourse as opposed to the huge concerns around violence and abuse.

The sixth chapter takes us deeper into other aspects of embodiment as I examine the lure of the promises and some of the traps offered by technology, science and biotechnology. I follow the work of Donna Haraway and others on cyborgs.[3] I take up some issues that are beginning to worry me in relation to embodiment in development as poor people, particularly women's bodies and 'disabled' bodies, have become the testing ground for many new technologies. I enter into the bioethical debates about the gender dimension of new bio-technologies (especially in assisted reproduction), the implications of nanotechnologies, how disabilities are now viewed, and trafficking in body parts.

I conclude the book by going back to some of my original questions and unease around FGM, opening up questions about how gender and development could better answer the many critical issues raised by body politics.

Overall, the book aims to illustrate how body politics informs the broader social, political and economic discourse of development. It aims to inform both those that are new to the field of gender and development, and those who work in one area of gender and development but would like to learn more about debates in other areas. As such it covers a wide range of issues in relation to body politics: reproduction, care, violence and violation, sexuality and technology. I situate these issues against a backdrop of the last twenty years of debates in gender and development, using the lens of my own experience to ground the arguments in passionately held convictions felt by the women and men engaged in body politics in development.

Notes

1 Throughout the book I use the terms Global North and Global South. With the end of the Cold War and the emergence of the current form of economic globalization, these are the terms used when referring to the rich countries in the geographic North (Global North) and poorer countries (Global South) which tend to be geographically located in the South. These terms are used rather than the earlier First, Second and Third World terminology, with its implied ranking of different regions of the world.

2 Different parts of that research have been published in two issues of the journal *Development*: 'Power, Culture, Justice: Women and the Politics of Place' (Vol. 48, No. 2, June 1998) and 'Place, Politics and Justice: Women Negotiating Globalization' (Vol. 45, No. 1, March 2002) and in an edited collection (Harcourt and Escobar 2005), which was also published in Spanish in 2006. In addition, a CD-Rom and a leaflet were issued and we held workshops with different academic and activist audiences in India, Italy, Tanzania and the USA (see <www.sidint.org>).

3 See my chapter 'Cyborg Melody' in the edited collection *Women@internet, creating cultures in cyberspace* (Harcourt 1999) which came out of a research project with UNESCO that looked early on at the potential of the Internet for mobilizing women's groups, particularly in the Global South.

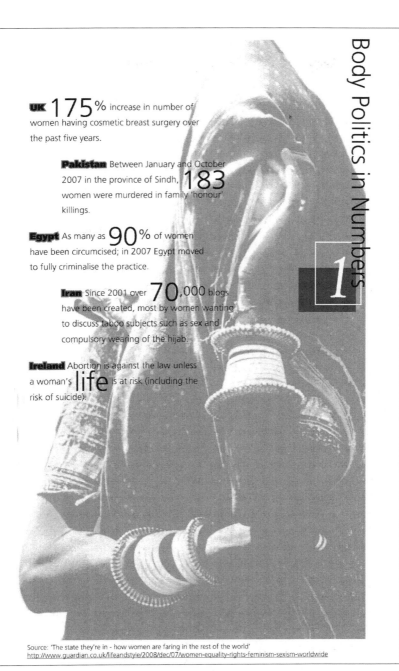

UK 175% increase in number of women having cosmetic breast surgery over the past five years.

Pakistan Between January and October 2007 in the province of Sindh, 183 women were murdered in family 'honour' killings.

Egypt As many as 90% of women have been circumcised; in 2007 Egypt moved to fully criminalise the practice.

Iran Since 2001 over 70,000 blogs have been created, most by women wanting to discuss taboo subjects such as sex and compulsory wearing of the hijab.

Ireland Abortion is against the law unless a woman's life is at risk (including the risk of suicide).

1

Source: 'The state they're in - how women are faring in the rest of the world'
http://www.guardian.co.uk/lifeandstyle/2008/dec/07/women-equality-rights-feminism-sexism-worldwide

One

What is Body Politics?

Setting the scene

As someone working in international development I spend a lot of time on planes, mostly on the way to conferences, seminars and workshops, with excursions to countries to observe and discuss other people's lives and bodies. Although the topics are often painful – disease, exploitation, violence, death, inequities and injustice – the conversations are usually conducted in considerable comfort. I listen to rather than experience the pain. I do not feel it on my body, though I may see, imagine and write about it. Often participants in the various meetings raise questions about the incongruity between the actual places where the subjects of development live, and the places and types of policy discussions that are held about them. It can seem incongruous to speak about pain and violation in decorous workshop settings. The contrast between the lived bodily experiences of the violated women and the comfortable lives of women leading gender and development debates evokes an eerie sense of dislocation. And for many it raises questions about whether such gender and development discussions, often held thousands of miles away from the subject of debate, actually contribute to real change for the women and men we so earnestly talk about.

When reading for this book the literature on bodies from anthropology, human geography, sociology, feminist theory and philosophy I was cheered to see that in academia there was no such hesitation about the worth of discussing and writing about bodies. Indeed, unlike when I was doing my PhD twenty years ago, the matter of bodies has become a recurrent theme in many disciplines. Just writing about bodies is deemed a political act in the academy.

Yet I still think it is important to focus on the question: whose bodies are seen as worthy of scholarly attention?

How do our embodied realities implicate our understanding of bodies? What is the politics of writing about bodies? To begin with, which bodies are producing knowledge about which other bodies? What are the connections and differences between academic feminist writings and the activities of the people advocating for sexual rights, reproductive rights and health, or those fighting for better public health care, an end to violence against women, and scrutiny of nano- and biotechnologies? Such advocacy and policy conversations usually refer, not to leading philosophers and writers such as Judith Butler, Michel Foucault, Donna Haraway, Gayatri Spivak and Liz Grosz, but to United Nations documents breezily known by the names of the places where the final negotiated documents were signed: Rio, Vienna, Cairo, Beijing, et cetera.[1]

Unlike academic texts such documents do not carry authors' names. The negotiated processes are hard to follow and are steeped in bureaucracy, political plays and power games often completed during late-night and early-morning haggling. The processes that mediate the impact of these statements and policy agreements on embodied experiences of the men and women who are living far away from such discussions are not entirely clear. What is clear is that the subjects of the debates do not have access to the social and economic resources or the languages that would allow them to participate in the negotiation processes. The issue here is that the stated aim of UN discussions is to improve the embodied lives of 'the poor': their health, rights, living conditions and security, and even their intimate, sexual expression. But where do the voices of people defined as poor and marginal fit into a discussion on body politics? There are uncomfortable contradictions at the centre of the body politics of development where those defined as economically poor are treated as objects rather than subjects of their own lives. On paper development is delivered in interventions that are clean, modern, politically free, based on modern technical knowledge, sound public health systems and comprehensive economic planning. The reality is far, far messier.

In this chapter I go deeper into these questions by tracing body politics in feminist texts on the body and gender as well as reflecting on key moments for body politics in gender and development discourse. In this discussion I deliberately keep coming back to the jarring unease I feel about who speaks for whom and to my questions about the methods and proceedings of international development. I try to balance out the positive and negative impacts of the development process. My point is not to decry the efforts to establish good public health systems, education, medical services, reproductive health, functioning economies and prosperity, but to examine the modern development apparatus through which they are meant to be delivered. I hear and see the damage done to local people and places, and the frustrations and difficulties expressed by those involved in the political struggle around the body in gender and development discourse.

The chapter has four main focal areas. After a short introduction on gender and feminism as pivotal terms in the book, I pick out what I see as useful feminist analysis and theory on the body. I then give my version of body politics in gender and development. This leads to an engagement with feminists working in the World Social Forum space who provide some key guidelines to addressing body politics on gender and development. These four main themes set up the key questions and approaches for the rest of the book. If I meander a little in the telling, please bear with me. Given the complexity of the subject, I cross several borders of knowledge and experience as an insider and outsider or, perhaps more honestly, someone trying to reside between feminist theory and politics.

Gender

Gender is a key analytical term in body politics. Gender refers to the psycho-social, political-cultural, scientific and economic reading of sexual difference that informs all human relations. Gender is lived differently in different places, bodies and locations (Connell 2002; Sjoberg 2007). Rather than thinking about gender as a biologically determined division between male and female, it is more helpful to see it as a fluid construct that provides the social inscriptions that enable us to identify, learn and live as male or female in the places we inhabit.

Feminism

I choose to use the term 'feminist'. I recognize from many conversations that the term feminist is not always easily accepted. Sometimes I am asked why I do not use the term 'humanist', for example, particularly as it seems more easily inclusive of men. Feminist for some conjures up images of white elite angry women, and somewhere bra burning hovers in the background. As many stories in this book show, however, a feminist viewpoint excludes neither men nor facets of masculinity, nor is it confined to elite women of the Global North.

Feminism started from struggles against various forms of women's economic, social and cultural oppression (around the world) and recognizes and builds upon (diverse) women's creative resistance to oppression (Basu 1995; Grewal and Kaplan 1994). In doing so it takes into account the many ways women and men relate to their different gender roles. It also questions the binaries that construct men and women as biological and cultural polar opposites, and asks for a more fluid understanding of gendered roles that embraces transgender and other ways of expressing embodied identities. Gendered identities, including those inscribed on the body and sexualities, are variously constructed through languages and a range of cultural, social and economic institutions. In trying to understand and challenge gender power relations feminism has had to move beyond any easy understanding of an essential sexual being and identity, whether woman or man. Feminism queries concepts such as women, female bodies and femininity, and the gender relations constituting these concepts. Imbedded gendered power relations determine women's and men's lives: their identities, behaviours and sexualities. Feminism, in challenging gender power relations, necessarily also shifts understandings of men, male bodies and masculinity (Andermatiz, Lovell and Wolkowitz 1997).

Feminism, then, is a broad political positioning that looks at how to change gender relations, taking into account different gendered aspects of people's lives. Feminism views gender relations not in terms of two opposed poles but as a continuum. In feminism there is ample scope for different expressions of gender identity. Unsettling the apparent norms around male and female lives, it understands biology as a social construct like any other. Reconfiguring sexuality and identity, it opens up ways for new gender positionings and possible pathways for social transformation. This reading certainly helped me understand my surprise when, in a temple in Jojakarta, Indonesia, I was asked by my host if I thought the dancer was male or female. I had assumed the beautiful and graceful person in front of me was a woman, but was told that this was neither woman nor man, but a member of 'the third sex'. I later learned there were many cultures that held a revered space in the arts for such people.[2]

Heteronormativity

Recent feminist theory questions the binary givens of male and female. Recognizing that gender is constructed, feminist theory proposes that gendered bodies exist along a continuum from male to female with various permutations in between. For example some individuals feel themselves to be male or female even if biologically they appear to be of the other sex. Queer theory recognizes the different gendered expressions of sexuality: heterosexual, homosexual, bisexual, intersexual and transgender. Anne Fausto-Sterling (2000), for example, proposes that such 'gender variation is normal and, for some people, an arena for playful exploration'.

Going beyond binaries of male or female allows us to consider people who have identities and lifestyles that do not conform to heterosexual norms. The term 'heteronormativity' allows us to question the assumption that 'natural' sexual relations are defined as only between men and women of certain ages and suitability. It highlights the legal, religious, social and political discrimination that assumes we are all heterosexual and all sexual unions are only for reproduction. Feminist analysis brings in the views and experiences of lesbians, gays, bisexuals, transsexuals, intersexuals and queers (LGBTIQ) who challenge and confront reproductive heteronormativity and the sexual oppression that follows from it.

Going beyond essentialism

There is a huge literature on what gendered bodies, sexualities and identities mean in academic writing. Like the term heteronormativity, such feminist writing unsettles what is apparent and obvious about concepts we take for granted. After all, we all have bodies, but in feminist readings of bodies we see that the gendered body is not so easy to define, but instead is a very fluid concept.

An important debate in feminist literature concerns the need to go beyond essentialism, or reducing women or men to a biological essence determined by their biological, maternal or procreative sexual functions. I have been asked why I want to write about embodied experiences, with a focus on women's lives or what others call 'fleshly' feminine experiences. Those asking me are concerned that I will slip into speaking about female embodiment only and reinforce an essentialist notion of women as defined primarily by their biological differences to men. It is precisely this unease around female bodies as determining an essence of women that I want to question. The female body is not as straightforward as it appears. It is a highly complex category constructed in sexual scientific discourses and other social practices. By looking at how gender relations are inscribed on bodies, and then defined in binary categories as male or female, I want to question dominant views of female embodiment. I see this questioning as a strategy that helps us go beyond essentialism. My feminist vision sees understanding more about embodiment and the concepts informing female embodiment as a strategy that uncovers sources of oppression and also of power.

Body politics refuses to see women or men or those genders in between – and all their diversities of history, race, experience and age – as 'being lashed to their bodies' at one remove from a 'true' self as Adrienne Rich (1979), a US feminist poet and writer, described it. Rather, it is in itself a nexus of power and knowledge.

Bodies as a source of oppression and power

To return to one of my earlier questions: which bodies matter? Liz Grosz (1994), an Australian feminist philosopher, takes us further into why female bodies are a source of both oppression and power in her discussion of volatile bodies and corporeal feminism. In her view, the female body is a site of both normalization and resistance where social norms of being female are inscribed on the body. She queries the commonsense understanding of bodies as given biological identities. Instead she analyses them as sites of social experience and political resistance. In this understanding of body politics, power is not always possessed as such, with hegemonic forces determining what one does or does not do. Bodies may endure physical torture, beatings, stonings and rapes, but in the normative construction of gender it is everyday life or micro-politics that shapes our knowledge and experience of the lived gendered body. These constructions include the language and practices of caring, parenting, sexual relations, health, and medical and biological scientific processes. If we analyse how gendered bodies are constructed in different discourses we can then challenge norms and oppressive practices, and understand how to exercise different forms of power that can transform and change such conditions.

Rewriting the truths of the body

An important strategy in looking at female bodies as a source of oppression and power has been to retell narratives about embodiment that unsettle concepts of biological sex and gender. Judith Butler (1993), a US-based academic, asks us to look at which bodies come to matter, and why. She suggests we look for the interesting questions that arise from the gaps between the values and interests of women's lives and those that inform dominant conceptual frameworks. How do young women living in urban slums in Nairobi, for example, experience the values of the Catholic Church, which condemns the use of birth control? Such decisions are lived by these women, who are thereby exposed to chronic poverty marked by overcrowded homes, no water and increased risk of AIDS. Some may have to choose sex work or abortion as ways for themselves and their family to survive, yet be practising Catholics. Such apparent contradictions can be closed by looking at how women's realities are grounded in the sexual specificity of the female body. For example, the 'given' understanding that femininity is linked to the womb is a major way in which heterosexual privilege is presented as the norm. In order to challenge some of the oppressive practices around female bodies, such as judging a woman for becoming a sex worker, it is important to look at the tensions and gaps in the assumed truths around bodies from different situated viewpoints. While it is not enough just to record lived experiences, such knowledge is vital to open up hegemonic ways of seeing. In addition to these narratives based on women's lived experiences it is also necessary to reread the conceptual frameworks that bind male and female embodied experiences tightly into dominant frameworks of politics, economics, culture and society (Scarry 1985; Adebon 1993; Grewal and Kaplan 1994; Butler and Scott 2002; Harding 2006). It is not enough just to tell the story of the sex worker in a slum; one should also position it in the debates around population and development, the George W. Bush administration's policies opposing family planning, and all the macro-economic reasons why those women are living in slums in the first place.

Butler's account of narratives as strategies to reclaim female embodiment raises the troubling questions of who writes, who speaks, who is recorded and by whom. For example, in 2000 the World Bank did a major study on *Voices of the Poor* (Narayan 2000),[3] recording in great detail the difficulties of living daily with hunger, deprivation, illness, risk and uncertainty, and concluding that good health is a fundamental need of the very poor. In assembling these hundreds of voices, the World Bank became the owner of important knowledge of embodied experiences and used it to frame itself as the leading expert on poverty, which since 2000 has become 'the' development concern. We need to understand in which context, and why that knowledge was gathered. The World Bank as a powerful Bretton Woods institution now dominates development policy on poverty and decision making over resource provision for community health. *Voices of the Poor* is an example of the troubling use of experience and narrative to support the policy bias of the World Bank. Critiques have addressed the manipulation of the data as well as the ethics of using specific experiences of poverty to form generalized abstract notions of 'global poverty' that undergird World Bank development policy (Rademacher and Patel 2002: 169).

Colonialism, racism and feminism

An often silenced issue in international development is how racism is lived alongside sexism. Indian-born, now US-based academics Gayatri Chakravorty Spivak (1987 and 1999) and Chandra Talpade Mohanty (2003) challenge the unmarked white gaze informing different discourses, including feminist writings. Mohanty warns us to look at the interwoven processes of sexism, racism, misogyny and heterosexism. She specifically points out the need to question the sexist and racist imperialist structures that determine that the fertility of women from the Global South is a central focus of development. Mohanty argues that the focus on fertility speaks volumes about the predominant representation of non-Western women in the social and scientific knowledge underpinning concepts of gender and development. Both Spivak and Mohanty point to the unresolved tensions between tradition and modernity that are in play when instrumental biological representations of women are embedded in neo-colonial development processes that cast non-Western women as an international reservoir of cheap labour in industrial, domestic and sex work.

Such blindness to racism is not new. Feminist writing has pointed out that perceptions of different female bodies are not only socially inscribed but also historically constituted (Hermann and Stewart 1994; Diprose 1994; Conboy *et al.* 1997; Shildrick 1997). The histories of colonialism show how understandings of bodies, sex and race are embedded in imperial and colonial medicine and science (Harding 2006). These historical inscriptions of bodies are still reverberating in international development, where European male bodies reign as the 'true' fully fledged human type. It is very difficult to break down these givens in development discourse, based as it is on an economic theory which poses modern, rational man as its subject. There have been some very interesting attempts to challenge this masculinist approach by feminist economists like Irene van Staveren, who directly critiques the male subject of development discourse (van Staveren 2001).

It is important to recognize how deeply gender and race have been worked into the apparently natural body of biology and science, and through those discourses into development. It is also important to contextualize why the interest in bodies, including my own interest, emerged in the 1980s and 1990s along with key political and social changes in demography and age, patterns of disease, new technologies and feminisms. Female embodiment associated with women's health activism and body politics in the 1970s in the Global North (the USA, the UK, Canada, Australia and New Zealand) is now embedded in state bureaucracies and global processes that determine development. Like all political processes, these social constructions of female bodies developed through battles between groups for competing political interests.

Foucauldian understandings of body, knowledge and power

In the literature on the history of bodies the late French philosopher Michel Foucault is a continual reference point for feminists and others. Foucault's concept of biopolitics as set out in *The History of Sexuality* (1976) is an influential text on female embodiment (Macleod and Durrheim 2002). Foucault presents modern power not just as hierarchical and oppressive but also as horizontally produced and, in complex but hardly visible ways, embedded in our language and practice. Biopolitics is the politics of the administering and governing of life through processes that modern Western society takes for granted. For example, we do not question the concept of collecting statistics to produce the 'average' weight or height. Foucault argues that this measuring of life is a historically specific political process. The process of biopolitics measures and analyses the body in an array of strategies that then produce the modern sense of gendered individual and social subjects. Foucauldian biopolitics understands bodies not as static givens, locked into certain biological rhythms, but as fluid sites of power and political contestation. Population statistics, medical records, thumbprints on our passports, identity cards that state our height and eye colour, magazines that advertise ideal bodies, are all part of biopolitical strategies that categorize modern bodies. In development discourse many biopolitical strategies around the body intersect. The language and practices of family planning, medicine, public health, population and reproductive rights produce gendered bodies as an interesting set of objects and subjects of study.

Another useful Foucauldian concept is biopower. The concept of biopower helps us to go further in understanding how body politics works in modern society. The strategies of biopolitics are by no means neutral. The specific set of meanings is determined by institutions framing how society understands gendered bodies. It is not a vertical use of power, where the US Government, for example, decrees that male security guards at the airport must treat with suspicion all veiled women who come into the airport. Biopower refers to the minute practices of power relations. Foucault sees power as immanent in everyday relationships, including economic exchanges, knowledge relationships and sexual relationships. Micro-level practices of power are taken up in global or macro-level strategies of domination. These power plays are made not through centralized power, but through a complex series of infinitesimal mechanisms. These mechanisms of power continually change, linking micro and macro levels of power. Modern administration and government are exercised through a whole range of institutions, procedures, analysis, reflections, calculations and tactics. They compose a complex system employing a variety of modes to achieve a particular end – for example, the oppression of women or the emancipation of women. A border security guard detaining a veiled woman in a New York airport is caught up in biopolitical power play that seems to him, and to the woman he is hassling, a natural order of things.

Bodies, science and technology

Questioning dominant views of embodiment using feminist analysis helps to unpack how tradition and modernity are played out on the lived body. US feminist scientist Donna Haraway's *A Cyborg Manifesto* (1992)[4] unpacks, with its wry humour, the ways in which Western science and politics are woven through racism and colonialism into the language of development, underdevelopment and modernization. Haraway suggests, somewhat hopefully, that in the early twenty-first century there is now a breakthrough in knowledge, with new technologies opening up the possibility of questioning the body in new ways. Offering a more positive perspective than many, she sees the new communication and bio technologies as fresh sources of power to be harnessed by feminists. Borrowing the term from the famous Boston Women's Health Collective's bestselling manual *Our Bodies, Ourselves* (2005) Haraway sees female bodies as maps of power.[5]

Bodies and power

Feminist analysis, as set out in a complex and intriguing literature, and no doubt in many unrecorded conversations, email exchanges and workshops, importantly challenges whose nature and whose reason decides the properties, qualities, identities and realities of female bodies. When this challenge is posted, the lived experience of the female body ceases to be an obstacle to knowledge, and becomes a vehicle for making and remaking the world (Bordo 1993; Weiz 1998; Haraway 1997b).

Such feminist analysis encourages us to go deeper into a vision of bodies removed from essentialist, naturalistic and scientific modes of explanation in order to position bodies as sites of contestation in a series of economic, political, sexual and intellectual struggles. If we understand that knowledge on bodies is irreducibly interwoven with other discourses – social, colonial, ethical and economic – we can strategically reconceptualize bodies as cultural products on which the play of powers, knowledges and resistances are worked out. Rather than fearing that reclaiming bodies erases other aspects of women's reality, we can move away from the concept that women are their bodies in ways men are not. Particular aspects of female embodiment (such as pregnancy, rape and aging) become privileged sites of significance bearing on how female experience is lived and changed (Flax 1992; Fox Keller and Longins 1996; Shildrick 1997; Shildrick and Price 1998).

Women and the politics of place

An example of how this analysis is used in feminist practice is a research project which I coordinated with US-based Colombian anthropologist Arturo Escobar in the early 2000s. The project, entitled 'women and the politics of place', looked at place-based struggles of women who challenge 'globalo-centric' frameworks of development (Harcourt and Escobar 2005). The project explored how women act as conscious agents in the challenge to neo-liberal global economic systems. Such women are keenly aware of the conditions of their embodiment, including health, sexuality, security, the right to pleasure and rest, and the need to care for community and environment. As women mobilize for change around the body, home, local environs and community, we argued they were creating a form of politics which we call 'place-based', with the body as the first 'place'.[6]

The findings of this project offer some useful entry points for a deeper understanding of bodies as a place for political mobilization interconnected with other sites of resistance and political action. This project suggests that bodies are not external to political processes but firmly enmeshed in them, even if they are not necessarily the defining site for action. The lived experience of the body, the identity and definitions attached to bodies, inform and are connected to all political struggles. In the women and the politics of place project we found that oppressive experiences of the lived female body – the confinement, the violations, the invisibility – were often resisted in struggles for citizenship, environmental and land rights. Women engaging in broader ecological or political resistance were often in the process needing to challenge bodily violations, and legal or cultural discrimination. One story in the book, from Papua New Guinea, illustrates this. Yvonne Underhill-Sem, a Pacific Island researcher, describes how a young Papua New Guinean village woman copes with changes in her bodily experience. When she first meets the young woman her body visibly bears the marks of disease, violation and pregnancy. Having left her village after domestic abuse, she is beaten and alone, searching for a job as a domestic worker in the town. Later, the young woman reappears in the narrative as a healthy young mother. Her body, but not her spirit, is marked by the experience of violation and pregnancy. Underhill-Sem uses that story to look at how Pacific Islanders have negotiated Christianity and its regulation of their bodies, particularly maternal bodies, in the process of development in ways that mixed tradition with modernity. Through their trangressions of Christian teachings and Western medical hegemony she illustrates how they were carefully manoeuvring the webs of power in their community (Underhill-Sem 2005: 21–30).

Understanding the body as the place 'closest in' and working from the micro-practices around female bodies to the broader picture helps to demonstrate how bodies are embedded, sometimes invisibly, in macro development discourses (Beasely and Bacchi 2000). Examining the ways in which lived bodily experiences are negotiated as politicized domains discloses the norms associated with the universalizing and essentializing of female bodies (Nast and Pile 1998; Howson 2005).

The body in this sense is an important political terrain or 'place' for feminist politics. Bodies are not separate from politics; indeed, their embodiment – their corporeal, fleshly, material existence – determines political relations. In calling attention to bodies as political subjects, feminists recognize that 'we are our bodies'. The political self is not distinct from the body. Our experience of ourselves, our cultural, political and social identity, is an embodied one, determined by our relations to other bodies. In order to lodge bodies in their physical and social particularities, theoretically we have to move from the instrumentalizing of the body as an object, to understanding the body as a subject, central to power, gender and culture, by acknowledging the fleshly bodies of women – in birth, breastfeeding, menstruating, their material experience of sex, pregnancy, violation, rape – and thus bringing the experiences of bodies into political discourse. This understanding reverses the suggestion that bodies are 'mired in biology' (Beasely and Bacchi 2000) and are therefore disqualified from politics. It also underlines that 'other' bodies that do not 'conform' to the male heterosexual norm (such as female, lesbian, black or disabled bodies) should not be constructed as having biological 'limitations' to overcome or to be negotiated; their fleshly embodiment is present and integral to political realities.

Body politics in gender and development

These insights into political meanings of fleshly and gendered bodies as well as the Foucauldian concept of biopolitics and biopower give an analytical context to political struggles around bodies in development. They suggest why body politics is often where women first find themselves mobilizing for their rights, in the process finding their political voice in the field of gender and development.[7] Through body politics the embodied experience of the female body became an entry point for political engagement (fighting for abortion rights, 'reclaim the night' marches, protesting against the use of rape as a weapon of war, and protesting against beauty pageants). Gender differences are marked out on the body in cultural, social, economic and political positioning. Such external markings – bruises and scars from violations; poisoned systems and worn-out limbs from exploitation in the field or factories; tears and prolapses from too many pregnancies; culturally induced physical restrictions caused by high heels, breast implants or the veil – are as much part of a gender political struggle in development as the demand for equal pay for equal work, gender quotas in parliament or drinkable safe water.

The body plays an invisible and yet also contested role in development discourse, even if most people working in the field would ask what the body and even gender have to do with the 'hard-core issues' of trade, security and economics.

In this book I tell very specific stories of gender and development practice around reproduction, caring, violence, sexuality and technologies. Those stories are vignettes set against the much broader panorama of gender and development policy and practice. My major focus is on the policy and practice of gender and development as constructed through the UN arena. I look at the shaping of the gender and development agenda by governments and UN agencies, funding foundations, academic research centres and policy institutes, as well as the contribution of the civil society groups which imploded during this period.[8]

Gender and development as an evolving strategy

It is difficult to categorize gender and development as a set of stable institutional arrangements. To begin with, the strategy of having specific gender focal points as well as gender mainstreaming throughout development has led to overburdened and underfunded 'experts'. On the one hand they are singled out as doing 'gender', something often not understood by their colleagues, while on the other hand they are asked to be experts in all areas of development in order to 'mainstream' gender. Beyond being set a difficult political and technical task, gender and development experts often feel they are marginalized from the mainstream debates and funding arrangements, and offered little in the way of human and funding resources. They see themselves as struggling to survive in an unfriendly environment. Many move in and out of different institutions to survive. At the same time, people outside the institutional arrangements of the UN and governments, or large NGOs, are often critical of gender 'experts' inside the mainstream institutions. These groups distance themselves from the gender and development mainstream, yet they accept funding and work with those inside the institutions to negotiate policy. In this sense gender and development is fluid in practice. Though the 'technical' practice and aims of gender and development are set by various conventions at the UN and government level, it has shifting targets, and many of those working on gender and development move in and out of jobs at various levels of engagement.

This is not surprising, because the practice of gender and development is itself part of a very fluid set of arrangements known by some as the 'development industry' (Cornwall 2006; Cornwall, *et al.* 2007). The first time I stepped into a Society for International Development (SID) meeting, as described in my Introduction, I saw how the term development itself is under continual scrutiny. There were heated debates among the leaders in the international development community about how to understand development: various measures included economic growth, meeting basic needs, fulfilling human welfare, putting in place sustainable environmental development, keeping the peace, and redistributing wealth among rich and poor countries. There were differentiated positions among those working for development in the Bretton Woods institutions, UN agencies, governments, communication, academic and policy institutes, and those working with what were called grassroot organizations ('NGOs' – non-governmental organizations – was not yet a universally recognized term). There were marked differences between those living and working in the South and those based in the North, and very few voices from business sectors or from the East. At the edge of the discussions in a pre-conference session was the section on 'women in development'.

Civil society as an agent in development

My book covers the twenty-year period from 1988 to 2008, partly because those are the years in which I have been engaged in development but also because this period marked the end of the Cold War and the rise of civil society as a major player in international development. It was in this period that the women's movements emerged as one of the main protagonists in the UN sphere. Spaces opened up for dissent as the development project first envisaged as state planning to engineer and lift the world from poverty had floundered. As the discussions in the SID New Delhi Conference indicated, the international development community could no longer confidently propose easy 'universal' (in reality Western) models and solutions for state-led development.[9] What was debated in 1988 was the need to move from state public-sponsored programmes to private solutions and market demand-led policy, increasingly subject to policy conditionality led by the IMF and World Bank, and to pro-market orientation and economic liberalization.

The questioning of the success of development and the failure of the state to deliver, as well as the end of the Cold War, opened up entry points for civil society groups to become politically engaged in UN global processes. These movements, clustered under the umbrella title of NGOs, emerged in the 1990s as a third actor in the development community.

The strength of civil society as a political actor in development debates became visible in the first half of the 1990s with an intense series of UN conferences held in the wake of the fall of the Berlin Wall. It was a hopeful period, with talk about the peace dividend, human global security, and sustainable development. During these UN conferences development shifted from the concept of aid and progress from North to South (by delivering technology and resources that would lead to economic growth and, eventually, institutionalized state development) to a much more politicized concern with delivering human rights and a more holistic concept of development.

For women's rights activists this was an exciting period when 'women in development', the marginalized 'pre-conference' of the SID gathering, became a much stronger political force in shaping 'human rights' and 'sustainable development' agendas. Campaigns over trade, agriculture, water, debt forgiveness, human rights, gender equality, climate, violence and conflict, and sexual and reproductive rights became a modern form of political action led by civil society actors in the UN 'transnational arena'. In these debates at UN conferences, and in the policies that emerged in response to the participation of women's rights and feminist groups, gender and development policy was framed.

The 1990s UN conferences

This book highlights the interactions of UN agencies and policies and women's rights groups in these debates in order to trace some of the key themes of the international gender and development discourse: the human rights framework, economic and social justice, political and legal rights, and, within these themes, global body politics. In particular, I look at some of the debates around the UN conferences on environment and development in Rio de Janeiro in 1992, on population in Cairo in 1994, on human rights in Vienna in 1993, on social development in Copenhagen and on women in Beijing in 1995.

These conferences on different facets of development were key international events that consolidated gender and development practices. As they moved through different topics, so did the gender and development expertise expand from the environment to rights, population, social development, habitat, women, food, trade and finance. Women, as both objects and subjects, became part of the public sphere of development discourse.

As the chapters on reproductive, productive and caring and violated bodies will discuss in detail, what emerged in these discussions was a complex set of assumptions about female and male embodiment. These assumptions were built into a series of discursive practices that created the gender and development wing of the development industry.

Even while protesting at the disempowering impacts of development, producing counter-knowledge and proposing other practices, women (and some men) engaged in 'gender and development' were tied into a Foucauldian array of micro strategies. In other words, the procedures, analysis, reflections, calculations and tactics around the UN arena defined female bodies as subjects of development. These discourses simplified the vastly different experiences of women around the world who come from hugely varied cultures and backgrounds. Through the UN official texts, background reports, statistics and evidence, these experiences became the generic gendered female body – poor women with an expertly understood set of needs and rights. They were depicted in various guises.[10] They were characterized as victims in need of aid, then as working subjects with productive potential, willing and useful agents for development. These messages, often not so hidden, reinterpreted the women's rights movements' arguments for autonomy, rights and gender equality. The complex links between health, reproductive life cycles, the caring economy, the market economy, the environment and what was increasingly summarized as globalization were repackaged by technical expertise into understandable development concerns. They were put through the UN machine of debate and policy making and came out as the issues that governments could agree to, but lacked the resources and capacity to carry out in reality.

The gender and development discourse, despite all of the attempts to connect social, economic and gender justice, smoothed away the links in its practice and language. In the biopolitics of the management of gender, women's rights, the female body, women and gender issues remained as the 'soft' issues of development. So, when it came to why there were no real reforms that took these concerns into account – or why there was less and less money to train women, provide health services, or counter violence against women – the answer could always be that there were other more pressing concerns to deal with: war, failed states, internal conflict, economic crisis, restructuring, liberalizing markets, security, trade agreements . . . In the end, it seemed, these did not have much to do with women's demands, figures and case studies, which were mostly still considered as micro-level adjuncts to the 'hard' macro development issues.

As this book discusses in each of its chapters, the attempts of the global women's rights movement to bring women's multiple needs and concerns into the development discourse became translated in the process of development body politics into an essentially passive productive, reproductive and sexualized female body. This female body was managed and understood through various mechanisms created in development discourse as engaged in particular types of work with specific health and education needs, as well as needing special protection from conflict, violence or unfair work practices, and sexual exploitation and domestic injustice.

In this sense the female body (roughly understood in the 'different' characteristics of 'women in' the 'Global South': South Asia, sub-Saharan Africa, the Arab region, Central and Latin America, East Asia and the Pacific and Eastern Europe) was there to be measured, counted and compared across regions. Discussions were held on what the ordinary woman could expect in the diverse regions from different experiences during moments in her life cycle. In this way development policy could predict, monitor, and try to change and better her life with more education, better health, more solid investments and more advantageous markets and trade regimes. Women who lived in North America, Europe and Australasia (the Global North) were not part of this set of biopolitical strategies. Nor were migrants or indigenous women, who were self-defined as 'Fourth World' women and were largely outside official UN gender and development debates, as were transgender people and queer activists. Women from the 'Global North' were lumped together as the 'developed woman' representing the wealth and values of the

West. It was assumed that they did not need 'developing' as they had, more or less, the money, access, rights and status for which these other groups of women in the rest of the world needed to strive.

Beijing 1995

The Conference on Women in Beijing in 1995 marked the peak of women's rights interest in the UN as a political space (Razavi and Miller 1995). Apart from the numbers actually attending Beijing – 40,000 in total at the official and NGO conferences – there were many thousands directly in contact with the discussions through media and the new information and communication technologies. Over 100,000 hits were made on the official website during Beijing (Harcourt 1999) and the resulting document, the Beijing Platform for Action, remains the benchmark for global women's rights. Peggy Antrobus, a vocal feminist leader from the southern research network Development for Women in a New Era (DAWN), recollects that in Beijing:

> Women ... had moved beyond a narrow definition of women's issues to advance women's perspectives on a range of global issues – macro-economic policy, environment, human rights, population, poverty, employment, food and trade ... the Conference and the NGO Forum were celebrations of the women's movement ... it was, in a sense, a showcase for the international women's movement. (Antrobus 2004: 63)

In the decade following Beijing, development took on a different political dimension (Petchesky 2002; Sen and Corrêa 2000; UNRISD 2005). High-level roundtables, commissions and expert-group meetings replaced the big UN conferences and NGO fora attached to them in a UN-wide process after 2000 that reduced the development agenda to the Millennium Development Goals (MDGs). Since 2000 the MDGs have become the primary global development framework within the UN system.

The overall goal of the MDGs is to halve global poverty by the year 2015, to make donor countries more accountable, and to live up to all the promises of the UN conferences (Sachs 2005). The MDGs are eight measurable and defined goals (with 48 indicators attached) and a host of UN mechanisms to ensure them – national reports, global campaigns, research projects, and

UN-wide monitoring and statistical assessments. Women's empowerment is measured in Goal Three by the level of girls' primary and secondary education and another goal aimed at reducing maternal mortality. For the rest, gender is stated as a cross-cutting theme in areas of concern such as health systems and human rights, though none of these have clear indicators. Issues highlighted in earlier UN conferences – such as economic justice for women, sexuality, reproductive rights and health, and violence against women – went missing.

Body politics in the new social movements

With the reductionist agenda of the MDGs in the early 2000s, feminist activists shifted their focus away from the UN as the only site of social transformation for women's rights. They began to engage more with social movements, in particular the protest movements against the IMF, World Bank and the G8 that exploded in Seattle in 2002 and continued to meet and grow exponentially in the various World Social Forums (WSFs) (Kerr *et al.* 2004; Harcourt 2006). The World Social Forum emerged as one potential site for feminists to engage in the attempt to build an autonomous space for social movements and civil society around campaigns on trade, poverty, climate change, food and security, gender equality and human rights under the slogan 'another world is possible'.

In the WSF process a group of feminist networks met in a series of Feminist Dialogues (FDs)[11] which have positioned the body as central to feminist analysis and cultural, social, economic and political struggle (Jones 2005; Vargas 2005; Feminist Dialogues 2007). The focus of the FDs in the World Social Forum has been on the rise of fundamentalism, cultural and economic repression, and violence. Specifically, they are interested in understanding the impact of global capitalism on gender relations and resistance to an assortment of hegemonies – the George W. Bush administration, the Vatican, the Islamism of Bin Laden, the Catholicism of Latin America, Eastern European regimes, Hindu fundamentalism in South Asia – and how from this analysis it is possible to build a new form of radical democracy. Feminists in the WSF challenge the binaries that simplify complex gender relations into public and private, nature and culture, biology and technology, men and women, and the norm of heterosexuality in gender relations.

The Feminist Dialogues

In the FD debates, as this book will show, the technical focus of gender and development on delivering programmes to ensure women's human, social and economic development is challenged. Instead, the dialogues look at how to transform relationships between people – with their diverse bodies and sexualities – into new forms of social and political relations that are not dominated by political and economic hegemonies. Rather than looking at how to 'empower' economic female or male subjects of global capitalism, the FD project is to create conditions that allow lived bodies with diverse social, cultural and political expressions to flourish. Body politics implies politicizing the private sphere, revealing the close, lived relationship between sexuality and democracy. Naming the politics of personal/interpersonal relations is a way both to democratize the private sphere and to bring daily life into the political sphere. This understanding of body politics, explored in the following chapters, is a critical dimension of newly emerging paradigms which are being fostered in the interactions between autonomous feminist movements and transnational economic, environmental and social movements.

Body politics as counter-culture

Body politics, in this setting, is part of a counter-culture that makes visible the invisible and names what is uncomfortable in gendered relations. The body becomes an 'impertinent way of knowing'. Talking about violence in the home, rape, repression and homophobia, or challenging 'traditions' – those that veil women, put their feet in high-heeled shoes, condone and institutionalize inequalities in the workplace or in the public meeting spaces that silence women, and build on male fears – these are impertinences to the givens, to the norms and the unspoken social and cultural rules.

Body politics is one contribution of feminism to a construction of counter-power that confronts hegemonic culture and economy. This hegemonic power has made the body a war zone, violated and plundered in the case of women, children, lesbians, homosexuals and transgenders. A wide range of violations map out the war zone: women raped in armed conflicts; denial of sexual and reproductive rights; racism that discriminates because of skin colour; ageism that stereotypes and uses young bodies. Body politics in these struggles emerges as a strong movement of resistance and expansion of rights linking the political dimension of the body with a radical form of democracy.

Feminist body politics at the World Social Forum

Feminists in the World Social Forum put several key issues of body politics on the political agenda. The first issue is women's reproductive capacity as the historical mechanism for subjugating women in economic, political, social, cultural and sexual spheres. They argue that reproduction is a right and a pleasure when it is freely decided. It is a source of pain, stigma and intolerance when this freedom is constrained by religious teachings, moral influences, or economic limitations. The feminist struggle aims to liberate reproductive rights from the framework of reproductive health, which is sustained by the traditional role of women in heterosexual relations, leaving aside other sexual diversities such as reproduction among lesbian women. Another key struggle in this framework is to overcome the legal and cultural systems that deny women the right to decide on abortion.

The opening up of the debates on sexuality has led to a growing recognition and celebration of the diversity of genders. The Feminist Dialogues see masculine, feminine, transvestite, androgynous and intersex expressions of sexuality as available to everybody and permanently in flux. At the core of these discussions is the theorizing around sex work and the politics of desire as debated in queer theory.

Today's global industry of pleasure is built on the sexualized body, creating in the process desire as a product to be developed, sold and consumed. Through diverse channels the market turns sexual freedom into a profit-making enterprise and ends up objectifying sexual relationships. Sexual pleasure is stigmatized and subject to stringent prohibitions. This is especially true for women, young people and those with 'other' sexual orientations. Monopolized by the specific vision of masculine sexuality, sexual norms can be repressive for women and all people whose bodies do not fit the hegemonic heterosexual norm. Pleasure is rarely the subject of development discourse, yet it informs many of the latter's interactions and concerns, as the chapter on sexualized bodies shows.

Another political concern is the new reproductive technologies and new stimulants for good sexual functioning. On the one hand, these technologies offer the potential to liberate; on the other hand, they are often dehumanized by profit and commercialism. The political struggle is to reject the commercialization of the new technologies, and look at how to democratize the use of scientific technologies so that they extend rights. Examples are discussions on the rights of lesbians to have access to reproductive technologies or rights to reconstruct the body. Yet, as the chapter on technobodies indicates, it is urgent to have controls in place and to alert the public about the threat of the dehumanizing potential of the new technologies and their ethically worrying profit motive.

Going beyond the rhetoric

I have described how I define body politics through my engagement with feminist academic theory, gender and development policy debates and transnational feminist political struggles. It is not easy for me to divide these three sets of understandings and practices of body politics into neat categories. All three have informed the way I have experienced/lived global body politics in gender and development. The contradictions and overlaps are evident in the chapters that follow. I, like many others, am tired of the unexamined rhetoric surrounding gender and development.

To quote Andrea Cornwall:

> The dominant thinking about women and development has become mired in a progressive-sounding orthodoxy that fails to engage with the realities of women's experience and aspirations around the world . . . feel good talk about women is gaining ground: one that puts women at the forefront of achieving peace, prosperity and democracy. Empower women, the story goes, and they will become the motor of development. (Cornwall 2007)[12]

Cornwall's image of gender and development masquerading as the 'real thing' through policies of 'empowerment lite' shows tough feminist questions and policies turned into a simulacrum. Such policies conflate power with money (the mantra is, Give the poor money and all is solved) and assume away the difficulties of changing social norms, institutions and relationships that are part of gendered realities.

It is politically important to refocus attention on the personal experiences of the women and men who are subjects of development and on what they have learnt from their own travels along diverse pathways of empowerment.

I include as subjects of development feminists like myself in the Global North who contribute to the theory and practice of gender and development and share responsibility for its framing, funding, success and failures.

This book, then, is about turning the gaze on feminists' engagement with gender and development around body politics. As Cornwall states:

> Feminists have long recognised that it is when women recognise their 'power within' and act together with other women to exercise 'power with', that they gain 'power to' act as agents. Feminist experience has shown that this is a process that may take a diversity of pathways, but for which there are rarely the kind of short-cuts envisaged by the proponents of empowerment-lite. (Cornwall 2007)[13]

The book aims to cut away the tangle of assumptions and stereotypes that have filled the field of gender and development. Starting from the lives of women as they feel and experience political, social, economic and cultural change on and through their bodies, it brings under critical scrutiny the taken-for-granted assumptions about what Cornwall calls gender and development 'empowerment-lite and democracy-lite'. Gender policy tools for institutional design do little to redress the power issues that lie at the heart of the cultures and conduct of politics itself. Opening up a feminist debate on development means asking new questions about what politics is about. It is not only about getting women and minority groups into power. It is about a body politics that shifts the meanings of the private and public spheres that relate to reproduction, care and work, sexuality, pleasure, violence, science and technologies.

Notes

1   Rio hosted the UN Conference on Environment and Development in 1992, Vienna the UN Conference on Human Rights held in 1993, Cairo the UN Conference on Population in 1994, and Beijing the fourth UN Conference on Women in 1995.

2   See *Development*, Vol. 52, No. 1 (March 2009) on 'Sexuality and Development'.

3   In 2000 the World Bank collected the voices of more than 60,000 poor women and men from 60 countries, in an effort to understand poverty from the perspective of the poor themselves. This participatory research initiative is called *Voices of the Poor*, and chronicles the struggles and aspirations of poor people for a life of dignity. See <http://go.worldbank.org/H1N8746X10>. For another way of understanding health and poverty, published in the same year, see the study *Dying for Growth* by a group of Harvard doctors and scholars (Kim *et al.* 2000).

4 The full text of Donna Haraway's 'A cyborg manifesto: science, technology, and socialist-feminism in the late twentieth century' is available on the Internet. See <http://www.stanford.edu/dept/HPS/Haraway/CyborgManifesto.html>.

5 Published in over 20 languages, the current (twelfth) edition of *Our Bodies, Ourselves* was published in 2005. The Boston Women's Health Collective offers a range of other books, along with a detailed website fostering a cyberwomen's health movement through blogs, reviews of medical journals and regular postings of up-to-date information on a range of women's health issues. See <http://www.ourbodiesourselves.org>.

6 Specific examples given in the book from the lives of the writers include: setting up the first women-led media in Tanzania; training women in Central America to conserve their local environments; and how women from Jordan use embroidery to maintain their local culture and history as they move to live in new places.

7 In a conversation with women from India, Malaysia, Kenya, Peru and Mexico at the Feminist Dialogues in Nairobi, January 2007, we remarked on how all of us entered into feminism through volunteer work at rape crisis centres, and how we all in the process shared intimate stories with women from different class, sexual identity, race and cultural backgrounds about female health issues and violence against women.

8 See Petchesky 2002; Antrobus 2004; Charckiewicz 2004; Kerr *et al*. 2004; Riccutelli *et al*. 2004; Fraser and Tinker 2004; UN 2005; and Harcourt 2006 for more detail on different shifts in women's rights movements and global body politics.

9 There are many important books that give this critique in detail, and it is one the journal *Development* has explored over the last two decades. Two of the most influential writers are Wolfgang Sachs (who edited the journal before I did) and Arturo Escobar, with whom I have worked with since 1993 and who has been a key influence on both development scholarship and the direction of the journal. See *The Development Dictionary* edited by Wolfgang Sachs (1992) and Escobar's *Encountering Development: the Making and Unmaking of the Third World* (1993). One of the issues of *Development* that captures this debate succinctly is *Development* Vol. 47, No. 1 (1997), entitled 'Violence of Development'.

10 As Betsy Hartmann, environmentalist and feminist research activist based in the US, argues in her paper 'Eve is black, primitive and pregnant and her reproduction is the Original Sin', published in the *Indian Journal of Gender Studies*, the negative images have a reservoir of core stereotypes that resonate deeply in the psyche of believers – in this case, the religious power in the United States concerned about overpopulation (Betsy Hartmann 2005b, email correspondence, 20 May 2005).

11 I refer to the Feminist Dialogues in other chapters of the book. For more information and statements about the FDs, see the website managed by ISIS International Manila: <http://feministdialogues.isiswomen.org/>.

12 Andrea Cornwall is a fellow of the Institute of Development Studies at the University of Sussex, England who has helped shape much of the new thinking on sexuality and development through her writings and research with notably Susie Jolly – and the DFID project Pathways of Empowerment – I refer to their work in more depth in Chapter 6.

13 Taken from the contribution of Cornwall to the Open Democracy Blog on 28 July 2007, <http://www.opendemocracy.net/trackback/34188>.

Venezuela There are 60,000 births a year to women under 15 years of age.

USA 30% of US girls become pregnant before the age of 20.

Bulgaria Youngest first-time mothers in Europe (average age 24.7 years).

Bangladesh Around half of all girls are married by the age of 15; 60% are mothers by the age of 19.

South Korea It is estimated that 50% of women in their twenties have had cosmetic surgery.

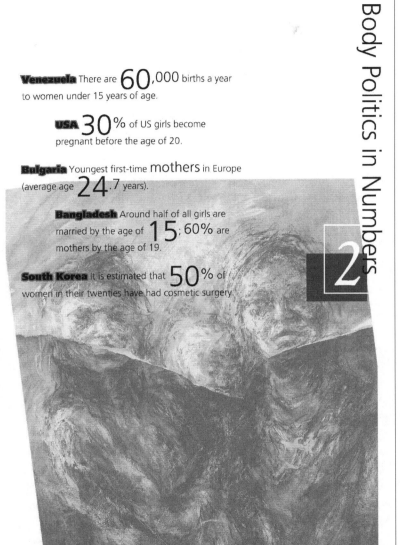

2

Two

Reproductive Bodies

Population and development: four entry points

The biological ability to give birth, to be a mother, is one of the most unquestioned or apparently 'natural' concepts associated with the female body. It is certainly one of the most powerful social and cultural constructs of feminine identity. It is also a concept feminists have long opened to scrutiny (Rich 1979; Nakano Glenn *et al*. 1994; Dinnerstein 1999; Chodorow 1999). There have been many books devoted to various aspects of reproduction, from celebrations of the biological ability to give birth as the most exalted task of womanhood to dissecting motherhood as a form of biological oppression (Firestone 1979). In this chapter I look at how being aware of embodiment can unsettle naturalized assumptions about reproduction in gender and development policy; in doing so I examine shifts in population and development discourse in the past two decades.

I try to understand body politics in population and development debates via four entry points. The first is the transnational effort to build and maintain what became known as the 'Cairo Agenda', with a focus on reproductive rights and health, in the early and mid-1990s. The second is the strategic shift to maternal health and mortality with the introduction of the Millennium Development Goals in 2000. Both of these engaged development policy experts and feminist movements in a series of transnational processes focused around the United Nations Conference on Population and Development held in 1994, together with subsequent reviews and policy mutations. The third, which overlaps with the first two, is the debate about the health of the population, what has been termed the Malthus Factor. The last, which is

38

perhaps more a question than an entry point, is the silence about the reproductive male body and the non-reproductive female body as the subjects or objects of reproductive policies, practices and engagements.

Biopolitics and population and development

As discussed in Chapter 1, Foucault's concept of biopolitics situates power in modern discourse as more than a vertical set of relations where people are forced to obey authority. It is also a more complex set of power relations 'over life' that are horizontally produced and embedded in language and practice. In development discourse many biopolitical strategies around the body intersect and cross-pollinate. In this chapter I look at how biopolitical practices of family planning, medicine, public health, population and reproductive rights mobilization in the 1990s and 2000s produced gendered bodies as contested objects and subjects of both micro-level practices of power and, at the global level, macro-strategies of domination.

Cutting right to the core of the issue, let us look at the promotion of contraception as an example of how biopolitics is played out in population and development policy. Contraception is understood in many ways, as immoral, liberating, oppressive or emancipatory. In population and development policy practice, contraception has become part of the modern, natural order of things.

Contraception

Contraceptive choice, at least in my heterosexual experience, has never been entirely straightforward, even if as a Western educated woman I have had knowledge of and access to family planning facilities since I was a teenager. Nevertheless, I found the idea of the pill disturbing, condoms not exactly reliable and the diaphragm, well, uncomfortable. However, I tried out at various times all three and was lucky enough to choose successfully the timing of my two pregnancies. I considered such choice a right, though not always an easy right to exercise. Choices and services were available and it seemed to me that my private individual choices were reasonably respected. I remember being mildly amused when I moved to Italy and a Catholic doctor suggested my use of contraception caused uterine fibroids. I was annoyed that diaphragms and spermicides were not available in Italy, but these adjustments were nothing I personally could not handle. No doubt my choices and medical visits are recorded in medical surveys somewhere, as are the births of my children. I consider myself lucky to have steered my way reasonably successfully through what is offered by public health services in three countries of the Global North. But this modern sense of choice in the Western elite setting I enjoy was not what I came across in my first visit to sub-Saharan African countries in 1990.

I vividly recall a week's visit to Ruhengeri, a city in the North Province of Rwanda. I was visiting a variety of women in development projects and my (male) guide in Ruhengeri interpreted my request to meet local women as visiting various clinics which he ran as a family planning doctor and a representative of the United Nations Population Fund (UNFPA) office. I was taken to a rural village not far from the Congolese (then Zaïrian) border where – after an early morning session with hoes, planting yams and eating some grassy goat guts and plantains on skewers which the men accompanying me washed down with beer and I with lemonade – I finally met some of the women. They lined up politely and I was invited to ask questions. At this point, feeling somewhat queasy after the skewered goat guts, I asked my guide to introduce women. To my embarrassment as I filed down shaking each of their hands, he told me not their names or opinions but how many children they had borne, what type of contraception they used, if they had had miscarriages and if they had had their tubes tied. They smiled proudly as he described their reproductive history to me, and the one young man at the end of the line positively beamed when I was informed that he had had a vasectomy after two children. I was then ushered into the clinic, which, unlike the thatched huts housing the people, the butcher shop and the meagre store, was brick with glass windows, colourful posters on the walls, and a large chart which detailed various contraceptive methods. Underneath the chart were white wooden benches where women sat waiting to see the clinic's nurse. I was shown the equipment and the register of all the people who attended the clinic, with its careful detailing of the number of condoms, pills and operations performed. Rwanda, I was told, as I was whizzed back to my hotel, had far too many children, leading to poverty and preventing development, and my guide was on the front line to reduce these numbers.

Somewhat in contrast to my own contraceptive and reproductive history, this anecdote shows how 'targeted' women's lives and choices in poor 'over-populated' countries were reduced to numbers and charts that measure 'population goals'. Though these women were no doubt benefiting from reproductive health care, its top-down delivery through modern medical interventions with funds for population 'control' is in strong contrast with other aspects of their lives.[1] The focus is on delivering the quotas set by the UNFPA programme and approved by the government, rather than on the rights and choices of the women and men involved.

Building the Cairo Agenda

The historical event which helped to unsettle and question such practices, while some would argue also confirming them, is the International Conference on Population and Development held in Cairo from 5 to 13 September 1994. In my reckoning this was one of the most fêted international development events in the 1990s, led officially by UNFPA, which managed the intergovernmental negotiations. Cairo, as it is usually referred to in gender and development debates, mobilized many thousands of women's health and rights movements to come together, and it produced the Cairo Programme of Action, which set the agenda for population and development policy for the next decade.

Cairo has had major implications for all those involved in women's health and rights movements. This history is still unfolding and is certainly one that overlaps with other discussions in the book. Cairo was an important event because it gathered together many groups and brought feminist voices directly into the public debate regarding body politics. Cairo was itself the result of a long process linked to other major events, beginning with the first UN population and development meeting in Mexico in 1984; it was closely linked to the Conference on Women's Human Rights in Vienna in 1993. These processes gave the women caucausing in Cairo knowledge and skills to push their agenda further and shift the population paradigm from numbers to women's sexual and reproductive rights.

Women's networks proclaimed in a strategy meeting held in Rio de Janeiro just before Cairo that:

> Reproductive and sexual rights are about self-determination in matters of procreation and sexuality. . . . Reproductive rights are about us being in charge of our bodies/ourselves, our freedom to express ourselves sexually and to be free from abuse. (Women's Voices '94, 1993)

It was exciting to me and many others that once-tabooed topics were on the table in an international arena. Much has been written on the story of Cairo from a transnational women's movement perspective.[2] I am not going to repeat here the official texts and agreements;[3] I am more interested in the analysis of the different positions in the debate, particularly those thrashed out by women's health and rights movements.

Consensus or compromise?

The Cairo Agenda contained within it some major contradictions. It was heralded as a huge gain for women's rights and gender and development, but also as deeply disappointing and problematic. In part this is obvious: it relies simply on moral suasion, because the final outcome was a declaration rather than a legally binding convention. What it promised and what was put into action are two different things. Even if Cairo still retains a sense of major achievement as a negotiated and agreed text by governments with important inputs by women's movements, the sense of it making a difference to actual lives has unravelled – as I explore below – even as the Agenda is defended.[4]

Cairo was the third population conference organized by the UN and represented a paradigm shift in the discourse about population and development. The Cairo Programme of Action, endorsed by 179 countries at the conference and preceded by many months of national and regional negotiations, was heralded as a comprehensive way forward for international and national population policy. It was the first international policy document to promote the concepts of reproductive rights and reproductive health. It marked an unusual moment of consensus among population and environment activists, demographers, women's movements and medical and public health experts and development bureaucrats. The conference saw a significant shift from a decades-old paradigm focused on population policies designed to reduce fertility and population growth to one that emphasized the reproductive health and rights of women.

Let me give a quick indication of what the Cairo Programme of Action covered. Following the Preamble and the Principles, chapters are divided into three main areas:

1. *Population and development concerns* (such as interrelationships between population, economic growth and sustainable development; international

into action the promises made. They pressured their governments to place reproductive health high on the political agenda. After a long battle creating public opinion to force the government to make good its promise to 'save women's lives and to respect women's reproductive rights', on March 2002 the Nepalese bill to legalize abortion passed through the House of Representative with 147 votes in favour and one against.

Uprety saw this as a victory for all who had worked hard to put into action the reproductive health and rights agenda through networking, media, dialogue, writings and research. Her challenge continues as she disseminates information about the new law and the facts about safe abortion to doctors, health workers, advocates, law enforcement officials and politicians in order to ensure that services are available for women in rural areas, that the legal boundaries are respected, and that sex-selective abortion is avoided (Uprety 2005).

Others who have written for the journal *Development* on the topic saw the unravelling of Cairo as part and parcel of the rapidly increasing social fractures and insecurities. Working in a Ugandan women's communication NGO, ISIS-WICCE, Ruth Ojiambo Ochieng described how post-Cairo projects on adolescent health failed due to 'lack of qualified staff with minimal skills in handling sexual and reproductive health issues within the community, lack of remuneration and cultural limitations' (Ojiambo Ochieng 2003). Farida Akhter from UBNIG in Bangladesh underlined that post-Cairo governments gave priority to population control programmes by reducing funding for basic primary health services in order to fulfil conditionalities set by donors (Akhter 2004). The official preoccupation with contraception and sterilization ignored other factors that influence fertility and health. The cost of an imported injection of Depo Provera (a questionable form of contraception rarely used in the Global North) is close to 4,000 rupees per year per woman; such an expensive item competes with essential life-saving drugs.

Economic insecurity, loss of livelihoods and the loss of state services opened the way for the strengthening of fundamentalism – religious right-wing groups that are sexist, racist, xenophobic and plain dangerous for women's rights and health. Internationally and nationally, the political economic and cultural disruption of these fundamentalists (whether in the US or other parts of the world) in this period dismantled women's rights to express their sexual and reproductive rights and to have access to resources that assure life choices leading to health and well-being.

Reproductive health, rights and choice were ultimately subsumed in the broader macro-agenda of development: trade and economic growth. Cairo defined 'reproductive rights' as the right of women 'to decide freely and responsibly the number, spacing and timing of their children and to have the information and means to do so'. Yet as Rosalind Petchesky, a US professor, key activist and writer in this field, pointed out, how can a woman

> avail herself of this right if she lacks the financial resources to pay for reproductive health services or the transport to get to them; if she is illiterate or given no information in a language she understands; if her workplace is contaminated with pollutants that have an adverse effect on pregnancy; or if she is harassed by parents, a husband or in-laws who will abuse or beat her if they find out she uses birth control. (Petchesky, quoted in Nair and Kirbat with Sexton 2004)

Cairo failed to address macro-economic inequities and the inability of prevailing neo-liberal, market-oriented approaches to deliver reproductive and sexual health for the vast majority. These failures blocked any real progress in transforming the reproductive and sexual health and rights agenda from rhetoric into policies and services. Public health activists such as the Indian Professor of Public Health Imrana Qadeer went further, arguing that the Cairo Agenda converted women's health into issues of 'safe abortion' and 'reproductive rights' and thereby 'marginalized the issue of comprehensive primary health care, social security and investment in building infrastructural facilities' (Qadeer 2005). Her colleague Mohan Rao adds that 'under the rhetoric of reproductive rights, the rights of the vast majority of women to access to resources, the most basic determinant of health, are being denied'. When reproductive rights are divested of rights to food, employment, water, health care or security of children's lives, and taken out of the contexts of women's and men's lives, they fit in well with the neo-liberal agenda of the day (Rao 2005).

Putting reproductive health and rights at the centre of population policies maintained the focus on women as reproductive bodies ('women reduced to their wombs') to the neglect of their wider economic and social roles, and of the conditions that could advance health for women.

The Millennium Development Goals and maternal health

The dissatisfaction with the Cairo Agenda pushing a reproductive rights and health agenda and not embedding it within the larger macro-economic picture was evident in the next set of strategies the women's reproductive rights and health movement engaged in: the Millennium Development Goals (MDGs). The focus of the MDGs on maternal mortality is the second entry point into the population and development debate.

The MDGs are, as explained in Chapter 1, a UN multilateral world-wide programme to halve global poverty by 2015. The stated aim of the eight MDGs, with their associated indicators and mechanisms, is to bind countries in a global partnership to eradicate extreme poverty and hunger; achieve universal primary education; promote gender equality and empower women; reduce child mortality; improve maternal health; combat HIV and AIDS, malaria and other diseases; ensure environmental sustainability; and develop a global partnership for development. Gender is considered a cross-cutting theme, though there are no clear indicators as with the other goals.[9]

Unlike the ownership expressed in the Cairo negotiations and in Vienna and Beijing, the engagement of the global women's movement with the MDGs was characterized by closed doors. UN agencies dispensed with big civil society consultations and instead funded a UN-led civil society campaign and committees of experts, with those 'in the know' advising behind closed doors. Their reports join the proliferating number of UN documents on the array of websites that the United Nations maintains as its official face to the world on the MDGs. With no open consultations, many of the women's groups at national, regional and international levels felt they were sidelined in the MDG process (Barton 2005; WEDO 2005).[10]

Engaging in the MDG process

I was invited in 2005 to do a review of the MDGs and civil society, specifically in relation to gender and development issues. In my interviews with experts and bureaucrats in the MDG process I was struck by the cynicism and the number of 'off the record' conversations I had about what really worried people, none of which I was allowed to print. As I observed more than once in and out of print, it seemed that the MDG process was doomed to failure largely because it was taking a technocratic, if not bureaucratic approach to an infinitely complex world. It seemed to be leaving the negotiating politics to others or at best to the UN corridors, while relying on 'campaigns' and 'experts' to calculate the figures and then sell the strategies to governments and civil society. No one could fault the aim to end poverty. But what kind of poverty was being addressed? Could figures and targets capture all that is needed to provide for a person's well-being? I never did receive straight-forward answers to my questions.

The narrowing down of the development agenda led to a highly selective set of topics on which development agencies and funding would focus (Sen and Corrêa 2000). What emerged as the key gender and health narrative in the MDGs is maternal mortality disengaged from the more feminist lens of reproductive rights and health. The headlines focused on the 50 million mothers suffering unnecessary ill health or death. Despite medical progress half a million women continue to die annually of pregnancy-related complications, 99 per cent of them in developing countries, the vast majority in Africa and South Asia. Maternal morbidity affects many millions more. Women and adolescent girls living in desperately poor communities continue to face overwhelming sexual and reproductive health problems. In addition, poorly managed pregnancies and deliveries result directly in millions of infant deaths each year, most of which could be prevented (Ravindran and de Pinho 2005).

Those gender and development individuals and groups who rallied around the MDG discussions politicized to some extent the technocratic approach of the MDGs by taking maternal mortality as an entry point to tackle inequalities in the health systems. They argued that maternal mortality and morbidity are not about lack of bio-medical know-how, nor simply lack of resources, but are determined by a complex mix of economic and socio-cultural factors that lead to gender discrimination, neglect and deprivation, and ultimately to the denial of women's rights to well-being (de Pinho 2005; Freedman *et al.* 2005).

I was involved in these attempts by women's groups to use the MDGs to promote a policy focus on maternal mortality. UNFPA and the Global Fund for Women gave my organization SID and partners in South Asia a grant to examine maternal mortality in the region. We looked at how to use the MDGs in order to catalyse change in the approach of South Asian governments to women's health, within which we strategically placed sexual and reproductive health. The slogan of our programme was: 'women's health, from cradle to grave'. We looked at strategic ways to deal with some of the difficult issues – now missing from the MDGs – that sexual and reproductive rights and health raised. Our language moved away from the Cairo language of autonomy and rights and instead became a much more technocratic language focused on providing services. For example, we could talk about abortion by arguing that it was an important medical service that would save mothers' lives, given that botched abortion was one of the primary causes of maternal death.

The language that suited the MDG environment was not about sexual and reproductive rights but about reducing maternal mortality and ensuring women's well-being, health and rights. The focus was on advocating for the provision of health facilities and care systems rather than women's choice, and to propose changes in funding priorities as part of shifts in national and international policies. It was about operational results, efficient use of resources and private–public partnerships. The meeting in Lahore was eye-opening in how well the NGOs shifted to fit their demands to the MDGs; it was strategic manoeuvring, but it was also a far more conservative and wary approach.

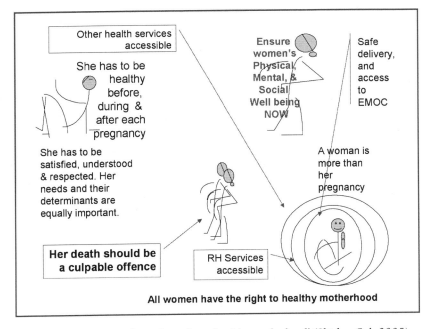

Figure 1 'All women have the right to healthy motherhood' (Shirkat Gah 2005)

This is complex, given how discussions on technical and systemic issues can blur a rights perspective. An interesting diagram taken from papers presented in Pakistan at the SID meeting on the MDGs and maternal mortality in Lahore shows a brave attempt to fuse the technical gaze on the maternal body while trying to keep women's health and rights central (see Figure 1).

This image drawn up by Karachi-based public health researcher Kausar Khan centres the reproductive female body within the social and economic development agendas. Rights of the individual woman are linked directly to social and economic development agendas. In these images the sexual and reproductive rights and health agenda is presented as a technical and managed strategy to enable poor women to access reproductive health and service provisions during pregnancy. The focus is squarely on a pregnant body that requires outside intervention, it being the professional responsibility of the health expert to ensure it.

The context that is missing in the diagram and the MDG debates is how maternal mortality is an outcome of poor general health and socio-economic constraints. The MDGs fitted in with a market-led health policy logic that is about creating new areas for investment and expansion of biomedical goods and services rather than about women's rights or health *per se*:

In the Lahore meeting this logic was challenged by Imrana Qadeer who provided the wider context to the MDG focus on the maternal body:

> maternity services are one of the most privatized and highly profitable services . . . the rising trend of Caesarian sections and sex determination tests is well recognized. . . . Micronutrient prescriptions, vaccines, contraceptives, and pregnancy diagnostic kits create a flourishing market for the medical industry. . . . We need to identify these links with the market and the conceptual distortions of public health used to justify them, within the larger political economy of the region. . . . The Bretton Woods institutions and other international funding agencies, while trans-forming the South Asian governments into stewards for the private sectors, also push them into becoming buyers through the imposition of WTO conditionalities. These mechanisms may be necessary for the promotion of global markets and multinational interests, but certainly not for the people of the region. (Qadeer 2005: 122)

Conservatism was evident in the funding agencies as well. I was totally taken aback when, after years of being given funding by UNFPA, my report on the Lahore meeting to discuss maternal mortality was carefully scrutinized. It was read not for readability or even credibility, but to ensure there was no mention of anything that would upset the right-wing George W. Bush administration and its cronies. All mention of abortion was deleted. This was March 2005 and I was high up on 42nd Street in the UNFPA New York headquarters, watching the skyline while the officer in charge of my project listened to closed UN negotiations around the Beijing +10 agreements, with his computer open on the website of conservative fundamentalist US groups, reading their instant reporting on what was being said while he struck out offending sentences. We were in a different game altogether.

Public–private partnerships

The last project I did with UNFPA funding was on public–private partnerships as part of achieving the MDG goals on reducing maternal mortality in South Asia and East Africa. For many involved in the project the proliferation of public–private partnerships in primary and reproductive health seemed to end hope of civil-society-led reform. The focus had shifted away from providing comprehensive sexual and reproductive health services towards medical treatment and, underlying this, how to increase demand and stimulate new markets for drugs. In many cases this had meant by-passing existing public health services and promoting foreign training and funding through top-down programmes which did not have equity as a priority. The project pointed to the evident contradiction between market-driven reform processes and the reforms required to deliver sexual and reproductive health by health systems that are rights-based and equitable. Long-term quality care such as training local nurses and midwives was not high on the list of priorities for market-driven health care.

The results of the project were presented in Colombo, Sri Lanka with the Minister of Health opening the event in front of a large gathering of the local development establishment. After completing a rousing critique of public–private partnerships to end maternal mortality and morbidity, a rather astonished panel, myself included, were presented with gifts from the multinational company Colgate Palmolive – who, it turned out, were the local sponsors of the meeting.

Such an anecdote helps to show just how difficult it is to push the revolutionary agenda required for true reproductive rights and health that Corrêa speaks about. The MDGs and in particular the public health specialists who contributed to the Millennium Project findings (Freedman *et al.* 2005),[11] were only too aware that the well-being of poor women who are at high risk due to high-maternal-mortality health systems requires comprehensive care throughout their life cycle. Defeating maternal mortality and morbidity requires systemic change to ensure health, access and finance for health. Maternal health is in this context a political and economic policy issue rather than a technical 'medical' issue. Beyond financial provisions a strong health system must take into account how neglected health is the 'norm' for poor people – and therefore be seen as not just a delivery system, but a core social institution that can tackle the complex issues around equity, social exclusion and gender bias.

Cairo dilemmas

As the unravelling of Cairo shows, there was a dilemma at the heart of the consensus. On the one hand, the negotiations around Cairo led to women's reproductive rights and health emerging as development issues where women's movements were able to bring into international debates core political feminist issues around embodiment. On the other hand, this was done at a time when these rights were immediately challenged by the neo-liberal economic discourse and conservative governments, as well as progressive groups concerned that embodied and women-centred rights would deflect attention from social and economic issues. Reducing the issue to maternal mortality did little for the sexual and health rights agenda. It played into a technical discourse that pushed for service provision and health system reform, which, given the unavailability of money, led to a privatizing of many services.

The Malthus factor

The third entry point into the population debate is neo-Malthusianism, which also helped to remove reproductive rights and health agendas from the fore-front of population and development policy.

Neo-Malthusianism refers to the work of Thomas Malthus, an Anglican priest who, at the turn of the eighteenth century, was one of the first to study human population. His principal tenet is that population will always outstrip food supply. Surfacing as neo-Malthusianism, this theory persists, linking poverty to environmental degradation and most recently to climate change (Ross 2000; Lohmann 2003; Hendrixson 2004; Hartmann 2005a). Put simply, the neo-Malthusian assumption is that when poor people grow in numbers they destroy their environment in an effort to survive; then, as the environment fails to sustain them, they move on to even more marginal environments, and destroy them as well. This leads to a vicious cycle of poverty, environmental degradation, migration and rising violence and conflict over natural resources. In this theory, poor women (surprise) play a negative role in relation to population growth, as breeders of environmental destruction, poverty and violence. It follows that controlling their fertility becomes the magic bullet solution.

Indian doctor Mohan Rao describes neo-Malthusianism succinctly in relation to India:

> Ten years after Cairo, despite a 'paradigm shift' in population policy, despite a liberal democratic framework, despite a commitment to gender justice, what we nevertheless see is the painful imprint of neo-Malthusian thinking surfacing in various new policy initiatives in India. What makes this so easy a part of commonsense, of everyday discourse, is a neo-liberal agenda that has also come into dominance, where the poor and marginalized are children of a lesser God. Accompanying a profound contempt for the poor is the overwhelming belief that they are responsible for their own poverty. (Rao 2005: 24)

As UK activists Melissa Leach and James Fairhead comment, it is not enough to refute such neo-Malthusian arguments. It is important to look below the population pressure, paying attention to how these narratives arise and become entrenched, and how they serve the institutions and individuals who deploy them (Leach and Fairhead 2000).

UK academic Eric Ross adds: 'the illusion that the poor's economic and reproductive behaviour is the source of most of their misery, and that capitalism and private resource ownership is their only source of hope, continues to be propagated. The claim that their reproductive behaviour is largely irrational continues to obscure the actual determinants of fertility' (Ross 2000).

Overpopulation fears

US-based professor and activist Betsy Hartmann writes about these concerns in her work on racist eugenic policies in the US.[12] She sees both the possibilities and the limitations of a reproductive health strategy as set out in the Cairo Agenda, and she points to the persistence of neo-Malthusianism and the dangerous intersections between it and the conservative assault on migrants, women of colour and the economically poor.

She raises the alarm about how the neo-Malthusian view has merged, since 2001, with the 'war on terror' security agenda. The story then goes that the cycle of poverty leads to conflict and to a rise of migration to urban areas, the creation of slums and the youth bulge. A high proportion of young men in urban populations around the world are then blamed for escalating crime, political violence and terrorism. This viewpoint leads to a pathologizing of the poor in the sprawling urban cities of the Global South (and to a lesser extent in the Global North). Hartmann in her critique of neo-Malthusianism raises several concerns around instrumentalizing women as well as the negative influence of the US administration on sexual and reproductive health agendas in the last decade. Fears of 'over-population' are enduring in both academic and popular thinking, obscuring the structural and systemic roots of poverty, inequality and environmental deterioration. In an interview published in *Development*, Hartmann warns that it is important to move a human rights agenda, not a repressive agenda, forward. 'Women's reproductive rights are worthy of pursuit in and of themselves; they should not be deployed as a neo-Malthusian instrument of national defense. Blaming the Third World poor is one of the oldest games in town; it draws on and reinforces racism both at home and abroad and does not illuminate the deeper causes of poverty, environmental degradation and insecurity' (Hartmann 2005b: 17).

As well as positioning the control of women's bodies as the answer to social and economic crisis, neo-Malthusianism is the ideological glue that reinforces racism within the popular belief that population causes poverty, environmental degradation and political instability. Such beliefs have pervaded many social arenas, especially in the era of George W. Bush. For example, influential mainstream US environmentalists such as Lester Brown of *WorldWatch* and well-known writers Paul Ehrlich and Herman Daly blame overpopulation for the environmental crisis and fail to address the environmental and developmental effects of the industrialized world's production and consumption patterns.

To quote Ehrlich's 1960s 'population bomb' theory:

> The causal chain of the deterioration is easily followed to its
> source. Too many cars, too many factories, too much detergent,
> too much pesticides . . . too little water, too much CO2 – all can
> be traced easily to TOO MANY PEOPLE . . . [and the] year-
> round sexuality of the human female. (Ehrlich 1969, emphasis in
> the original, quoted in Lohmann 2003)

Neo-Malthusianism leads to grossly distorted views of the sources of
conflict in the Global South and, in the post-9/11 world, provides military
and intelligence agencies with a justification for surveillance and intervention.
The portrayal of refugee women as having extremely high fertility and the
attack on single mothers in welfare reforms in the US are examples of neo-
Malthusianism, which naturalizes racism and the politics of exclusion.
Lohmann, referring in his 2003 essay on 'Rethinking Population' to Ehrlich's
earlier work, puts it well:

> The history of 'population science' is full of technocrat-tourists
> who see, hear, smell and sympathize with, but tend not to
> converse at length with, the poor. Thus Paul Ehrlich in Delhi:
>
> > I have understood the population explosion intellectually
> > for a long time. I came to understand it emotionally one
> > stinking hot night in Delhi, a few years ago. . . . The streets
> > seemed alive with people. People eating, people washing,
> > people sleeping. People visiting, arguing, and screaming.
> > People thrusting their hands through the taxi window,
> > begging. People defecating and urinating. People clinging to
> > buses. People herding animals. People, people, people,
> > people, people . . . since that night I've known the feel of
> > overpopulation. (Lohmann 2003, quoting Ehrlich 1969)

If reproductive health remains within a 'population' context, then it is
riddled with contradictions. The concern with 'the female body' centres on
women's biological ability to give birth, linked to a range of social evils. The
assessment is that there are too many poor people and the focus remains on
providing contraceptives for them but in circumstances that are far away from
notions of individual sexuality and choice of procreation. I take this up in
Chapter 6, where such scientific logic leads us to other related issues around

technology. It can also be seen in the hype around climate change and the food crisis that has made world headlines in 2008 (Hällström 2008).

Biopolitics and the Cairo Agenda

The shifting debates and interests around population and development cannot simply be described as eugenics or population control gone underground and re-emerging as neo-Malthusianism, though this might be part of the story. Feminists call for sexual reproductive rights and health focused on the individual demand to choose secure and safe sexual behaviour, health care and safe birthing. The drawback is that those very valid demands are hard to meet in almost all societies given the many medical, technological, legal and cultural constraints. Nevertheless, that demand was registered by the inter-governmental system through various mechanisms, including the Cairo Programme of Action.

The biopolitics that produced the Cairo Agenda worked with and helped constitute a modern reproductive body with rights that required access to legal, medical and health practices. The assumption was that reproductive rights could be granted and acquired through modern technical, state and legal institutional arrangements. Such institutional arrangements were administered by agencies such as UNFPA and service NGOs that were to retrain nurses, doctors and administrators in the principles of the Cairo Agenda. In such service delivery systems and institutional arrangements modern reproductive bodies were produced, managed and administered. The modern delivery of population and development policies was assumed to be part and parcel of modern Western medical, technical and legal practices. Non-Western practices were placed as outside the modern development discourse dealing with what was required to produce healthy, functioning, modern reproductive bodies.

In order to ensure the sexual and reproductive health of individual bodies investments were made in administrative requirements to measure modern medical and technical services. Such assessment processes were often removed from the context in which these services were delivered, in economically constrained areas marked by poor infrastructure and little modern medical training. The health of the population or 'social body' was measured by the level of maternal mortality, live births, numbers of doctors per patients, clinics per town or rural area, et cetera, ignoring the social, cultural and economic context. Funding required such technical reports in order to hold administrations and governments accountable to the international system. As well as not taking into account the economic and social realities, in these accounting systems health interventions outside the modern system were seen as outside the modern biopolitical operations that deliver services, so governing and managing the reproductive body.

The shift in the MDGs to focus on maternal health and mortality was partly due to a strategic decision that there was strong cultural resistance to the sexual and reproductive rights agenda. It was easier to speak about maternal death in a technical medical way that could be measured, rather than enter into the messy and politically more radical sexual and reproductive rights agenda. A biopolitical strategy that focused on modern management and administration and measurement of the reproductive female body as a reflection of the health of the social body fits well with a neo-liberal agenda where governments were encouraged to make compacts with 'more efficient' businesses. Trained in the latest modern administrative techniques, businesses could help the state to manage and administer, alongside selling products and services. A sexual and reproductive rights agenda focused on poor women's autonomy to negotiate their needs was not such an interesting investment proposition as the delivery of modern medical services, high-tech machinery and pharmaceutical products. It makes sense in this logic that maternal mortality emerged as a key area to be supervised, managed and administered through the goals and indicators agreed to by technical experts.

Replacing reproductive rights with maternal health also narrowed the focus on women's reproductive role to her biological ability to give birth (sexual rights and reproduction could after all refer to men, or bodies that are not pregnant). Placed within the 'reduce poverty refrain' it also removed the agency aspect of sexual and reproductive rights for all women. The focus is on the poorest women in dire need or dying, whereas sexual reproductive rights are about all women, even those in rich countries. The decline in numbers of women dying can be measured, whereas the achievement of reproductive rights for all is far less precise and has far greater implications.

It is important to point out that within Cairo and population policy there is no hidden evil agenda of rich companies or countries trying to wipe out poor people. The reason why Ehrlich and others are convincing is because the biopower that is operating is all about security, safety, management, modernizing, data collection and reassuring people they are part of a larger system that is about the public good, progress and modernity. Many doctors, bureaucrats and policy makers are doing what they see as an important job both for the women to whom they administer and for their own profession.

There are real and valid concerns raised by many of the women's health and rights activists working in the Global South about the extremely gloomy macro-economic picture in light of which transnational corporations, rich states, the World Bank and the IMF impose conditionalities, reversed aid flows, unfair trade and a global system that benefits donor countries rather than the countries they purport to support. Put simply, money, expertise and knowledge to ensure good public health systems are clearly vital everywhere, rich countries included. There are without doubt major inequities in the global governance and economic system that are skewing and preventing attempts to bring about any real change. But I am also concerned that dropping the sexual, reproductive rights and health agenda, or seeing it as subsumed within the maternal health arena, is buying into an essentializing view of mothers, and giving power to experts and managers. It totally loses Cairo's powerful appeal to women's agency. The critique of the maternal health paradigm has a strong economic North versus economic South component. The North is seen as continually ripping off the South. Reproductive rights and health programmes are therefore considered as eugenic control of the North over the South. I spoke to several people in South Asia who made it clear that elite feminists imposing their family planning agenda on poor women was worse than meddling. If we move away from seeing all-powerful elites from the Global North imposing their agendas on the South, and instead see that population and development policy and practice are enmeshed in biopolitics, we are able to change the rules of the game by changing the practices we are all engaged in. This means challenging some of the expert technical and management practices that make up biopolitics and enmesh us in particular understandings of reproductive bodies. We need to push beyond seeing women as primarily maternal bodies and instead see health and reproductive rights as a key political entry point for women to seek their own agency.

Beyond maternity

The last entry point is to ask where are the non-maternal bodies in the population and development debate: where is the male reproductive body? In this period male bodies and specifically male sexual organs did become a focus in the discourse around HIV and AIDS. But though it was soon recognized that HIV and AIDS were spread by heterosexual sexual behaviour, and thus by reproductive sexual behaviour by men and women, the focus of family planning was not on regulating the male sexual organ. The closest one comes to it is in discussions in relation to HIV and AIDS on how to protect vulnerable women from infected deviant men, specifically married men who have sex with men or drug users. I look at those sexualized bodies in the later chapters. HIV and AIDS did bring in a concerted focus on penises, or rather on condoms covering them up, but this was not about men's reproductive responsibility for children; it was about the consequence of their pursuit of sexual pleasure. Indeed the sexual health and reproductive rights agenda and the HIV and AIDS agenda appeared to have missed the chance to work together, as both were taking different gendered bodies as their subject of interest.

Within the population and development discourse, the focus remains implicitly and explicitly on female bodies. A wonderful statement is made by Hugh Gorwill, a Professor in Obstetrics and Gynaecology at Queen's University at Kingston, Canada, who stated in reference to reproduction: 'We know more about what makes females work than what makes males work. That's only because females create population problems. . . . The common pathway to turn off having people is females' (quoted in Lohmann 2003).

So even if it takes two to tango, and for now we leave out any technological assistance, it seems that male bodies are not in the picture. What is spoken about in the Cairo Programme of Action is 'male responsibilities and participation'. The five paragraphs devoted to this subsection of Chapter 4 (of 16 chapters) are entitled 'Gender Equality, Equity and Empowerment of Women'. This is not a short but detailed description of male sexual and reproductive behaviour; rather, it is aimed at improving relations of men and women from the familial to government level. Men are encouraged to take responsibility, in the abstract, for their sexual and reproductive behaviour and their social and family roles. Governments are asked to encourage men to undertake responsible parenthood, practise family planning and avoid unsafe sex. The emphasis is on their role as fathers who are supporting their children financially and ensuring their education, including respecting and treating girl children equally with boys. There are no discussions of male reproductive bodies. It is their active behaviour which needs guidance. It is considered within their power to make changes; they need to be encouraged and suggestions for their consideration are offered. The focus is on shifts in communication so that men will take up a more responsible role in family life, and that includes within the family bed. Unlike with discussions of women's reproductive behaviour, levels of fertility, morbidity and mortality, there are no studies or numbers attached to these paragraphs. The tone is one of respectful distance. Men, it is noted, are powerful in all areas of life from family to government: they need to share that power. They should participate in gender equality but they are not subject to reproductive health and rights issues as heterosexual family men. The assumption, reading between the lines, is that it is, of course, their choice and right to have sexual relations, to have children. What is limiting them is the health and well-being of their partners and children. The family planning agenda post-Cairo talks about men's 'responsibility' and promotes an 'involving men' agenda, but it stops short at awareness raising: male bodies do not need to be under scrutiny or control.

It was noticeable that there were very few men in Cairo unless they were there as population experts, doctors or bureaucrats. There are many more men in HIV and AIDS, social justice and environmental movements. Reproductive rights and health is seen as a women's issue; it concerns their bodies, their rights. Male agency and choice are a given. In the reproductive health debate no one speaks about controlling male reproductive urges. There are no diagrams of penises at the centre of public health discourse. When male bodies are spoken about in relation to population and numbers they are considered as workers and as soldiers, not as fathers, husbands and lovers. The lack of male reproductive bodies tell us that the embodied reproductive body in gender and development is essentially female.

There is something of an irony in the failure of the reproductive health and population lobby to focus sufficiently on men's responsibility for fathering children as a reproductive right, as in many cultures men are seen as the providers of children; indeed, legally they are seen as owning children. The construct of parenthood in these cultural contexts gives women few or no rights over their own children. Gender and development, instead of looking at the parenthood of both sexes, is caught in seeing motherhood as the primary role of women, one that is biological and natural; the chance is missed to look at how to balance between the genders, seeing the rights and power of parenthood as a social and cultural responsibility rather than a biological given.

Similarly, the issue of infertility is missing in gender and development. The assumption is that family planning in development policy is about controlling fertility, rather than about assisting infertility. This is a major body politics issue, as in parts of the world where family planning agencies have been pushing contraception some women are still desperately struggling to have children, particularly male children. But these reproductive rights choices, which are recognized in the Global North, are not of concern in gender and development when speaking about women in the Global South. The focused gaze on the reproductive body obscures those non-reproductive bodies of women, who as a result are often socially rejected, losing husband, family and sense of identity, and as a consequence having to spend their life energies as well as their savings trying to become pregnant. The fact that those women's 'choices' are not considered hollows out the rhetoric of family planning and raises questions about whose choices are determining which population services are provided.

Notes

1 Tragically, the area I visited was at the heart of the Rwandan genocide three years later. I know the doctor and his family who showed me around managed to leave the country and made it to Brussels. I can only surmise that the women and children of the village were lost in the genocide.

2 See Sen (1997); Silliman and King (1999); Singh (1998); Nair and Kirbat with Sexton (2004); Corrêa with Reichmann (1994); Bandarage (1997); Petchesky (2002); and Ravinran and De Pinho (2005). See also many newsletters and policy journals, for example *Reproductive Health Matters*; *Development* ('Reproductive Health and Rights: Putting Cairo into Action'), Vol. 42, No. 1 (1999); *Development* ('Globalization, Reproductive Health and Rights'), Vol. 46, No. 2 (2003); *Development* ('Sexual and Reproductive Health and Rights'), Vol. 48, No. 4 (2005). Valuable sources include numerous websites: AWID (Association for Women's Rights in Development), <www.awid.org>; CRR (Center for Reproductive Rights), <www.crlp.org>; EngenderHealth, <www.engenderhealth.org>; ICRW (International Center for Research on Women), <www.icrw.org>; IPPF (International Planned Parenthood Organization), <www.ippf.org>; RHO (Reproductive Health Outlook), <www.rho.org>; WHP (Women's Health Project), <www.wits.ac.za/whp/index.htm>; AMANITARE (African Partnership for Sexual and Reproductive Health and Rights of Women and Girls), <www.amanitare.org>; ARROW (Asian-Pacific Resource and Research Centre for Women), <www.arrow.org.my>; ISIS Women's International Cross-cultural Exchange (ISIS-WICCE), <www.isis.org.ug>.

3 These can easily be accessed through UN websites that keep the key documents online; the annual issues of the State of the World Population Report are also excellent resources on the ongoing debates: see <http://www.unfpa.org/swp/>.

4   Speaking in early 2008 with a Canadian gender expert working on population issues, I was reminded that the Cairo Agenda has been subject to many governmental UN negotiations and in the process has lost ground continually over the years, despite the defence put up by people like her. She had been in Cairo as a civil society advocate and had run (unsuccessfully) for Parliament to defend the agreements reached in Cairo and later in the Beijing Fourth World Conference on Women.

5   The oral statements and reservations published officially with the Programme of Action – from Catholic Latin and Central America, and Muslim West Asia and Middle East countries – were all reservations around sexual health, abortion and family values, made on cultural and religious grounds.

6   The definition of reproductive health in the Programme of Action is:

'a state of complete physical, mental and social well-being and not merely the absence of disease and infirmity, in all matters related to the reproductive system and to its functions and processes. People are able to have a satisfying and safe sex life and they have the capability to reproduce and the freedom to decide if, when and how often to do so. Men and women have the right to be informed and have access to safe, effective, affordable and acceptable methods of their choice for the regulation of fertility, as well as the access to health care for safe pregnancy.'

The reproductive rights stated in the Cairo Programme of Action are:

• The right of couples and individuals to decide freely and responsibly the number and spacing of their children, and to have the information and means to do so;

• The right to attain the highest standard of sexual and reproductive health;

• The right to make decisions free of discrimination, coercion or violence.

7   Empowerment is understood in this context as a social action process that promotes participation of people, organizations and communities in gaining control over their lives in their community and larger society. Empowerment is not characterized as achieving power to dominate others, but rather power to act with others to effect change (Stein 1997: 6).

8   After The Hague, I coordinated a series of regional reviews with women's rights health groups in which we explored the impediments to making Cairo work. The co-hosts of the meeting were: ODAG (Alternative Development and Global Justice), DAWN Africa (African network of the Development Alternatives with Women for a New Era), TAMWA (Tanzanian Media Women's Association), CEPIA (Cidadania, Estudo, Pesquisa, Informação Ação), the KCWH (Key Centre for Women's Health in Society), University of Melbourne, Australia; and WOREC (Women's Rehabilitation Centre), Kathmandu, Nepal. A series of short reports from each of the dialogues are available on-line and in leaflet form: 'Arab Regional Dialogue: Building Alliances for Women's Empowerment: Putting Reproductive Health into Context', Catania, Italy; 'Africa Regional Dialogue: Building Alliances for Women's Empowerment: Globalization, Empowerment, Reproductive Health and Rights', Dar es Salaam, Tanzania; 'Latin American and the Caribbean Regional Dialogue: Reproductive Rights, Violence Against Women: Boys and Men's Roles and Responsi-bilities', Rio de Janeiro, Brazil; 'South East Asia and the Pacific Dialogue Reproductive Rights, Political Mobilization and the Law', Melbourne, Australia; 'South Asia Dialogue:

Political Disruption, Women's Empowerment and Health', Nagarkot/Kathmandu, Nepal. See the summary leaflet 'Working Together in Solidarity for Gender Equality and Social Justice: Overview of SID-UNFPA Policy Dialogues on Population, Gender Equality, Reproductive Rights and Development for Alliance Building. Held December 2001–November 2002 in support of the International Conference on Population and Development Programme of Action': <www.sidint.org>.

9 All of these documents are available on the Web: see <http://www.un.org/millenniumgoals/>.

10 After the 1999 protests in Seattle some women's health movements chose to search out alliances with other social movements – environmental justice, migrant rights, human rights, fair trade and economic justice – in order to defend reproductive and sexual rights in non-UN spaces (Barton 2005; Harcourt 2006).

11 The Millennium Project, directed by Jeffrey Sachs with UN funding, brought together many experts on the different MDG subjects. The Task Force on Child Health and Maternal Health, who produced the report on maternal mortality, included sexual and reproductive rights experts from civil society, UN and academia – notably Lyn Freedman, Helen de Pinho and Meg Wirth, who were the lead writers (Freedman *et al.* 2005).

12 Betsy Hartmann is the Director of the Hampshire College Population and Development Program and a member of the advisory committee of the Committee on Women, Population and the Environment. She is a longstanding activist in the international women's health movement and writes and speaks frequently on population, environment and development issues (see Hartmann 1995; 2005b).

Armenia More than a quarter of women have experienced domestic violence.

Kyrgyzstan Up to half of all marriages are the result of 'bride kidnapping', a practice also common elsewhere in central Asia and the Caucasus.

China The 1979 one-child policy has led to an estimated 400m fewer people. The fertility rate is between 1.7 and 1.8 births per woman, below the 2.1 births needed to keep the population at a stable level.

Russia At least one woman dies every hour due to domestic violence: 14,000 women are killed every year.

Caribbean Around a third of women suffer domestic violence. UN crime trends surveys suggest that three of the region's small island states are among the 10 countries with the highest incidence of rape worldwide.

Body Politics in Numbers

3

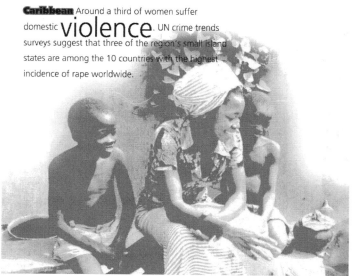

Source: 'The state they're in - how women are faring in the rest of the world'
http://www.guardian.co.uk/lifeandstyle/2008/dec/07/women-equality-rights-feminism-sexism-worldwide

Three

Productive and Caring Bodies

Toiling female bodies

A major focus over the last 30 years of gender and development policy and analysis has been to underline women's important contribution to economic production. The images of gender and development projects are of women's 'productive bodies': either rural women toiling in the fields, bearing water on their heads and gathering firewood, or the new nimble-fingered factory workers, often young women, bent over assembly lines or sewing machines in export processing zones. Women's bodies in those visual images seem uncomfortable. They are toiling under heavy loads of wood, cramped in factories sewing toys and cheap garments, breathing in toxins of the heavily sprayed cut flowers for rich women's tables thousands of miles away. These pictures are designed to show how women are critical to economic development, literally bearing the burden of economic growth. The case studies and statistical reports measuring the progress and contribution of women – conducted by government, UN and non-governmental networks – emphasize, often with a catchy title, that women are 'good investments' in business, government and development projects. The millions of women entering the new global markets in the 1980s and 1990s confirm that, indeed, poor women from the South are a source of globally flexible, docile and cheap labour (Wichterich 2000).

Since the first study on women's economic role in development by Ester Boserup in 1970, a huge amount has been written about the feminization of global labour,[1] establishing the importance of women's work globally.[2] In this chapter I reflect on the embodied lives of women who are engaged in productive and caring work. I look at the contradictions between women's productive and reproductive roles in the various places where they toil as paid workers and as paid and unpaid care givers. I examine how women's gender role as care givers overlaps and maps onto their working lives. My interest is in how women manage their family role as primary care givers of households, children, elderly workers and husbands. What are the costs to their health? How is this burden of care work marked on their bodies?

Three approaches to production and care

I focus on three aspects of productive and care work that are slightly off-centre to mainstream gender and development: feminist analysis of the care economy; the work of women migrants who provide care; and care as a form of 'alternative' economy based on the conceptual insights that emerged from the women and politics of place project mentioned in Chapter 1, and particularly in the work of J. K. Gibson-Graham on community economies (1996; 2005 and 2006).

These three approaches to women's productive and care work open up possibilities to see women's work in a more nuanced way. I look at these issues not as an economist might do, in order to understand how to revalue women's productivity and role as carer, seeking more comprehensive data to align the topic with mainstream economic accounting and analysis.[3] Rather, I look at the implications of the overwork of women in many parts of the economy in the Global South and the sense of crisis emerging as tired and exploited female bodies fail to cope. It is curious to me that the embodied lives of women in their homes and communities and in informal economies – the spaces in which the majority of the poor survive – are largely invisible in mainstream analysis of the global market economy. This is the case even if the entry of large numbers of women into the workforce has been central to global economic shifts in recent years. It points to conceptual gaps in the mainstream economic analysis informing gender and development policy and programmes. Similarly, I am interested in considering the implications for gender and development of the many women migrating to take up jobs in the new global economy, and how that growing phenomenon is challenging assumptions about how to understand economic and labour trends in development policy.

Most of all I am interested in how the productive and caring working lives of women overlap and create new forms of relations among women. What has been dubbed a 'care chain' has been forged as women migrate for work and in the process often leave their families in order to care for others, while other women (largely educated and wealthy) benefit from the care 'gain'. The flexibility and fluidity of women's work, taking into account both productive and care work, whether in the Global South or North, make it complex to analyse. Factors to consider include whether women are engaged in formal or informal work, or in care work, paid or unpaid; whether they live in cities or on farms, in their home community or outside it; in their own home or other people's homes; what sense of personal security they have; what family and travel arrangements are made for them to work. The stresses and strains of juggling different roles and modes of working are marked out on women's bodies. The need to factor in these conditions underlies the difficulty of speaking about women's productive as well as paid and unpaid caring in a world where the dominant understanding of work is as a male occupation performed for contracted and negotiated wages between worker and employer, a company or the state in the global capitalist system.

Women and work: changing trends

There are complex shifts and trends and differences among women living in the Global North and South, yet their lives are integrating more and more in tangible ways through 'care chains' and 'gains'. As Gita Sen stated in 1995, 'women are at the crossroads of production and reproduction' (Kabeer 2007: 9). The focus of gender and development is on poor women, but their working lives intersect also with the economic and social lives of the growing numbers of the global middle class (whether in India, Italy or Poland). Their labour is evident. There are the toys sewn by women's hands in Chinese factories that fill the rooms of wealthy children throughout the world. African women enduring long hours to meet foreign supermarket deadlines prepare the cut flowers and fruit thousands of miles away from the tables where the fruit is eaten and flowers are displayed. Asian women in sweatshops stitch the cheap cotton clothes and sports shoes that are sold at huge profit by the label owners around the world. The connections are there, if invisible. More visible are the increasing numbers of migrant women from poor communities who migrate to work in the homes of elite families to care for children and the elderly, to clean houses and walk the dogs.

It is important to unravel the complexities of these connections even while underscoring the very different experiences according to the work performed. Balancing productive paid work and family and care work is a core struggle for many middle-class women. US economist Folbre (2001) shows how educated US women struggle to do paid work and also cover the housework and care work expected of them, and experience a considerable amount of guilt if they hire people to support them. The issue of child care for women, particularly those living in heterosexual nuclear households in the Global North, can be difficult to organize when they cannot rely on extended family or proper state provision. Where I live in Italy the huge decrease in birth rates is largely to do with inadequate child care. In a study I undertook on the working conditions of women scientists in Europe in 2006, among the Italians interviewed child care was the biggest factor determining career choices of the young women scientists working in laboratories (Harcourt 2007).[4]

Gita Sen's observation that women are at the crossroads between production and reproduction, between economic activity and the care of human beings, implies that the two roles are rarely considered together. But as any working woman can tell you, she spends a lot of time organizing ways to fulfil both roles. Naila Kabeer points out that the feminization of labour markets is forcing a long-term change in the domestic sphere:

> Markets today not only operate on a scale that is unprecedented in history, they also penetrate spheres of life that were once considered the antithesis of the market principles: the spheres of family reproduction and the domestic economy. (Kabeer 2007)

Economic restructuring and the feminization of labour

The impact on women's lives of major restructuring in the global economy by the neo-liberal agenda is well documented (Elson 1991; Sparr 1994; Sassen 1998; Delahanty and Shefali 1999; Rowbotham and Linkkogle 2001; Razavi 2002; UNRISD 2005; Rai 2008). With the imperative for countries to compete in a global economy the older, state-led nation building processes have been replaced by a drive for profit where labour is treated as another commodity. In order for countries of the Global South to compete in the global market as dictated by international institutions such as the World Bank and International Monetary Fund, 'structural and institutional constraints' were removed. In order to improve 'efficiency', governments were forced to cut price subsidies, public investments on infrastructure and social expenditure on education, health and public services. Women were a plentiful supply of cheap and docile labour for the new industries. At the same time women were expected to supply the labour and care necessary to sustain families and communities, compensating for the cuts in state support (Razavi 2002: 9). In rural economies, alongside farm work or paid formal work, women supplemented incomes through a whole range of informal work. Increasingly women had to move to find paid work outside the home and community. This necessitated them travelling long hours to work, moving to urban areas or migrating to other countries. In the drive to compete in the global economy huge numbers of women were employed in export manufacturing sectors and performed the semi-skilled and lower-level tasks in production processes and expanding service sectors.

The conditions under which these poor women entered national and global economies in such large numbers have been a major focus of gender and development policy, feminist movements and feminist economists. Case studies have shown how women absorbed the shock of structural adjustment and shifts in agricultural and global manufacture by working longer and harder in and outside the home. Export goods were produced at the expense of women's time, health, well-being and household security. Health, education and social security were privatized with the dismantling of welfare provision and labour market regulation. Where these markets did not exist, provision of these services devolved to women, adding to their work burden (Sparr 1994; Cagatay 2003; Kabeer 2007).

As Peggy Antrobus of Development Alternatives with Women for a New Era (DAWN) argues, the neo-liberal economy is 'grounded in a gender ideology which is deeply and fundamentally exploitative of women's time/work and sexuality' (Antrobus 2004). According to Imrana Qadeer, an Indian public health specialist, with the implementation of neo-liberal economic policies 'women's relative access to economic resources, incomes and employment has worsened, their burden of work has increased, and their relative and even absolute health, nutritional and educational status has declined' (quoted in Nair and Kirbat with Sexton 2004).

As British feminist economist Ruth Pearson points out in her study on the globalization of women's work (2008), labour-intensive export industries target 'women's nimble fingers' to achieve flexibility, productivity and responsibility. There is an increase in intra-regional trade – between higher- and lower-wage economies, and between East and West Europe – and most new jobs for women are in the unregulated informal economy. Much of this work is in personal services – care and cleaning work both in homes and in public offices, as well as work in the entertainment, leisure and sex industries. Feminization of work is about informalization/deregulation, as by their nature sub-contracted supply chains tend to reach out well beyond the formal sector. In today's global economy capital migrates in search of cheap female labour and women migrate to find work, both as part of the global care chain and as migrant factory workers: Burmese workers in Thailand, for example, or rural workers who migrate to south-west China.

Pearson and others argue that the rise of China and the other BRICs (Brazil, Russia, India and China) has created lower-cost competition for many sectors that employ women to produce for export markets – in Central America, Eastern Europe and South-East Asia – thereby reducing employment opportunities for women, pushing them into the unregulated sector and the more exploitative conditions of house factories, workshops and home-based work (Wichterich 2007). The global demand for agricultural and mineral products has pushed developing economies away from producing food and wage goods for their own people, increasing the burden of women seeking basic foodstuffs for their families. This situation has led to a focus on survival amid a frantic search for wages, and made it harder to push for services or what Pearson calls 'the reproductive bargain' – for public provision of education, wages, housing, sanitation, utilities and pensions, all vital to people living in poverty.

Negotiating work and family

These findings seem contradictory to the premise that economic development is the pathway to progress and that earning an independent income enhances the social standing of women in the household and the society. The problem is not simply material reward or the type of work in which women are engaged, but the conditions under which they undertake the work, whether in the formal or informal sector. Equally important is how they are able to perform their care work in addition to their paid work, as well as whether they control their earnings. This is not to say that working in paid, recognized jobs cannot improve the quality of women's lives, but that the type of job and its compensation is important, and that women's lives as workers cannot be separated out from their lives as carers and household managers.

Production needs to be understood in relation to gender relations and social and cultural norms, as well as national and global economic trends (Robinson 2006: 326). Wage labour is not necessarily emancipatory when taken on with reduced earning capacity when compared to men, alongside ongoing responsibilities for caring work and in the context of economic crisis.

Markings on the body and in the family

As feminist geographers like Yvonne Underhill-Sem (2002) remind us, corporate globalization and fundamentalisms are leaving deep marks on women's bodies. The embodied work experience, the strain of work in factories, the inappropriate working spaces for women in environments that do not cater for specific female bodily needs, the increased exposure to health dangers – all these map the underside of productive work for women.

These shifts and adjustments play out differently depending on the type of work performed and the changes within households and families. In her study of globalization, marriage and masculinities Kabeer (2007) details the emerging crisis in care work which she calls social reproductive work.[5] Kabeer proposes that on the whole the entry of young, unmarried women into paid work tends to be positive, with a greater sense of control over their own lives. Married women's entry into the workforce, however, is more ambiguous and they encounter greater resistance (Kabeer 2007: 16–20). Married women have to negotiate their time and labour in order to soothe husbands' fears and prejudices. Kabeer cites a range of resistances by men reluctant to give up their male privileges. These resistances range from an increase in marriage breakdown, drink and depression to higher suicide rates and domestic violence as men insist on women's responsibility for domestic care work. Almost universally, when compared to men, women have longer working days due to the combination of their paid and unpaid care work. Kabeer adds wryly: 'Clearly there is something about the masculine identity that makes men deeply uncomfortable about taking on care work even within the privacy of their own homes' (Kabeer 2007: 50). Men struggle when they are unable to live up to hegemonic models of masculinity which promote the idea of men as the power brokers, the providers and household heads of society.

Kabeer concludes that 'marriage appears to have become increasingly unattractive to both women and men in many parts of the world', and she speaks of the 'invisible feminization of responsibility like feminization of work' (Kabeer 2007: 26–7). She argues that women's labour has been stretched to breaking point and that there are serious economic and social costs when women's care work and responsibilities are not taken seriously.

The physical strain women experience is revealed in the ill health that accompanies poverty and exploited work conditions. In terms of the 'markings on the body' of poorly paid working women, there are many issues that determine their well-being which have to be considered alongside the potential economic gains of paid work. The production of gender hierarchies within work relations and in the wider economy are played out on their bodies. As the studies show, for the majority of women working in global multinational company factories, work is characterized by low wages, long hours, insecurity, irregular returns, fines for misdemeanours, stress to meet imposed deadlines, health hazards and monotony. In addition from a gendered dimension they endure sexual harassment; lack of respect of supervisors; poor security at night (a critical factor given often mandatory overtime); restricted toilet breaks; for mothers, problems with child care and difficulties with part-ners; and, for single women, impairment of social status in their home com-munity. Extended working days cut into women's time for sleep and leisure.

The hazards of the workplace – along with poor living conditions, low access to food, discriminatory treatment and domestic violence – show up in higher anaemia, gynaecological complications and general ill health among women. High levels of ill health occur where pregnant and lactating women are engaged in endless, backbreaking and hazardous work; their vulnerability is greatest when they are undocumented workers.[6]

These women's working lives are complex, constantly changing and shifting according to familial and social pressures. Yet even though the global economy relies on women's productive work in large multinational companies, they are the lowest-paid, most insecure and most poorly organized workers. They are also hit hardest by the macro-economic structures and austerity measures involving cutbacks in social services on which they rely, and they bear the greatest burden in terms of household work and care for families and communities. Within both the workplace and home their needs and rights are subsumed under notions of male breadwinners engaged in formal employment. In mainstream economic and development policy almost no account is taken of the networks of relationships and responsibilities that exist within and outside the home that allow women to cope, and policies rarely take note of the power struggles inherent in domestic relations ruled by gender bias and gender blindness.

Who cares? Feminist analysis of the care economy

Feminist analysis has tried to rectify this gap in recent years with studies of the care economy, mainly in the Global North (Bigo 2004).[7] In countries in the Global South the paid care sector is not yet well researched as it is mostly informal, largely employing poor women in urban contexts where the 'contract' is verbal.[8] That being said, women's solidarity movements do valorize and acknowledge women's care roles in political claims for better conditions and support for women's work in their demands for justice and equitable distribution.[9]

Care work is at the core of domestic activities and is the area where gender divides seem hard to change. Caring is both the set of pragmatic tasks of providing physical care and the critical role of ongoing emotional support, where it is difficult to separate out the emotional bond from domestic duties. Housework, child rearing, volunteering and care for the elderly and infirm, whether paid or not, are crucial to human well-being and to the economy. The unwritten assumption is that mothers, grandmothers, aunts, sisters and wives do not expect to be paid because the care work they do is an expression of love. In short, they care about their families. The modern state is built on the concept of the male-headed heterosexual nuclear family where the male head of household is paid a wage that can support children and a full-time wife and mother who performs domestic and care work without pay. Care work is part of the fabric of society; it is relied on in economic development even if it is not counted. There are limits to how much women can absorb and society can rely on the motivation and commitment of overworked women. As Diane Elson commented, 'even if care is done for love, we do not necessarily love doing it' (Elson 2004).

One of the limits to women participating in productive work outside the home is their role as main care providers. The question then is who does the care work when women work outside the home? Traditionally other women in the family are expected to take on the task, or less well-off women are paid to come and work in the home.

Paid and unpaid care work

The global shift of women to productive work outside the home and the growing commodification of care means care work is now coming to the forefront in feminist economic thinking. Feminist economists like Nancy Folbre, Diane Elson, Ruth Pearson, Gita Sen, Bina Agarwal, Nifular Cagatay and Naila Kabeer,[10] in their studies on the changing working patterns of women globally, have made visible the unpaid care aspects of the processes by which life capabilities and the labour force are reproduced on a daily and generational basis (Kabeer 2007). This analysis is an important correction to the strong focus on women's productive capacity in gender and development which since Boserup (1970) has highlighted women's economic importance in developing economies.[11] Gender and development has had a strong productionist bias, underscoring women's role in production and making visible the previously unvalorized work that women did as usually unpaid family labour. Even if women's productive contribution to export-oriented agriculture and subsistence economies and capitalist enterprise was recognized, the mainstream focus of development still excludes care work from an assessment of economic production (Razavi 2007).[12] There is a tendency to treat the domestic sector as a bottomless well able to provide care regardless of the resources it can receive from other sectors (UNIFEM 2000).

In making the care economy a visible area of economic analysis feminist economists stress that the failure to tackle gender hierarchies within the labour market and in the home means that women continue to be employed in casual, irregular and poorly paid jobs, while in the home male authority and privilege are upheld. The undervaluation of women's paid and unpaid care work, combined with the assumption that women can endure unlimited long working hours in the home and outside, is reaching unsustainable levels. Women's entry into the paid workforce as a near global trend has squeezed time that was allocated to the care of family and friends on an unpaid basis.

As care work has become commodified, feminist economists have begun to measure and evaluate care in their analysis of the connection between the market-based commodity economy and the unpaid care economy (non-market-based social reproduction). What emerges is that the paid care sector is a significant employer of women. It is, like many sectors associated with women's work, underprivileged and badly paid. A vast amount of care work continues to be done unpaid, and how care is addressed is inextricably intertwined with other structures of inequality, race and social class.

Valuing care work

There are strong tensions in feminist economics about the need to support and value care and yet at the same time to liberate women from its confines and enable a more active presence of women in the public sphere. The gender analysis of labour markets draws attention to family care and welfare arrangements that interlock with the labour market system, and to unpaid caring responsibilities as an obstacle to the expansion of female employment.

As Sharai Razavi, who leads the gender programme of the UN Research Institute for Social Development, observes:

> ideally society should recognize and value the importance of different forms of care, but without reinforcing care work as something only women can or should do given the well-known and adverse consequences of such gendering, women's financial precariousness and their exclusion from the public domain. (Razavi 2007: 2)

Women are entering jobs in the paid care sector in a range of roles such as domestic workers, child care workers, teachers and nurses. Women from the Global South take up the care job deficit in the Global North and women from disadvantaged racial and ethnic groups provide care services to meet the needs of middle classes in the Global South. In both cases their own needs for care are downplayed and neglected. Migrant women are at the core of the new transnational working arrangements. Their work is part of the infrastructure of jobs involved in running and implementing the global economic system, in the same way that export agriculture and export manufacturing have mobilized large numbers of people into wage labour.

Care gain, care drain: migrant women and care work

Women migrating to take up care work are a feature of the global landscape. The second approach of this chapter is to look at how migrant women's work is at the crossroads between global production and reproduction. Despite their contribution to the family and communities where they work and the families and communities back home, women migrants are often outside mainstream discussions of gender and work. This absence is partly because their time and identity straddle different worlds and partly because they do not fit the current categories of mainstream economic measurement and analysis.[13]

I remember in 1991 attending a meeting in Colombo called by the Asia Pacific Development Centre to broker better conditions for women engaged in what was then called the 'domestic maid trade' within Asia, including West Asia. These mostly rural village women were trained as domestic workers and nurses and then sent out in controlled numbers from the Philippines, Sri Lanka and Indonesia to Taiwan, Singapore, Thailand, Saudi Arabia and Kuwait. The meeting was attended by members of women's rights organizations, researchers, government and UN policy makers. There were no migrant women present at the meeting.[14] On my way back and in subsequent travels, I became used to seeing large numbers of young women wearing tags and identical tracksuit jackets over saris holding plastic or straw baskets full to the brim with carefully wrapped packets. They were shepherded on and off planes and disappeared through customs lines.

I attended in 2007 a well-funded meeting on migration and development in Rome opened by various Italian government ministers and European Commissioners, and addressed by high-level researchers. Detailed studies of various migration flows were explained in highly complex graphs and numbers. Screen after screen indicated the huge numbers of people involved and the billions of dollars flowing, the profits made from remittances and by telephone companies, financial services and state governments. While it was noted that nearly 50 per cent of the migrants were women working and producing for so many different economies, tellingly there were no migrant women among the speakers. Nor was gender or the close-up lives of those women discussed as a specific issue by the researchers.[15] It seemed as if all those experiences lived by women had disappeared again, this time into numbers.

Gender and migration remains an under-theorized area in gender and development. One reason is that those who have moved are by no means the poorest or least-educated. On the contrary, they are the women who are willing to take risks and move away from difficult home situations. Nor, as Laura Agustín (2007b) and others have pointed out, are the reasons for moving unambiguously about economic gain. In the Philippines, where divorce is illegal, migration can be one way to move out of an unhappy marriage. For young women it can be a welcome way to move from the confines of the village; a way to escape the patriarchal traditions of their communities.

The global care chain

It is interesting to consider how the formation of transnational households is changing women's lives. Migrant care work is being carried out as an integral feature of globalization. The numbers involved in the flows of people migrating transnationally are huge; it is estimated that 200 million people in today's world have left home to look for a new life. Of those, 50 per cent are women, many of them moving to provide various forms of care work. Paid domestic service, which had nearly disappeared in many European, Australian, Canadian and US middle-class homes, has returned in a significant way as educated working women turn to the paid labour of other women migrants who are moving to take up those opportunities in the US, West Europe, Taiwan, Japan, Singapore and other high-growth countries in Asia and Latin America. The supply of a migrant labour force willing to do the work that citizens of wealthy countries are not willing to do reflects the existence of wide and widening global disparities in wages and living standards. Filipinas who earn the equivalent of US$176 a month as nurses, teachers or clerical workers in the Philippines, earn US$450 in Hong Kong or US$1,000 in Italy or US$1,200 in the US in the less-skilled work of nannies, maids and other services (Summerfield 2007).

Moving countries to provide care services, often in vulnerable and exploited situations, cannot be described in cut-and-dried economic terms. Care work is not easily compartmentalized into neat divides between emotional engagement and professional work. Transnational families change the lives of those offering the services and the families relying on their work. They enable affluent women to work and their affluent men to continue not to take up their fair share of child care responsibilities.

Migration studies offer mixed findings about how families cope. Migrant women and those employing them present a challenge to public perceptions of ideal mothers. They are blamed for the bad behaviour of children left with nannies, or those left behind. It is seen as unnatural if a mother leaves home to work, but not when a father migrates for work. Both migrants and their employers have to negotiate these feelings of distress and ambivalence.

Race, class and gender tensions

In her study on domestic work, Taiwanese feminist scholar Pei-Chia Lan presents a detailed study of how migrants and employers cope through interviews and vivid ethnographic detail. She presents a nuanced look at the boundaries between workers and employers in a changing Taiwan. She gives a sympathetic account of the contradictions and difficulties for both domestic workers and their employers. The survival strategies of the domestic workers are described, including a detailed look at their dress, their food and their disguises. In one case she depicts how a domestic worker would deliberately change look, from humble employed maid to star of the disco scene, every Sunday. She also relates the surprise, but not condemnation, of the employer when she finds out. Lan sees such disguises as a way for a domestic worker to mark boundaries that enable her to keep her dignity and sense of self, often in confined and potentially intrusive spaces. Lan describes how domestic workers carefully draw the line between their feelings and the employing family, politely listening but not being involved emotionally in the wife's or husband's sometimes intimate confessions. On the other side, she relates how middle-class Taiwanese women are employing migrant workers as a modern working mother's survival strategy. In the absence of their husbands' help they turn to paid domestic workers to support them. The changes in Taiwanese family life as the three-generational households break down also mean that domestic workers are employed to cater for the shifting responsibilities of the mother-in-law who increasingly no longer takes up the traditional role of caring for children. What Lan brings out are the inner struggles of employer and employee alike as they try to negotiate caring roles, paid and unpaid, within small domestic spaces and with uncertain rules as to what is an acceptable level of emotional engagement on both sides. Though obviously more sympathetic to the domestic workers, she presents carefully the predicament of hard-working young middle-class mothers who hire domestic workers in an effort to move outside of tradition, often spending all their income to pay the domestic worker.

Her study of how care work is stretched beyond borders, through the use of mobile phones to keep mothers in touch with their family back home, is a particularly interesting aspect of long-distance parenting and caring. It touches on the uncomfortable issue of migrant work as an aspect of our consumer globalized world, where a mobile phone call once a day serves to bring families closer, as mothers work for years away from their children to provide schooling and housing that the state fails to deliver. Too often what is not commented on is how the considerable profit of all those phone calls goes to multinational phone companies.

Lan's narratives reveal how race, class and gender relations are changing, for good or for bad, in response to global migration. As an Australian living in Italy I have directly experienced how migration is about relationships across different borders that are shifting and changing gendered roles and identities. While it is true that the ebbs and flows of people have been an enduring feature of many of our histories and places, what the studies of care work show is that women need to negotiate different arrangements as our globalized lives interlink within the complexities of global capital. The stark levels of inequality, violence and uncertainties that dominate and curtail migrant women's lives may be in the shadows, but they are not so far from all of our lives. The economic and social factors that are leading 200 million migrants to search for another life demand a reconsideration of what living in this transnational world means for our sense of self, community, belonging and home. Whether we are migrants or tourists, cybersurfers or newspaper readers, workers or consumers, and the layers in between, all of us live far more global lives today that demand the deeper feminist analysis.

Sharing paid and non-paid care work

On a very personal level through my contacts with Filipina migrant groups in Rome I have employed for nine years (through a state contract that ensures holidays and a pension) a Rome-based woman from a Filipino family (she is the eldest of six children all of whom have migrated with their parents, who are in their late forties). Trained as a computer specialist, she earns far more working as my babysitter in the afternoons and caring for an old lady in the mornings. She and her father are the main breadwinners in the family. As dutiful daughter and observant Catholic, she gives her earnings to her family, though she lives with her equally hard-working Filipino partner, whom she met here in Rome. They want to be married traditionally in a church back home where most of his family is based. Her reasons for being in Rome are largely financial, but she and her family feel they are part of Italian as well as Filipino life. Certainly being in Rome has exposed the family to different opportunities and difficulties, with her and her siblings taking the chance to move beyond the confines of traditional family life. One of her younger sisters, for example, is a single mother and is living with a female partner, a source of continual concern to the family. Her brothers are struggling to pass the Italian high school and her mother endures chronic ill health. As the eldest daughter she is expected to help family members navigate all these issues, including the crackdowns imposed on migrants by the increasingly racist local and national Italian governments.

How her life intertwines with mine is very palpable. Her work in my home gives me time to be engaged outside the home in my feminist work. She and I share the care work of my children. We try to negotiate financial and emotional balances between the care 'chain' and care 'gain'. I find it puzzling how such relations and connections are separated in gender and development analysis. In one organization I have been involved in for nearly two decades, Women in Development Europe (WIDE) – headquartered in Brussels with a programmatic focus on gender and development, trade and women's rights – it is only now that the careful divide maintained between what happens over there in the Global South and what happens here in the Global North has been broken down.[16] Despite WIDE's focus on gender, globalization, work and trade, for many members of the network once poor women arrive in the Global North they somehow disappear from gender and development analysis and therefore from the vision of WIDE. The lives of female migrants are not seen as part of the gender, trade and development nexus.

Questions arise about where migrant workers belong. To which countries? Which households? Which families? How do they live their lives across different cultures and borders? How do they find time to rest, enjoy the money earned but usually sent to others? How do they relate to the women with whom they work? Where are their voices in the debates? These are all vital issues for feminists and gender and development work. It is not simply an issue of workers' rights and casual border crossing; it is a vital issue that requires us to make care work a basis for rethinking gender and the global economy.

Women and the politics of place

In the third of the three approaches in this chapter, I return to some of the issues raised in the first chapter on what is body politics. Specifically, I look at ways to think outside gender and development discourse in order to understand how globalization changes women's productive and care work in both positive and negative ways. Studies on the care economy and women migrants take the household as a key category in order to analyse gender relations and how they determine global economic processes. The project 'women and the politics of place' (WPP) presents another way of understanding globalization by examining the overlapping ways in which women mobilize politically in four 'places': the body, home, community and public space. As with work on care economy and studies on the lives of women migrants, WPP looks not at globalization as grand-scale narratives of 'world-scale capitalist penetration and dominion' (Harcourt and Escobar 2005) but instead at how globalization informs and is shaped by local initiatives – especially non-capitalist economic ones – described as 'the community economy' in the contribution of J. K. Gibson-Graham, a geographer and an economist writing together as academic feminists for the last twenty years.

J. K. Gibson-Graham's interest in countering dominant economic thinking is similar to the work of feminist activists and economists' studies of care work. The focus is on independent economic dynamics within household economies, the voluntary sector or neighbourhood economies as an exploratory practice of thinking economy differently.

Community economies

J. K. Gibson-Graham move away from the standard image of wage labourers as workers who sell their labour power to a capitalist employer in return for a monetary wage. Instead they propose that the most prevalent form of labour is the unpaid work that is conducted in the household, the family and the neighbourhood or wider community, predominantly by women. In these activities women contribute productive activities that sustain social existence.

They point to many other forms of paid labour that are outside the large globalization narratives. Self-employed workers pay themselves a wage, setting within the constraints of the success of their business their own wage level. Other people work in return for payments in kind, sometimes mixed with monetary payments. A share farmer works on someone else's land in return for a proportion of the harvest; a live-in migrant domestic servant works in someone's home in return for room and board and a small allowance of spending money that does not amount to a living wage. A minister or pastor performs caring labour in a community and is supported by in-kind payments

– access to a house, car, gifts of food and a small stipend. Residents of a community offer their collective labour to others at times of high labour demand – for example, a harvest, house renovation or house moving – in return for a reciprocal claim on labour at another time. J. K. Gibson-Graham see all these different ways in which social wealth is generated and deployed as representing a community economy (Gibson-Graham 2005).[17]

From local to global alternatives

Community economies are linking up through various global processes engaging social justice and alternative economic movements. These networks are re-socializing economic relations by giving them ethical values and political intent.[18] For example, fair trade networks connect Global South producers with Global North consumers, so that in the buying and selling of coffee, bananas or craft products transactions are not disembodied but are negotiated ethically in a quasi face-to-face manner. Farmers' markets, farm-share arrangements and local buying campaigns in community-supported agriculture, such as Italy's slow food campaigns, have sprung up in cities around the industrialized world to bring fresh produce to consumers at (higher) prices that allow farmers to stay in business.

The movements that aim to build and strengthen community economies know that the production and distribution of economic benefit cannot be left to chance. It involves a vision of the economy as an ethical space of negotiated interdependence rather than a self-regulating structure that produces (via the invisible hand of the market) increased social well-being as a by-product of the unfettered pursuit of self-interest.

Building community economies has a strong political component. In the last decade groups working for economic justice and alternative economies have come together to form a loosely connected transnational justice movement. The rapid transformation of companies globally has allowed new types of alliances among North and South trade unions, women's rights movements, movements of consumers, environmentalists and farmers' organizations. One of most visible global expressions of these new movements is the World Social Forum.[19] The World Social Forum process first emerged during the mass protests against the WTO ministerial in Seattle in 1999. These new social movements have a distinctly transnational viewpoint. Some have participated in the processes linked to the UN 1990s conferences, but many came out of local environmental and peace movements, women's movements, consumer campaigns, socialist parties and workers' rights movements. These movements came together to contest neo-liberal globalization and later post-9/11 anti-war coalitions. This broad alliance of movements is an attempt to break away from single ideological narratives of the traditional left such as Marxists, trade unions and ecologists, among others, and to build a new politics based on new ways of understanding economies from diverse points of view, struggles and tensions. They work in horizontal and decentralized structures or network structures aided by globalized communication systems such as the Internet, which are decentralized and built on an open cooperative infrastructure.[20]

Women's issues in alternative movements

Within this search for political and economic alternatives women's issues are at a crossroads where productive and reproductive bodies meet, though in a far more radical and outspoken fashion than that discussed within mainstream gender and development. In the gender and development discourse, solutions are premised on the idea that integration into the global markets offers the most effective route to livelihood security, but they offer little by way of challenge to the worst excesses of commodification and only piecemeal recognition of the synergies and trade-offs associated with women's location at the crossroads of production and reproduction. Feminists working in the context of broader social justice movements challenge global capitalism in a process that noted feminist theorist Saskia Sassen calls 'gendering the global economy' (Sassen 1998: 83).

The global feminization of work has altered gender relations, changing strategies of resistance to capitalism as a mobilized transnational female work-force forms cross-border feminist solidarities. These solidarities are 'negotiating the borders and terrains that connect powerlessness to power' (Sassen 1998: 100). Feminists in organized labour, peace, women's rights and community-based rights movements come together within the broader context of the global social justice movements. As within gender and development discourse there has been a struggle to include gender relations as an integral component of the broader movement agenda for social and economic justice. The challenge of how to engage the broader movement in discussions and actions that understand gender relations as transversal and cross-cutting – starting with the body – is frustrating. Feminists leading this challenge find themselves confronted with an engrained patriarchal gaze that fails to see gender equality or social reproduction, care work or women's specific experience of exploitation as part of the struggle.

Feminist alternatives

As mentioned in Chapter 1, in recent years I have been participating in a project of feminist 'cultural subversion'[21] in the WSF through the Feminist Dialogues. The FDs have been held prior to three WSFs in order to define and elaborate a transnational feminist agenda and also to understand the role of feminists in the larger social movements. Thematically they have focused on neo-liberal globalization, militarism and war, and fundamentalisms. Cross-cutting these themes is the body as a site of politics that acts as a mediator of lived social and cultural relations. In contrast to many UN and NGO meetings I have attended, these spaces are open to intimate and honest discussions on how women's productive and reproductive lives intersect and are experienced as fleshly markings on their bodies.

The FDs held in January 2007 in Nairobi brought 200 women together to discuss feminist visions and strategies to transform democracy (Feminist Dialogues 2007). The conversations focused on common experiences of women's changing economic lives with the impact of global capitalism. For example in Canada small fisheries are unable to compete with big high-tech industrial fisheries, with loss of local jobs and incomes. Women migrating from Latin America to Canada to take up jobs in the big factories in the process lose their citizenship and rights, community and family. In Korea, women once made a living by applying traditional skills in the local fabric industry, but with the rise of Chinese companies making the same fabrics and able to sell more cheaply, Korean women have lost their livelihoods. In Zambia a major concern is that the loss of jobs pushes rural women into sex work because they have no other means of livelihood available. In Pakistan, thousands of women who worked in the fishing industry in the coastal area of Karachi find themselves in very vulnerable situations as big companies from Dubai set up operations obliterating the local market (Feminist Dialogues 2007).

The stories shared over the two days on how women are surviving the dark side of globalization spoke not only of suffering but also of many alternative sources of income and social and cultural change led by women. These narratives were about how women are trying to safeguard women's livelihoods and access to the commons in local communities through resistance movements demanding that states promote pro-people economic reforms and resist corporate dominance in new trade and financial regimes. Resistance by women's groups is varied. Some strategies that emerged in the FDs include: organizing child care and more secure working conditions for women in big hotels in city tourist spots; providing soup kitchens run by mothers' clubs in Central America; pooling savings by Filipina migrant women to build houses in communities back home; creating self-help groups among women fishers for better compensation; working in small farm collectives to provide food security for communities; and preserving traditional ways of husbanding scare resources. The stories reveal how women are building community economies in their struggle to maintain self-reliant small industries pushed to the verge of extinction, retaining popular control over small local industries – such as fisheries, textiles, handicraft and fabric-dying skills – that are being taken over by multinational corporations.

Challenging the stereotypes of care work

Women are building new kinds of politics as they signal their discontent at society's failure to achieve a better integration between productive and care work. This frustration is evident in both analysis and action. Studies of the globalized economy and the care economy, and the recognition of the new transnational lives women are leading as migrants, help to provide ground for the cross-border solidarities being forged among transnational feminist movements.

Feminist analysis and action show how production and care work overlap in women's embodied experience. The assumption is that women who perform paid work are still to be relied upon to continue (paid or unpaid) care work of men, children and the elderly. Such responsibilities are not necessarily undesirable but can become unmanageable and oppressive when working and home conditions do not allow women to navigate their productive and reproductive roles. Despite so many women entering the paid workforce, it seems that men do not in the same numbers as women take up shared responsibilities for care work in the home. Nor are workplaces and conditions evolving to allow for women (or men's) dual roles. Studies on masculinity argue that men's greater involvement in caring may help break down the rigidities of male identity and that a greater caring role may be good for men's health, well-being and life expectancy, but so far they are rarely heeded.

Revaluing care

It is interesting to consider why, as a rule, it is hard to involve men in caring work, in sharing the burden but also the pleasure of care work. There are many answers, depending on the social and economic context, culture and age group. Part of the answer is that the caring work women perform is assumed to be not only as an extension of motherhood but also as a primarily 'biological' female task and therefore judged according to the hierarchies of patriarchal knowledge that stigmatize the 'lesser sex'. Female bodies, psyche and identity are assumed in patriarchal societies to be inferior socially and physically. Such norms are hard to break. For men to take on what is perceived as women's work – caring and running the family home, keeping the community together, changing the workplace to take into account women's bodily needs – would challenge concepts of masculinity, male privilege, power and ownership.

Patriarchal bias is a very difficult area to discuss, embedded as it is in so much of our lives. The story of women as the weaker sex is one patriarchal bias that is challenged by the lives of factory women whose work is 'feminizing' the global economy, the migrant women who are caring for families across continents, and the transnational feminists who are pushing for economic change that recognizes the value of women's care work in the home, the community and the global economy. While perceived as biologically more vulnerable, women in reality have to be physically and psychologically very strong to endure the level of stress and strain involved in working long hours, as they bear responsibility for both productive and care work. The question of why women rather than men take up the burden of care work, even when both are in productive work, is complex. Explanations abound, from the biological to the spiritual. But the point is that someone does have to care for others, and that society would and does break down when women are not there to step into the vital, if often unrewarded and under-analysed, area of care.

Valuing care work is a critical feminist strategy. This does not mean just monetarizing it, even if that is a highly useful exercise in terms of the 'reproductive bargain' when it is important to show to policy makers how much care work counts towards the 'efficient' working of economies. It is also important not to undermine the rewards of giving and sharing our lives in families and communities. Loving and giving care is a socially and culturally rewarding task, as well as hard work. It is also a traditional source of matriarchal power, one that many women, particularly in the Global North, are trying to reclaim by learning from other cultures that continue to recognize that power. I do not wish to romanticize care work, but the trend towards paternity leave in parts of northern Europe does at least engage men in some of the joys of caring for their own children, as well as exposing them to all that is required.

The growing global domestic crisis that Kabeer speaks about, caused by the huge shifts in social and family arrangements, needs to be acknowledged – but not in order to promote once more the 'women as victims of economic development' argument. Instead, it is important to build on the strength of women's resistance globally and the positive and creative ways in which women are handling very difficult situations. Most of all, the realities of migration, care work and the current transformations need to be taken into the core of gender and development work if it is to have any relevance to the vast majority of women's lives. Both in the Global North and the Global South, women's strategies are challenging the 'care chain' domestically and across continents. The crossroads of productive and reproductive work for women may be about to be recognized finally as a shared global playing field. The issue is not about creating work opportunities for women, or getting men to work more in the home, or ending migration, but about real commitment by societies to allow women and men to combine productive and reproductive work in non-exploitative and personally and socially rewarding ways.

Notes

1   For example: Waring 1989; Elson 1991; Folbre 1994, 2001; Beneria 2003.
2   For example gender budgeting undertakes to measure the work, paid and unpaid, women contribute to the economy in order to advocate for a more equal share of the national budget and aid budget to support women's work in homes, communities and paid workplaces.
3   In the style of New Zealand academic, parliamentarian and feminist Marilyn Waring's book *If Women Counted* (1989), which made an important breakthrough for early feminist economics and activist policy.

4 From my own personal experience in the late 1990s – I travelled with my children when I was breastfeeding them – child care would often be provided but only on request. The headquarters of the World Health Organization (WHO) told me it was the first time any one had requested it, and even women's groups made it clear this was an exception, not the rule.

5 Kabeer focuses mainly on very poor countries, but she does describe Italy, the country where I live, as undergoing a 'birth strike'. She examines the fall in births in Italy and highlights the gendered domestic division of unpaid labour. Italy spends 3.5 per cent of its GDP on child-related social spending, compared to 8 per cent in the EU as a whole.

6 See the International Labour Organization's work on gender and health and safety at work: <http://www.oit.org/public/english/protection/safework/gender/index.htm>.

7 Vinca Bigo in her Cambridge University PhD study examines the care crisis in the UK, looking at how care work is both undervalued in terms of pay and also idealized. She examines the crisis by looking at how the amount of time and personal attention given to care makes it an unprofitable investment. She extends the notion of care in a very interesting way to examine a gendered loss of care in the workplace. She has also undertaken an extensive review of the literature on care. In the review she looks at over 300 books and articles that cover mainstream economics on care, feminist economists, heterodox economists' measures of care and the concept of care as a public good. Her study compares literature on care in economics, sociology, politics, philosophy, psychology and anthropology.

8 Studies now being done by UNRISD in a team project headed by Razavi are beginning to document different forms of care work. Razavi, in setting out the plans for the research, argues that there is a need to find an economic strategy for caring if standards are not to deteriorate and care workers are not to fall further behind other workers in pay and working conditions. See the papers on the website www.unrisd.org on politics and social economy of care.

9 In the 1970s the Italian feminist, Mariarosa Dalla Costa (1972) promoted pay for women's domestic work, and there continues to be a push for pay for care work globally by feminists. See the website <http://www.globalwomenstrike.net/English/PRFEB16.htm> which calls every year for an international strike of women to demand pay for household work.

10 These are just a few of the better-known feminist economists working on gender and development; many of them are also associated with the International Association for Feminist Economics (IAFFE): founded in 1992, it now has approximately 600 members in 43 countries. While the majority of IAFFE's members are economists, the group also includes scholars in other disciplines, students, activists, and policy makers. See <http://www.iaffe.org/about/index.php>. For recent books by feminist economists, see for example the series 'Advances in Economics' published by Routledge with IAFFE, <http://www.informaworld.com/smpp/title~content=t729491036>.

11 Boserup (1970) argued that the subsistence sector and the modern capitalist enterprise were both dependent on women's productive labour.

12 This work has had some effect in 1993 with the system of national accounts revised to

include undercounted work (unpaid family work, as well as the home-based, self-employed, informal sector and hitherto uncounted subsistence work).

13 Though slowly, this is shifting, particularly as the amount of remittances sent home by migrant workers is now so large that the World Bank, among others, now sees it as major financial flow; in some countries it is larger than ODA. See the articles on remittances and women migrants in *Development*, Vol. 50, No. 4 ('Migration').

14 Papers from the meeting were published in the March 1993 issue of *Development*, Vol. 43, No. 1 ('Immigration and the International Division of Labour'), pp. 32–47.

15 An award-winning film was shown on that occasion which focused on young men travelling the Sahara to try to reach Europe. Migrant women in the audience asked where the women were. See Zarro 2007.

16 See WIDE's publications and programmatic directions at <www.wide-network.org>.

17 J. K. Gibson-Graham have written many articles together that explore the concept of community economies in detail. See their two major books: Gibson-Graham (1996, 2006).

18 Examples of different social movements can be found in 'Window on the world', *Development*, Vol. 51, No. 4 ('Movement of Movements').

19 The WSF has been held four times in Porto Alegre, Brazil and once in Mumbai, India. In 2006, the WSF was held as a polycentric forum, with three smaller fora simultaneously in Africa (Bamako), the Americas (Caracas), and Asia (Karachi). In 2007 the Forum was held in Africa and in 2009 the WSF was held in Balem, Brazil.

20 See the *Development* journal issue on the 'Movement of Movements', Vol. 51, No. 4, which has several contributions on how the WSF process evolved as a horizontal movement of locally engaged activists working on alternatives to global capitalism, many of whom have continued working together around 'climate justice'.

21 According to Virginia Vargas, a founding member of both the WSF and FDs, the WSF process aims to 'overcome the rigid separation between economy, politics, society, culture and subjectivity. It is creating thepossibility for agendas that aim at cultural subversion, including those of sexuality and equity, to be included as an integral component of the broader movement for economic justice and the deepening of democracy' (Feminist Dialogues 2007).

Serbia and Montenegro Maternity pay is
100% for 365 days.

Sweden Parents of newborn babies are
entitled to 16 months leave between
them.

Cambodia A third of the 55,000 prostitutes
are under 18.

Body Politics in Numbers

4

Source: 'The state they're in - how women are faring in the rest of the world'
http://www.guardian.co.uk/lifeandstyle/2008/dec/07/women-equality-rights-feminism-sexism-worldwide

Four

Violated Bodies

Gender-based violence

The struggle to end sexual and gender-based[1] violence has been central to feminist analysis and practice. It has been a major collective task to identify how sexual and gender-based violence is played out at all levels of power structures, within both the private and public realms. Gender-based violence is manifested in the home and the community; it is built into gender-blind legal systems and expressed in social, economic and political practices; most manifestly it is played out in violent conflict and war. The widespread violence of men against women, whether physical, sexual, or psychological, has its roots in patriarchal power structures, ideas and practices. As such, sexual and gender-based violence has a strong cultural component that is not easily surmounted through norms and laws. The depth and complexity of understanding required to identify and then transform sexual and gender-based violence have been an important feature of women's movements and are visibly part of gender and development policy projects and vision. In this chapter I explore some of the successes and difficulties of this complex and ongoing struggle.

My aim is to understand how sexual and gender-based violence emerges from the human rights discourse with its explicit statement of the rights to freedom of expression, protection from violence and guaranteed personal security. Another aim is to understand how prejudices and fears that are contained in racism and colonial hangovers, fundamentalism and xenophobia are also played out in gender-based violence, a topic rarely addressed directly in gender and development policy.

Indeed, writing and speaking about sexual and gender-based violence are difficult. On the one hand, these topics touch deeply personal experiences that form gendered fears and identities. On the other hand, acts of sexual and gender-based violence are among the major public subjects of our time – from scandalized newspaper reporting, films, advertising and pornography to state censorship, public moralizing and religious creeds. It is therefore important to tackle the subject aware of all the hype around it.

Two approaches

In the last two decades many strategies on how to counter sexual and gender-based violence have been proposed in the dialogues among women's movements and feminists that are part of gender and development discourse. In this chapter I take up two approaches. I first look at the issue of rape and violation of women within gender and development discourse, tracing how it emerged from silence and taboo to a subject of campaigns, debate and policy. I explore how sexual and gender-based violence has been 'mainstreamed' into gender and development discourse by its framing as a health and gender equality issue. I look at the use of media by awareness-raising campaigns to lobby governments into action and raise money for women's groups on the ground; at the attempt to involve men; and at the extensive work of UN agencies and women's rights activists in post-conflict situations to redress rape and sexual violence as war crimes through reforms to the judicial system.

In the second approach I go deeper into some of the uncomfortable issues unable to be 'mainstreamed' in a context that includes the war on terror, fundamentalism, racism and difference. I look at sexual and gender-based violence in relation to issues around war and conflict, fundamentalism and militarism, and am led deeper into issues of racism and sexual and gender-based violence that form an unspoken backdrop to gender and development policy.

Breaking the silence

More than any other in the book, this chapter is informed by my own feminist practice.[2] Like other feminists my first political entry point into feminism was through protests at violence against women. As an Australian student I joined others in the struggle for the right to walk safely at night on the university campus. We courted arrest marching in protest on the streets against rape in war. In my transnational feminist work I have met many women who have taken similar paths. We have begun working at local levels and then, over the years, fuelled by the global communication technologies and the increasing outreach of transnational networking, found ourselves working both locally and globally. From different local struggles we came together in thousands to the halls of the UN to exchange experiences and strategies and to push for international agreements that have made once-silenced issues such as rape in war recognized as an international crime. One of the main issues that brought us together despite our many different cultures and responses was sexual and gender-based violence. Many women's lives and those who are considered gendered 'others' to men (such as homosexuals and transsexuals) are shaped by the fear, experience and response to sexual harassment, battering, rape and abuse of different sorts by men in and outside the family. Sexual and gender-based violence remains one of the biggest issues in the women's movement although where one lives, the colour of one's skin, access to resources and social positioning determine greatly the actual experience on the flesh.

Rape as a public issue

Rape is one of the most difficult experiences to survive and to comprehend for many women, wherever they live. Rape is not about sex but about power and domination; it involves the loss of control over the body, sexuality and the core of self. In my teenage years in Australia it was one of the most shaming and therefore unspoken-about events. It is now almost shockingly public.

This was brought home to me when I was attending the 2004 annual meeting of the Human Development and Capability Association in Pavia in North Italy. I listened to Martha Nussbaum, the incoming President, giving her keynote address to a packed hall of around 200 professors and students.[3] She opened with a graphic description of being raped by her date when she was a graduate student at Harvard. It is hard to describe the shock and discomfort in the room when this elegantly dressed Ernst Freund Distinguished Service Professor of Law and Ethics spoke of such an act of brutality and then linked it to the violence experienced by women in Gujarat in the anti-Muslim riots in 2002. Certainly I found myself not wanting to look at the young male students sitting around me.

The experience raised the difficulties of speaking about rape and wondering if and how rape is a universal experience for women across cultures. It is clear that Nussbaum's talk was driven both by her personal experience and by her friendships in India, where she spends many hours listening to poor women talk about their daily struggles. Yet I felt the context and the reasons for making those connections were somewhat ambiguous. As a liberal feminist Nussbaum was calling attention to the fact that rape happens everywhere, even to rich US students, and that in today's modern world she was able to speak about it openly. At the same time, as a privileged US professor she was speaking about her rape as if that experience gave her a special authority to understand the violent rapes of the women in Gujarat, also one of the topics of her talk. I could not help but contrast her poise and ability with what I had read about the experiences of the women in Gujarat. They were subject to organized, state-condoned violence; many of them died in terrible ways. The bodies of pregnant women were slit open to remove the foetus. The gang rapes were of such brutality that the women died of the wounds. The social and individual shame meant that those women who did survive were doomed as outcasts. Those women could never openly speak about what happened to them. That being said, much has been written about Gujarat 2002 and the rapes are recorded and seen as integral to fundamentalist attacks.

Nussbaum showed courage to bring into an academic forum on economic capabilities the issue of sexual and gender-based violence. To women's groups however, the concept of date rape and the sexualized violence experienced in Gujarat are not new or surprising.

Mobilizing against gender-based violence

There are hundreds of campaigns set up by local women's groups to tackle the daily grind to end sexual and gender-based violence. Sexual and gender-based violence is now part and parcel of a public discourse that includes the gender and development policy discourse. Personal and organizational messages, reports, appeals, campaigns, stories of success and of dire violations criss-cross my computer screen daily. The many documents, books, journals, websites, leaflets and videos record how the opening up of what was once a taboo topic is one of the main achievements of transnational women's organizing and advocacy. The anecdotes I tell in this chapter indicate the collective strength of the transnational women's movements to prevent and change sexual and gender-based violence, with varying degrees of success.

I could point to the work of many excellent groups.[4] One that stands out in my transnational experience as a central vocal campaign that has linked women around the world working to end sexual and gender-based violence is the 16 days Days of Activism Against Gender Violence Campaign. The 16 Days Campaign was set up at the first Women's Global Leadership Institute sponsored by the Center for Women's Global Leadership based in Rutgers, New Jersey, USA in 1991. The 16 days begin with 25 November, International Day Against Violence Against Women, and end on 10 December, International Human Rights Day, in order to link symbolically violence against women and human rights, and to emphasize that such violence is a violation of human rights.

The 16 Days Campaign demonstrates how women's groups are creating tools to pressure governments to implement promises made to eliminate violence against women – with some success as different laws are pushed through, police stations set up, hospital services provided and trauma centres funded. Though awareness raising is hard to measure with precision, the numbers that have participated and use the campaign for effective advocacy work is impressive. Over 2,000 organizations in 154 countries have participated in the 16 Days Campaign since 1991. The website gives a long list of local activities undertaken over the years and highlights which UN and other international initiatives are supporting the work to end sexual and gender-based violence against women.[5]

As the numbers of groups involved indicates, a major transnational tool for women's networking and action against gender-based violence in recent years has not only been the UN space but also the Web and Internet as means to share information, campaigns and support to put pressure on governments for change, and to make public issues that then surface in the mainstream media and on the agendas of decision and policy makers (Harcourt 1999).

The V word

A highly visible and popular campaign has been inspired by Eva Ensler's play *The Vagina Monologues*. This V-Day campaign is a fascinating example of body politics on the margins of development. The 'V' in V-Day stands for Valentine, Vagina and Victory, linking love and respect for women to ending violence against women and girls.[6] Every monologue relates to women's experience through the vagina, be it through sex, love, rape, menstruation, mutilation, masturbation, birth, or orgasm. Naming the vagina is presented as a tool of female empowerment: the strategy is that women reclaim a sense of pride and self-fulfillment through embracing feminine embodiment.[7]

Since 1998 every year a new monologue is added to highlight a current issue affecting women around the world. In 2003, for example, Ensler wrote a new monologue 'Under the Burqa' about the plight of women in Afghanistan under Taliban rule.[6] In 2008, the play had been produced in 45 languages in 120 countries, in the process chanelling more than 50 million dollars into local women's shelters and safe houses, raising awareness, promoting legislation or establishing community anti-violence programmes by local groups.

When one reads the responses from around the world,[8] including the clandestine readings by women from Saudi Arabia and the banning in 2005 of the play in Uganda, *The Vagina Monologues* are breaking deep-seated taboos. They work with the pain and horror many women experience but also by linking women together through the monologues and through a sense of pride and fun in their own bodies.[10] Notably the V-Campaign is not seeking to institutionalize, but has rather evolved in a quirky *ad hoc* way that grows with the interest and need of those who participate. The V-Campaign links up to gender and development projects; for example UNICEF coordinated a V-Day event in the Democratic Republic of Congo.[11]

In an interview on 8 March 2008 in the *Toronto Star*, Ensler is quoted as saying:

> When I started this I had no idea of the [size of the] epidemic of violence against women. . . . I had no idea how women had hungered to have happy sexual lives and to be in their own sexuality and feel good about their sexuality and how far away some women are from living that life. . . . When women can't identify their genitals or their body parts, often they are disassociated from them, so they have no power over them and no rights over them. (Walker 2008)[12]

Ensler's is a one-woman vision which has spread and resonated with a lot of other women by the use of entertainment and creativity in unapologetic yet wryly funny ways. It is important to question the unstated assumption that just to speak about the body is enough: V-day strategies cannot address the complex global experience of poverty, violence against women and profound social and gender inequalities. Nevertheless, *The Vagina Monologues* work against the sexually saturated male pornographic gaze regarding women's bodies and provide the space for women's embodied voices. The V-Day campaign represent an interesting form of body politics that weaves in and out of the gender and development discourse.

Sexual and gender-based violence as a health issue

The experience and knowledge that women's movements and other movements in the LGBT and progressive men's movements have built, shared and acted upon is at the core of body politics in gender and development. It is this experience-based work that informs much of the analysis and research that informs the frameworks, modelling and policy at the more official levels around the UN.

Since the 1990s the World Health Organization (WHO), through the work of a dynamic team of women researchers linked to women's health organizations, has taken up domestic violence and health as a critical health issue (WHO 2006). It is a mark of how far the taboo around sexual and gender-based violence has been challenged. The statement on the WHO website is explicit: sexual and gender-based violence is 'one of the most pervasive violations of human rights in all societies [it is] a global concern . . . it exists on a continuum from violence perpetrated by an intimate partner to violence as a weapon of war'. These acts of violence have been codified by WHO as physical violence, sexual violence, emotional violence and intimate partner violence (also called domestic violence).[13]

One of the landmarks of the WHO's work that established how sexual and gender-based violence is a major public health and human rights problem is a multi-country study on women's health and domestic violence. The study is based on comparable data from over 24,000 women interviewed in Bangladesh, Brazil, Ethiopia, Japan, Peru, Namibia, Samoa, Serbia and Montenegro, Thailand and Tanzania. The study aims to establish the norms and standards for a health sector response to sexual violence. It sets out a series of guidelines for providing care to sexual assault survivors as well as a framework for health sector policies related to sexual violence. The WHO initiative that emerged from the study trains health workers and provides a framework for health policies with the aim of improving medico-legal services and to coordinate efforts of police departments, health services, prosecutors, social welfare agencies and non-governmental service providers such as rape crisis centres. These tools for the public health sector are based on a holistic response, one that places the psycho-social dimension alongside the physical treatment (WHO 2006).

The WHO approach is one of capacity building and service provision guided by evidence-based research. In its research and norm-setting work, WHO has successfully promoted awareness and change in the health, education, legal and criminal justice sectors. Hospitals, women's health movements and rape crisis centres have made use of a WHO-backed message in their work on countering and dealing with the trauma and pain of women who suffer sexual and gender-based violence.[14] These centres take very practical approaches such as training police, medical personnel and judges on how to deal with the victims of intimate violence, rape and other forms of abuse such as female genital mutilation (Garcia-Moreno 2001; Haque 2001).

Gender-based violence campaigns

There are several other UN agencies that work on sexual and gender-based violence such as UNICEF, UNFPA and UNHCR, to name a few. UNIFEM in particular sees its role as providing leadership and support to women's organizations in the fight against sexual and gender-based violence, and has become one of the major focal points for women's groups globally. UNIFEM[15] sees fighting gender-based violence as a major concern: 'one of the most widespread violations of human rights ... an epidemic that devastates lives, fractures communities and stalls development ... its horrendous scale remains mostly unacknowledged'.

One way that UNIFEM tackles the 'cycle of the violence against women ... rooted in gender inequality' is through information and advocacy campaigns, working with a range of partners. The Trust Fund to End Violence Against Women offers grants to small projects working to prevent violence that are run by community, national and regional organizations.

The UNIFEM report 'Not a Minute More: Ending Violence Against Women'[16] provides an overview of efforts by women's (and some men's) groups around the world to end gender-based violence. The report is a homage to the 'monumental' work of women's groups and activists to put the issue on the agenda: women advocates have 'transformed the way gender-based violence is understood, and have promoted international documents and treaties that recognize, for the first time, women's right to live free of violence'.

UNIFEM released videos accompanying the message of the report in 2007. They teamed up with the UN Trust Fund started by TV billionaire Ted Turner. Promoting private and public partnerships, the Fund aims to broaden support for the UN through advocacy and public outreach to end violence against women. The feature video of the campaign, 'A Life Free of Violence Is Our Right',[17] promotes the UN Trust Fund to End Violence against Women. Managed by UNIFEM, the Fund supports local groups to change laws and attitudes, provide shelter and social services, and offer protection and legal support to women. The film shows scenes of tearful mothers of victims, trafficked women, women with HIV and AIDS and sex workers all claiming their right to a life free of violence and the need for money to build their organizations and continue their campaigns. The message the video conveys is to support UNIFEM and the UN Trust to help these women survive and recover from the trickery and horrific violence in their lives before they are trafficked or raped again, overwhelmed by despair or murdered.

'Let's End Violence Against Women',[18] made by London-based advertising agency Leo Burnett, is another UNIFEM production with a striking series of images set to dramatic music. The core message of this one-minute video is that simply being born a woman is one of the biggest reasons for suffering violence – even more than war, racial discrimination or religious extremism. The viewer first sees graphic media images of violent war shots, street violence and incense-filled temples. These images are then followed by the words blocked out in black and white: 'rape', 'genital mutilation', 'domestic violence' and then the looming question: 'Who will be next?' The video closes with the answer that it could be your sister, daughter or mother, and that one in three women will be violated in their lifetime.

Though it is highly appropriate that UNIFEM should champion the need to end gender-based violence, I have several problems with the messages and images of the video. The film is aimed essentially at a male audience, as it assumes a male gaze (your sister, daughter, mother) and women are objectified as the victims. The assumption is that people need to be shocked into donating money to stop violence against women: it is a crisis which requires a charity approach to help the victims, rather than a human rights issue that needs to be addressed by governments and legal systems. It confirms the patriarchal stereotype that being a woman is the most vulnerable state of being, requiring the protection of others. It is also not useful to compare racism, extremism and conflict as somehow separate from a 'female' experience of sexual and gender-based violence, when in real life they are all combined.

Million Women Rise

To go to a national example which depicts women as victims of men's violence in need of protection: consider the British-based Million Women Rise campaign. As with the UNIFEM campaign I feel a strong sense of unease at the essentializing of women, even if the call is for grassroots action and marches rather than for policy change. Their website features pictures of abused Asian women, presumably migrants, alongside strident pictures of women protesting almost joyfully in colourful multicultural marches.[19] The 'million women' march to end violence against women and to defend women's and children's rights to live free from violence and/or the fear of violence. They attack the government, the media and most of all men, depicting men's violence against women as a 'global pandemic', including emotional, psychological, sexual and physical abuse, coercion and constraints. They call on women in Britain to express their outrage at 'the continued daily, hourly, minute-by-minute individual and institutionalized violence enacted against women worldwide'. The message mixes local with global as they speak out against domestic rape, commercial sex work, trafficking of young girls, foeticide, female genital mutilation, rape in wars, women living with HIV and AIDS, and maternal mortality. They also provide links to women's NGOs working on global issues and international human rights agreements. Though I have no quarrel with the importance of the issue, the campaign acts on anger and fears where women are victims, failing to see the broader social, economic and political context in which violations need to be placed.

Filmstar ploys

So what strategies do we use? Million Women Rise appeals to women's anger and fear. With more money and a less radical approach UNIFEM uses glamour. The film star and goodwill ambassador Nicole Kidman features in another UNIFEM video to launch an Internet campaign to say no to violence against women. Kidman in carefully filmed headshots with her peter pan collar slightly crumpled, and blonde hair held back, with just a wisp escaping, explains the need to say no to violence against women, and where to sign up. The campaign is backed up by an email blitz to UNIFEM supporters with a signed letter from Kidman.[20] I find that there is something unsettling about using Kidman to promote the end to violence against women in the same way as she promotes the perfume Chanel No. 5.

Engagement of celebrities is not new or unique to UNIFEM. The V-Campaign certainly uses them, and stars abound now in highly publicized development negotiations, the best-known being Angelina Jolie, Bono of U2 and Sharon Stone. UNIFEM certainly engages in meaningful ways to end violence against women and is supporting and building on the work of women's groups. But the way the campaign has been designed to reach a broad public indicates the difficulties and limitations of a global campaign led by UN agencies working through policy channels, governments and marketing methods funded by mainstream media. The reasons for choosing Kidman – a slim, white Australian Hollywood actress who is paid millions of dollars for her films and whose face promotes perfumes and glamour – might be that she is a good marketing tool and to ensure publicity for the Fund and UNIFEM, but the choice belies the far from glamorous violence and death that, according to UNIFEM, will be the reality of 'one in three' women. Feel good signs-ups on a website do not counter that.

I have a similar sense of unease and questions about how sexual and gender-based violence is taken up on film screens. Let us take the case of the Mexican border town of Ciudad Juárez, home to export-processing plants or *maquiladoras*. Since the mid-1990s the *maquiladoras* have primarily employed young women. As a result of the rapid and mostly uncontrolled economic growth, the high level of unemployment among men, and the arrival of migrants from different parts of the country, the social fabric of Ciudad Juárez has been torn apart. The city is now infamous for its organized crime and violence, and for the many young women who have been murdered there in the last decade. Since 1993 over 400 bodies have been found and many more hundreds of young women have disappeared. Through local and transnational organizing, these murders and disappearances – a graphic form of sexual and gender-based violence – have become a political issue in Mexico. Mexican women activists have called on women around the world to advocate that the Mexican state must comply with its obligation to protect and ensure women's rights and to prevent gender-targeted violence (Marchand 2004). It is an ongoing campaign as, despite past and current unsolved murders, in August 2006 the federal government dropped its investigation – and the murders continue.

The protests began with a group of mothers, families and friends of the victims, called Nuestras Hijas de Regreso a Casa (Our Daughters Come Back Home). Another organization, Voces sin Eco (Voices without Echo) was founded in 1998. They painted pink crosses on black telephone poles to draw attention to the problem. Since then it has been taken up by women's movements, Mexican and US journalists, singers and film makers. A major film release by Gregory Nava – *Bordertown*, with Jennifer Lopez and Antonio Banderas – was shown at the 2007 Berlin Film Festival. The message Nava gives is that the plight of these women is integral to globalized violence.

At a press conference in Berlin, Nava was clearly moved and disturbed by the plight of young women from Ciudad Juárez whose lives, as he pointed out, could be thrown away by their government in the interest of globalization. It took over eight years to make the film, and it is telling that he could only attract the money because he engaged Lopez. Lopez stated in the same press conference that until Nava told her about Ciudad Juárez she had no idea of the situation but was immediately deeply concerned and agreed to do the film. In Berlin, Lopez was given an award by Amnesty International. Though she accepted the award, to her credit Lopez named and publicly hugged the three members of Nuestras Hijas de Regreso a Casa who were there to see the première. But for the world press, these women remained in the shadow of the silver-clad star. Again the question is about if we should and can make change by using the power of Hollywood to bring attention to sexual and gender-based violence. Without a doubt we raise awareness, but do we risk confusing real-life misery and tragedy with the glamour and fictional lives of the stars? Are we just adding one more story to a billion-dollar industry based on violence and sexism?

Engaging with boys and men

With or without Hollywood, ending sexual and gender-based violence requires major shifts in gender roles. There are men in academe and activism who are engaging with the issue of sexual and gender-based violence in ways that interlink with gender and development. In key UN documents on sexual and reproductive health and rights there are many statements about male responsibilities, and funds have been made available for capacity-building exercises to train religious leaders, male police, hospital staff and judges. In the work I did in the follow-up to Cairo, for example, I came across campaigns working with policemen in Brazil and Suriname, with community leaders in Indonesia, and with religious leaders in Ghana with funding from UNFPA and others such as the MacArthur Foundation.[21]

One global network of organizations is MenEngage. MenEngage is a global alliance of non-governmental organizations that are involved in research, interventions and policy initiatives seeking to engage men and boys to reduce gender inequalities and promote health and the well-being of women, men and children. The MenEngage Alliance highlights how social constructions of masculinity impact on gender-based violence, reproductive health, sexual rights, fatherhood and caregiving.[22]

Another global campaign of men working to stop violence against women – one that overlaps with MenEngage – is the White Ribbon Campaign, so named because its members wear white ribbons in the same way HIV and AIDS activists wear red ribbons. One of the founders of the White Ribbon Campaign, the Canadian Michael Kaufman, has written very movingly about his work to end violence against women by engaging strategically with governments and UN agencies.[23] He sees the relationship of men to violence against women as multifaceted and very complex, one that touches all men directly or indirectly. His concern is that far too many men are committing sexual and gender-based violence, and that even the lives of men who do not use violence are still touched deeply by the construction of hegemonic masculinities that condone the use of violence.[24]

Violence and masculinity

I met Kaufman when holding a series of meetings that led to a journal issue of *Development* on violence against women and the culture of masculinity. In the process I met documentary film makers, NGOs and social workers from Australia, Brazil, Canada, India, Nigeria, USA and the Caribbean. These men and women came together to discuss with UNICEF and WHO staff how to change boys and men's perceptions of their gender role. Their work was a combination of awareness raising and analysis, going beyond the limitations of macho roles and learning from feminist methodologies on how to transform gender stereotypes and male identities that linked violence and sexual aggression to images of how to be a 'real man'.

I found the work with boys, adolescents and young men in the slums of Delhi and the favelas of Brazil intriguing, as the programmes aimed to reach men before they had hardened into violence and despair. It seemed uphill work, as some of the orphaned street boys were already locked into a life of survival and brutality at a very young age. These projects deliberately aimed to catch up on the years of engaged and rigorous research and work on women's lives and women's cultures in order to produce a textured understanding of the diversity of men's experiences, attitudes, beliefs, practices, situations, sexualities and institutions. Rahul Roy, in an article beautifully entitled 'The Eyes are Silent . . . The Heart Desires to Speak', put it like this:

> Violence against women and girls and violence, in general, is an issue, which almost all parts of South Asia have been forced to confront. If we pause to draw on the images of violence, it is almost certain that the images, which will flash across, will be of men as perpetrators of violence. This is not to suggest that all men are violent or that women are biologically non-violent. In fact the truth that most men and women are not violent gives us hope of changing the worlds we live in. (Roy 2001: 20)

Roy's documentaries provided a platform to initiate a discourse with young people, especially boys and young men, on the larger gender concerns without being didactic. The method he employed began from conversations about young men's life experiences in general, then moved to problems they encountered in relation to sexuality and gender roles, and then to a discussion of institutions such as schools, families, society, relationships, gender, conflicts, abuse, violence and HIV and AIDS.

Another contributor to the *Development* issue was Gary Barker, who works with boys and youths in the favelas of Rio de Janeiro. In these conversations he found that sexual violence is viewed as part of gendered sexual 'scripts'. In these scripts dating and domestic violence are justified by men when women 'betray' informal marriage and cohabitation contracts. Men may resort to violence when they are denied the 'benefits of patriarchy'. He found that young men sometimes condone domestic violence among their peers as part of mutual support for each other. Similarly, traditional 'machista' views about sexuality in which men view women as sex objects without sexual agency are closely associated with domestic and sexual violence. Poverty and a violent background lead to violence. One-third of male partners who used violence were out of work at the time of the violence. Boys in favelas are subject to higher rates of physical abuse in the home than girls, a factor that may be related to some men's subsequent use of violence in their intimate relationships. Men's silence about other men's violence also contributes to domestic violence. The majority of the young men said that they felt powerless to speak out against sexual and gender-based violence. As Barker stated, 'Overcoming the silence of men who witness other men being violent toward women is a key starting point for our work' (Barker 2001: 96).

In a later study for WHO in 2007, Barker and his colleagues (Barker et al. 2007) assess whether such projects with boys and men to break the silence have worked. Their evaluation of 58 projects shows that it is difficult to bring together policy agendas that shift men's gender attitudes towards sexual and gender violence and at the same time empower women. The nagging problem of the silence and complicity among male peer groups and within health, judicial and government institutions remains. None of these subtle factors can be 'measured' or considered in evidence-based methodology. Barker and his colleagues refer to many more experiences which they felt obliged to exclude from the study because the studies were much harder to measure or quantify. They question why a table or model is necessary in order to decide on a policy direction, given that much of what works in real life is based on intuition and risk taking. The not so surprising official conclusion of the study is that deeper long-term engagement in changing structural gender bias is required rather than small projects aimed at particular individuals or social groups. Barker is contributing to that work through MenEngage Alliance.

War, conflict, and sexual and gender-based violence in development

Sexual and gender-based violence has been integral to war and military regimes throughout human history.[25] Sexual and gender-based violence is employed as a weapon of war. Through the work of UN agencies and countless NGOs, acts of violence against women and girls during conflict and its aftermath are in the public domain; as war crimes, they can be legally redressed.

Wartime rape aims to destroy both the personality and the identity of women and girls, and also attacks the integrity of the community. In modern conflict civilians are often trapped in the fighting between militia groups and military forces. Such a situation leads to fractured families and communities, and to violence for girls, women and vulnerable men. Children and women are subject to sexual and gender-based violence by military forces, by police and security officials, local leaders, fellow refugees and displaced persons, as well as members of the host community. The consequences for individual women, their families and the community are profound and enduring, leaving social, economic, health and psychological scars. Sexual and gender-based violence is not limited to women. It is also used to humiliate men and boys in war. In Bosnia-Herzegovina ten years after the war, several thousand men were found to have been sexually harassed and raped in Bosnia (Çalışkan 2006).

Violence does not end with a declaration of peace. In the post-war period sexual and gender violence continues. The military part of 'peacekeeping' missions eats into resources for education, health and basic community, and studies now show that sexual and gender-based violence increases in such a militarized insecure environment, often in ways that condone violence as part of a nationalistic and patriarchal assertion of identity. There is considerable concern that children and women endure sexual exploitation and abuse at the hands of international peacekeeping forces or humanitarian aid workers.[26] In post-genocidal Rwanda rape is one of the most common violent crimes committed in the capital, Kigali. An estimated 50,000 to 64,000 Sierra Leonean women who were displaced within that country have suffered from sexual violence (Porter 2006).

The concern is not only with rape but also with sexual exchange for food, money or protection, as one of the only ways for displaced women to survive economically. Such transactions leave girls and women extremely vulnerable to HIV and AIDS and other sexually transmitted infection. HIV and AIDS are emerging as a deadly form of modern conflict. It is estimated that two in three women who were raped as part of the genocidal violence in Rwanda are HIV positive. In the Democratic Republic of Congo, Amnesty International estimates that some 40,000 women were raped between 1999 and 2005, and that up to 30 per cent of rape survivors may be HIV positive (Naraghi-Anderlini 2005). UNAIDS estimates conservatively that military personnel are up to five times more likely to be HIV positive than the general population.

Women's groups responding to survivors' needs

Community-level women's groups have to deal with trauma and pain following the horror of war and violent conflict. In research on post-conflict situations and the 'reconstruction' of societies, major concern has been raised about how women are left with very few resources to deal with traumatized children and family members who were combatants. Women's shelters have been set up to support women, meeting everyday needs while dealing with intense traumas, including the issue of war babies.[27] Women's local community groups provide a safe place to encourage rape survivors to speak out and help to change social attitudes to accept survivors. They provide post-rape care, including access to health care, psycho-social care, safety and, whenever possible, access to legal redress. These groups offer a community network for survivors and provide information for treatment and how to begin life again.

One example is Medica Mondiale, founded in 1992 during the war in Bosnia to protect and support the women who endured ongoing mass rapes in the armed conflict. Working with local women, the Medica Mondiale team set up a multi-ethnic therapy centre under war conditions for traumatized women and girls who had been raped, to give them and their children short- and medium-term assistance by specially trained female Bosnian experts. The experiences from war and its consequences of traumatization for women's bodies and souls led them to build up further interdisciplinary projects in Kosovo and Albania to support women in war-affected societies. They also link up with war-rape survivors in northern Iraq, India (Gujarat), Sudan, Turkey and Mexico (Çalışkan 2006).

Networking and sharing experiences, breaking silences and advocating for legal redress are the goals of The African Partnership of Sexual and Repro-ductive Health and Rights of Women and Girls (AMANITARE), made up of 50 or more organizations and individuals based in Africa and the diaspora.[28] As a member of AMANITARE, Isis-WICCE has documented women's experiences in situations of armed conflict in East Africa and the Great Lakes Region over the last six years, recording numerous cases of sexual and gender-based violations resulting from the war and violent conflict. The documentary video *Women, War and Trauma* tells of the experiences that have left the survivors physically ill and psychologically traumatized. In addition to the video, Isis-WICCE raises public awareness through drama and radio sketches on the effects of war on women's sexual and reproductive health and rights. They try to link these on-the-ground sufferings with possible redress following existing international conventions such as the Convention for the Elimination of all Discrimination Against Women (CEDAW).[29] What is revealed in such documentaries is the need to break down the women's strong sense of ethnic difference, anger and bitterness, as well as their isolation as rural women (Ojiambo Ochieng 2003).

Gender justice in modern wars

Training to build the capacity of women as leaders able to be involved in peace building and negotiations has been one of the major responses of the women's movement to redress sexual and gender-based violence. Beyond crucial on-the-ground grassroots initiatives (also dealing with the problems of widows – another major transnational networking effort),[30] a major achievement of transnational women's organizing has been the adoption of UN Security Council Resolution 1325, an important advocacy tool for women's groups to redress injustice against women in war or in the post-conflict transition, and to create the conditions for women's full citizenship and rights.

Resolution 1325 calls for gender equity in the transition to peace, recognizing the role women play as community leaders and active peace builders. Advocacy based on Resolution 1325 pushes for war crimes against women to be punished and to ensure that women gain political, policy and legal decision-making positions in the post-conflict situation.

Sanam Naraghi-Anderlini (2005) looks at the problems of achieving gender justice in the context of modern wars in which, she estimates, 90 per cent of casualties are civilians, women are systematically targeted with all forms of sexual abuse, and children are abducted and forced to murder and maim. She points out that after the war the victims and perpetrators have to live side by side again.

Much of the international community's engagement in justice post-conflict has been through judicial processes such as the International Criminal Tribunal for the former Yugoslavia (ICTY) and the International Criminal Tribunal Rwanda (ICTR). International tribunals and mechanisms have been highly problematic for women. Prior to the ICTY and ICTR, war crimes tribunals or truth commissions were totally blind to the gendered dimension of political violence and war. Naraghi-Anderlini argues that a sea-change took place with the formation of the ICTR and particularly the ICTY. Bosnian women's human rights advocates, together with international women's rights activists, demanded that sexual violence during the war be treated as a grave violation of international law, and not just a by-product of war. In the ICTY female judges were on the bench. With gender experts among the staff, the substance of proceedings and court procedures improved. Learning from this, the Women's Caucus for Gender Justice has influenced the design and statutes of the International Criminal Court (ICC). The ICC statutes recognize rape, sexual slavery, enforced prostitution, pregnancy and sterilization, as well as other forms of sexual violence, as crimes against humanity and war crimes.[31]

Such international judicial developments have helped remove the invisibility and silence surrounding sexual and gender-based crimes in war. Nevertheless, despite the millions spent, the overall effectiveness of such tribunals is still questioned. There is little sense of local ownership, and there is anger at the perceived bias of the court as key leaders of the war remain free. The tribunals have failed to have a significant impact on the lives of the majority of the actual victims. On the tenth anniversary of the Rwandan genocide, the ICTR had handed down just 21 sentences: 18 convictions and three acquittals. An overwhelming 79 per cent of those judgments contained no rape convictions. Looking at such international justice through the eyes of rape victims reveals that international criminal courts continue to overlook crimes of sexual and gender-based violence (Nowrojee 2005). The majority of men who rape and pillage are not brought to justice. No judicial system can cope with the sheer numbers of perpetrators. And no society emerging from war – attempting to heal, reconcile and move towards peace – is able or even willing to consider prosecuting the thousands (overwhelmingly men) who would be implicated in such crimes. Most of the victims who survived will never talk about the horror they had to suffer. Survivors are often willing to live with impunity for their attackers, either for fear of reprisals or because they believe that trials would jeopardize the fragile peace.[23] Women's participation in peace and security concerns around the world continues in mediation, conciliation, trauma counsel, healing and memory work, providing health care for survivors of rape and HIV and AIDS sufferers.

Going beyond the numbers

It is awkward writing about this level of suffering and the courageous struggles undertaken on so many different levels. These stories are about betrayals, pain and emotion as much as about justice and development and rights. Such experiences cannot be reduced just to numbers: the 'one in three' women so dramatically spoken about in the UNIFEM video; all those experiences hidden in the oft-quoted number of 20,000 women raped in former Yugoslavia; the unimaginable cruelty done to the 240,000 women raped in Rwanda. The list is absurdly and relentlessly long. The pain and emotions of even one person, let alone the devastating numbers mentioned here, are hard to analyse and describe without diminishing them in some way. Making something visible, bringing it to the attention of judicial and political structures that are not built to handle it, leads to huge disappointment, frustration and bitterness. Worse, the experiences can be twisted and misused. It is for this reason that many survivors of sexual and gender-based violence remain silent; even when the women are in great pain and in need of support. It is understandable that the issue seems too big to tackle. No doubt it is also why men close their ears and eyes.

The temptation to turn away from the subject as just too difficult is a response I feel even more keenly when I read feminist analysis on sexual and gender-based violence which asks awkward questions about women's role in violence. This analysis makes us question the stereotypes of women as victims and men as perpetrators of sexual and gender-based violence. They ask us to look at gendered subjects, and question the elevated role of women as mothers and peace makers. They point out that the hatred and cruelty of men is also shared by women, and how we need to confront the role of women in the military. They agree that violence is an abuse of power, and that sexual and gender-based violence disempowers women of all ages, religions, ethnicities and race – but also they force us to see that women themselves are implicated in the power structures, identities and histories of sexual and gender-based violence.

War on terror

The second approach in my discussion of violated bodies is to review feminist analysis and practice that looks at militarism, fundamentalism and racism, the subsumed subtexts to the gender and development discourse on sexual and gender-based violence.

I first drafted the chapter as a petition was going around global women's networks asking people to support an Amnesty International campaign to stop the death threats to six men and three women writers and human rights defenders and activists who have spoken out about irregularities in the Kenyan elections of 27 December 2007. Over 800 people were killed and at least 250,000 driven from their homes after the rigged presidential elections on 27 December, and human rights abuses continued to be committed by police and armed gangs throughout the country. Kenya until now has been held up as a darling of the development community, even if studies show a steady increase in inequalities throughout the country.[233]

Muthoni Wanyeki, Executive Director of the Kenya Human Rights Commission and a well-known activist in transnational feminist circles, describes the violence and climate of fear that is enveloping Kenya. She argues that words like genocide and ethnic cleansing are only fuelling the rifts and resentments already felt in political and economic exclusion and the widening inequalities (Wanyeki 2008). In an open editorial in the *New York Times* co-authored with Maina Kiai, Wanyeki points out that Kenya, as a willing partner in the Bush administration's war on terrorism, has received millions of dollars of military assistance. Weapons bought with that money have been used to kill Kenyan civilians with impunity (Kiai and Wanyeki 2008).

The war on terror, with its militarized approach to development aid and its 'civilizing' mission, is where sexual and gender-based violence is now embedded. But it is a far from simple relationship. Masculinisms, as feminist academic and researcher Ros Petchesky points out, combine militarism, nationalism and colonialism: 'men's sense of their own masculinity, often tenuous, is as much a factor in international politics as is the flow of oil, cables, and military hardware' (Enloe, quoted in Petchesky 2001). Misogyny goes hand in hand with state terrorism and extreme fundamentalism. Eisenstein outlines in *Sexual Decoys* how Bush claims that the US army is liberating Afghani and Iraqi women from the fundamentalist regimes of the Muslim world (Eisenstein 2007: 125). This US Empire fantasy continues a long history of colonial powers who justify military aggression in the guise of protecting subjugated women and bringing civilization and prosperity to natives who are unable to govern autonomously. The rhetoric around women's oppression symbolized by the veil reveals a deep hostility of the West's colonial gaze, which creates the orientalist 'other'. In these discourses women's bodies become the ground on which nationalism builds its discourse of power. Afghani and Iraqi women represent the essence of a culture/nation that needs to be 'liberated'. To remove the veil is a powerful metaphor for reaching and removing the heart of the 'other' culture.[34]

Abu Ghraib

In the modern-day playing out of the destruction of the other in the war on terror the military scandal of 'Abu Ghraib' in 2003 and 2004 became a global scandal when pictures of personnel in a US military prison in occupied Iraq included shots of US military women sexually abusing prisoners. The outcry against US abuse of both women and men soldiers made feminists curious about the role of US women in the military command chain. Cynthia Enloe (2007) points out that it focused attention on women as the subjects or the wielders of violence rather than its objects or victims, disturbing the given gender script.

These images of abuse were very differently perceived. Some, including the Bush administration, dismissed the abuse of it as the work of a few oddballs; others saw it as the downside of gender equality, when women start behaving like men; others saw it as the aggressive act of the corrupt imperial power playing out violent homo-erotic sexual fantasies where the ultimate humiliation is that a woman brutalizes a man (Eisenstein 2004).

Feminist analysis has taken apart the Abu Ghraib story as a racialized and gendered incident that is grounded in the colonial desires and practices of the fantasy of the war on terror (Richter Montpetit 2007). The US hegemonic national fantasy of the George W. Bush era is that by invading Afghanistan and Iraq the US was the first world 'self' bringing liberal democracy and civilization to the Global South 'other', incapable of self-determination. Such a new world order, even while speaking of democracy and reconstruction, depends on the deployment of military force. The fantasy is that the US and its allies save civilization from the troupe of rogue states who in this orientalist thinking inhabit the dark corners of the Earth. The rhetoric of the Bush speeches to Congress and the nation[35] is about the power of the US Empire that protects without possessing. The US, in this image, is the land of chosen people who defend others' freedom by bringing democracy, and in the process opening up their resources and economy to multinationals and US business interests. The Global North business people attending the World Business Forum in Davos every year, like their colonial predecessors, receive generous compensation for shouldering the burden of bringing civilization to others.

To feminist scholars and women's movement activists Abu Ghraib is of great interest yet not surprising: they know all too well the prevalence of criminal abuse by soldiers in war zones. Abu Ghraib was not an aberration in the behaviour of US military personnel; similar abuses have been reported in Afghanistan, Guantánamo, and in other US military and civil prisons where the majority of the prisoners are black (Enloe 2007).

What happened in the prison cells is a racialized, sexualized encounter between prison guards and detainees that mirrors the militarized ideology of manliness of the Empire. It is an ideology premised on violence, aggressive heterosexism, misogyny and racism, which are normalized as part of the civilizing acts inherent to the war on terror. The 1,800 pictures taken for friends and family of women and men soldiers smiling in front of tortured and abused prisoners, including a pyramid of naked prisoners used as a soldier's screen saver, have been compared by feminist critics to the trophy-hunting white colonial rulers who stood proudly over slain wild animals, guns slung over their shoulders. Like the postcards of lynching in the deep South, these are the visible signs that the torture of black and brown bodies is integral to the building of the 'land of the free' (Philipose 2007).

Rethinking bodily rights

Abu Ghraib is perhaps the first time that abuse by military women has been reported officially and in the media. The military women at Abu Ghraib disrupt global stereotypes about women as peace and community builders. Enloe (2007) and Eisenstein (2007) have contributed ground-breaking work on militarized femininities in the Gulf War and sexual decoys in the war on terror. While not denying the agency of military women, they aim to place their behaviour and the global media response to it as part of the ongoing history of the neo-liberal colonial self of the Western world. Such critical feminist discourse refuses to allow an easy understanding of the war on terror and how it implicates all our lives.

Petchesky (2005) has also contributed important work in her writing on the global 'war on terror' as exposing new forms of violations of bodies through sexualized, racialized and gendered techniques, as normalized parts of the military and foreign policy machinery. From Abu Ghraib and Guantánamo to refugee camps, armed conflict zones and increasingly policed borders, the evidence of violation challenges feminist assumptions that privilege women as the exclusive victims of sexual violence. It forces us to rethink the deep connections between militarism, racisms, gender hierarchy, homophobia and prejudice against transgender people, as well as the shifting dynamics of imperial power and national sovereignty.

Petchesky's critique forces a new look at the Vienna Conference slogan 'women's rights are human rights', which, along with Cairo and Beijing, put on the agenda the right to bodily integrity: both affirmative rights relating to sexual expression, reproductive choice and access to health care, and negative rights pertaining to freedom from violence, torture and abuse. She sees the violated male bodies of Abu Ghraib, Guantánamo, and Gujarat as mocking these basic premises: that women are primarily the victims rather than the perpetrators of bodily abuses; and that, as such, women are, or should be, the privileged beneficiaries of bodily integrity rights. She calls for a re-examination of the premises of bodily rights in the shadow of the 'war on terrorism', religious extremism, and practices of racialized, sexual, and often homophobic violence against men that emerge in wars and ethnic conflicts. In particular, she sees the war in Iraq as reconfiguring body politics, challenging the exclusive privileging of women in gender and development discourse as the bearers of sexual rights. Her intervention in the debate invites discussion of more inclusive coalitions of diverse social movements for the rights of the body.

A new global order

The implications of political conflict and its impacts on women, both as fighters and as civilians, unsettled the distinct binaries of war and peace, men as fighters, women as victims. Visiting Nepal in the early 2000s during the Maoist insurgency I heard differing stories about the role women played during the conflicts. Violence was experienced largely by women from socially marginalized groups, indigenous ethnic groups and the Dalit castes. These were among the women who joined the Maoist Women's Revolutionary Front, the women's wing of the Maoist movement. Their taking action, according to what I heard and saw, contrasted with those women traumatized and immobilized by the deaths of their husbands, fathers and sons, and reliant on charity from women's groups. It was difficult for me to understand fully the level of violence that permeated people's lives and the huge amount of frustration they felt at outsiders dictating terms in relation to development aid, solidarity work, service provisions or arms. Within those conversations my own script was highly limited and contained, representing as I did the neo-colonial development discourse that appears to feed on and exacerbate situations of conflict. Certainly I felt that the lines were blurred about what role outside intervention should play, whether military or in the form of aid, and if either promoted security.

This view is supported by development theorists such as Mary Kaldor who in her latest book of essays talks of 'new wars', the military and violent political conflicts intertwined with other global risks such as the spread of disease, natural disasters, poverty and homelessness. In her analysis new wars do not have a decisive beginning or ending. She warns that globalization is weakening territorial state-based approaches to security and creating global forms of insecurity. Globalization, according to Kaldor, has undermined the power and authority of states, reducing the role of state leaders to manage complex relationships with international institutions, other states, international companies and NGOs, as well as domestic interests and the wider public. She suggests that attempts to impose international relations and recreate national power such as the Bush administration's war on terror feed global insecurities. She opens up the question about how development is reduced to nation states' inclusion in or exclusion from the world market. In this Western understanding of development, the underdevelopment of what are perceived as weak, fragile and failing states invites intervention, through either military means or neo-liberal trade and economic development policy measures (Chandler 2008).

Fundamentalism

The rise of religious fundamentalism is also a feature of the 'new wars' and global insecurities. Fundamentalism should not be confused with religiosity. It is premised on highly specific interpretations of religious teachings which insist on a truth and create opposing views that need to be resisted, challenged and changed. Thus a religious 'other' comes into being, along with a set of norms and rules that ossifies groups in particular ways and sets them up against each other along essentialist lines of nature and biology. In this process a 'higher' authority (of whatever religion) is quoted in order to define what people can or cannot do. Throughout the ages, fundamentalism is essentially anti-women and against democratic rights; it opposes change and is hostile to cultural and social diversities.

Fundamentalism has taken a particularly virulent form in the last twenty years as women's human and sexual rights in private and public spaces are being undermined. Such undermining ranges from control over how women should dress to theocracies that condone stoning to death. Conservative and right-wing religious political forces are fiercely trying to maintain or reinforce traditional mechanisms of control over women's bodies, sexuality and mobility. Take, for example, the strong alliances forged among the US right-wing Christian groups, the Vatican and the Islamic states during the UN conferences held in the 1990s,[36] which collectively opposed and restricted women's right to control their bodies and sexuality.

Fundamentalism has taken many forms in these last decades. Christian fundamentalism is expressed in right-wing extremism in the US, Europe and Latin America: in the fight to block the legalization of abortion and the push to impose abstinence among youth as the way to fight HIV and AIDS, many women's lives have been lost and put in jeopardy. Islamic fundamentalist movements have been propagating customary practices in societies where previously they did not exist. In the name of religion, dress codes, the implementation of personal laws and moral policing are used as social instruments to control women's mobility and sexuality. Extreme forms of punishment for transgression include stoning for adultery as practised in Iran. There have been many courageous responses by women's movements to combat fundamentalisms.

Body politics and gender-based violence in Gujarat, 2002

The violence that exploded in Gujarat in 2002 is an illustration of Hindi fundamentalism and violence. Let me add to the voice of Martha Nussbaum that of Vasanthi Raman, an activist researcher based in Delhi who undertook a detailed study of printed official and unofficial reports.[37] She presents the Gujarat events as a complex combination of economic developments based on jobless growth and planned Hindutva 'social engineering' towards the creation of Hindu Rashtra, with support from the fundamentalists in state administration and in line with protecting their business interests and partnership with the state.

Women are central in Hindu fundamentalist elite, chauvinist and ultra-nationalist projects. Raman argues that gender was an important tool in sharpening Hindu identity and shaping the divisions among Hindus and

Muslims and Hindus and Sikhs. Integral to this form of Hindu identity was an 'othering' of both Muslims and Islam where the conflation of religion, culture and nation was central to the Hindutva project. Muslim women were targeted because they were perceived as the biological reproducers of the community and their bodies therefore symbolized the body of the community. In the atrocities of Gujarat in 2002, the Hindu men perceived it as their function and duty to violate the bodies of Muslim women. Women were gang-raped and then burnt on a mass scale, their sexual and reproductive organs were violated and their children, born and unborn, were killed before their eyes. These atrocities were pre-planned and condoned by the state. Hindu men and women participated in the killings. Rape became a weapon, compounded by murder and the most perverted forms of physical abuse of women and children in 40 cities and over 2,§000 villages (Raman 2008).

In extremist and fundamentalist murders neighbours turned against neighbours and in this Hindi women were also complicit. Raman speaks of upper-middle-class women preparing tea and snacks for the men who went out to pillage and kill. Eyewitness accounts tell of Hindi women abusing and burning Muslim women savaged by the men.

Women's complicity in the violence that erupts in expressions of extreme forms of fundamentalism is difficult to comprehend within some versions of feminism that position women as community givers, peace makers and defenders of rights. Women can be as caught up as men are in the complex combination of fear and insecurity that is whipped up by religious leaders – often, as in Gujarat, with the complicity of secular and economic power holders. As life becomes more insecure economically in many areas of the world, the need to belong becomes critical as the struggle over resources becomes more acute. The celebrated 'return to the roots' justifies class and gender divisions. The work of many women's groups has been to try to break down the sense of the other, whether in terms of class, religion, caste or ethnicity.

Women confronting fundamentalism

The violence that many women live with, and the menace of racism, xeno-phobia and fundamentalism, cannot be separated from other oppressions. In social movements, particularly those around the World Social Forum (WSF), it has proved difficult to make those connections outside of feminist analysis.[38]

In the Feminist Dialogues, which I have mentioned in earlier chapters, the 'cultural subversion' by feminists to include gender equality and sexuality as an integral component of the agenda of the broader movement for social and economic justice is uphill work.

Women Living Under Muslim Laws (WLUML)[39] is one of the networks belonging to the Feminist Dialogues coordinating group. WLUML is made up of individuals and organizations from over 70 countries and provides a collective space for women whose lives are shaped, conditioned or governed by laws and customs said to derive from Islam. One of the WLUML initiatives is 'The Global Campaign to Stop Killing and Stoning Women'. It addresses the misuse of religion and culture to justify killing women as punishment for violating the 'norms' of sexual behaviour.[40] Another group, WWHR-New Ways, has been working on issues around sexuality and sexual rights. In 2001 they co-founded the Coalition for Sexual and Bodily Rights in Muslim Societies, the first solidarity network of NGO representatives, academicians and researchers advocating for sexual and bodily rights as human rights in Muslim societies to eliminate honour crimes, sexual coercion and violence, marital rape, sexual harassment, restrictions on women's mobility, seclusion, forced/early marriages, 'imposed' dress codes and virginity tests.[41]

Stoning to death for sexual intercourse outside of marriage (*zina*) is a legal form of punishment in Afghanistan, Iran, and Nigeria (in one third of its 36 states), Pakistan, Saudi Arabia, United Arab Emirates and Sudan. It is mostly women who are condemned to death as discriminatory laws and customs assign more guilt to women. Men are more mobile and able to escape punishment; they are legally allowed to have more than one wife and can use this as a justification for sex outside of marriage. The campaign is ongoing and active, though the protagonists have been threatened and arrested. Stoning to death for adultery continues, mostly in Iran and among rural communities in Pakistan. Nigerian women activists have prevented cases happening and in United Arab Emirates international pressure has led to the overturning of the sanction. The campaign also takes on cases of what are called honour killings of women and girls, often at the hands of their own families (male relatives). WLUML records such killings in Bangladesh, Brazil, Ecuador, Egypt, India, Israel, Italy, Jordan, Morocco, Pakistan, Sweden, Turkey, Uganda and the UK.

In listening, reading, viewing and trying to understand sexual and gender-based violence over these years I see the power of the strong resistance of many women, including survivors of sexual and gender-based violence. Farida

Shaheed from Pakistan, working in Shirkat Gah, an institutional member of WLUML, has written widely about the different encounters of violence and extremism that women face. She underlines the importance of speaking out on behalf of the victims. She sees moments for those that survive as also a moment of opportunity created by the violence, and underlines how important it is to recognize how often women move from the role of narrators of sufferings to assuming leadership roles. She challenges transnational women's rights activists to extend the support needed to victim-led initiatives emerging out of political violence as one of the most important ways to face large-scale violence (Shaheed 2006).

Feminism, racism and difference

From where I am situated in Europe the spread of right-wing political parties and growing violence against migrants is indicative of the rising fear of a 'clash of civilizations', which is strengthening xenophobic attitudes linked to traditional values of white supremacy. The fantasy of Fortress Europe is based on a false sense of being cocooned in a safe 'European' space that needs to keep the others out. The reality of course is that Europe is historically, culturally and linguistically made up of many 'others', something that was brought home to me when listening to Enisa Eminova at an international feminist conference in 2005.[42]

In her wry and powerful speech on how she defines herself both as feminist and as Roma young woman, she spoke about her work as an activist challenging embedded cultural prejudice and developing new leadership networks within the Roma community. In her negotiations across race and culture in Europe she describes working across difference:

> As I travel and meet many people, I then go and ask Roma women in the West how they feel about this tradition. Many of them support it, they believe it is okay if our private bodies are a public metaphor for family purity and community acceptance.... This is not a 'Roma problem', this is a problem of the society, but people assume that if you are part of a group you do not object to any of the cultural practices present in that community. But, eventually Roma women from Eastern Europe decided to disagree with the idea of having to live in the past. They disagree being excluded

from exercising their right to education, freedom of movement and human development. (Eminova 2006: 36)

She challenges advocates for group rights of minorities to address women's rights in communities such as the Roma, and asks them and us to pay more attention to the differences within cultures. Specifically, she speaks of the need to support young women to continue schooling over their father's decision that they marry instead, to talk about domestic violence, to challenge patriarchal laws that impose on women virginity until marriage and exclusive care by women of children and elderly.

Her challenge is profound. She asks us to tackle fundamentalism, and at the same time to acknowledge the deep degree of fear of the 'other' that we carry:

> Only when I see that you are related to me in the 'we and the us' can I then understand that I should not harm you. This is true for racism, this is true for war, because if I harm you, I harm myself. So simple, and yet so difficult to attain awareness and more than that, practice, on this. The challenge then is, if we build the 'we and us' culture of shared responsibility, shared joys and shared pains, and shared resources especially, how do we also honour our differences? (Eminova 2006)[43]

Notes

1 I use the term sexual and gender-based violence rather than violence against women or gender-based violence. It is a term used by official UN documents and many women's groups since 2000. Sexual and gender-based violence includes much more than sexual assault and rape. It is rooted in individual attitudes that condone violence within the family, the community and the state. Overwhelmingly, the victims/survivors of sexual and gender-based violence are girls and women. *The Progress of the World's Women* (UNIFEM 2000) includes in the term homicides and abusive relations by intimate partners, coercion into sex, trafficking of humans world-wide, female genital mutilation, missing women due to sex-selective abortions, infanticide and neglect, mass rape in war, sexual slavery, rape and torture.

2 Some of the chapter is based on a publication I did for UNRISD and the Dag Hammarskjöld Foundation (Harcourt 2006).

3 The speech was published as 'Women's bodies: violence, security, capabilities' in the *Journal of Human Development Alternative Economics in Action* (Nussbaum 2005).

4 Every day I come across more. For example I recently met with the new director of the English office of Women for Women International (<www.womenforwomen.org>) and

read the gripping autobiography of its Iranian founder and president Zainab Salbi (Salbi and Becklund 2006) who set up this non-profit organization to provide women survivors of war with resources to move from crisis to stability and peace. She describes from her childhood days the use of violence including sexual and gender-based violence by the most powerful men in the inner circle of Saddam Hussein, and her own horrific rape within marriage.

5   See the details provided on the 16 Days Campaign at: <http://www.cwgl.rutgers.edu/16days/home.html>.

6   On 21 February 2004, Eve Ensler, together with Jane Fonda and Deep Stealth Productions, produced and directed a new series of transgender monologues. These three 'Transgender Monologues' have been added to the original production.

7   Examples of the original monologues are:
'I Was Twelve, My Mother Slapped Me': a chorus describing many young women's and girls' first menstrual period;
'My Angry Vagina', in which a woman humorously rants about injustices wrought against the vagina, such as tampons, douches, and the tools used by obstetricians and gynaecologists;
'My Vagina Was My Village', a monologue compiled from the testimonies of Bosnian women subjected to rape camps;
'The Little Coochie Snorcher That Could', in which a woman recalls memories of traumatic sexual experiences in her childhood and a self-described 'positive healing' sexual experience in her adolescent years with an older woman (in the original version, she is 13, but later versions changed her age to 16);
'The Woman Who Loved to Make Vaginas Happy', in which a dominatrix for women discusses the details of her career and her love of giving women pleasure;
'Because He Liked to Look At It';
'I Was There In The Room', in which Eve Ensler describes the birth of her granddaughter. See <http://en.wikipedia.org/wiki/The_Vagina_Monologues>.

8   See 'V-Day event by creator of The Vagina Monologues gets set to turn 10 in April', an interview by Susan Walker for the *Toronto Star*, 8 March 2008, <http://www.vday.org/contents/vday/press/media/0803081>.

9   See <http://en.wikipedia.org/wiki/The_Vagina_Monologues> for a list of the different critics of the V-Day from the libertarian Camille Paglia, complaining it is too negative, to the conservative right complaining it is too scandalous, to Global South feminists seeing it as too colonialist.

10 On a personal note, when writing this chapter I found myself discussing the terms vagina and vulva (they are the same words in Italian) with my two girls aged 13 and 9 both of whom refer to their 'patatina' (potato). They did not know until we spoke about it that I was speaking about the same part of their body when I spoke about the vagina.

11 See <http://www.vday.org/contents/vcampaigns/aame>.

12 See the *Toronto Star* interview by Susan Walker, 'Ensler continues fighting against violence against women', 8 March 2008 at <http://www.thestar.com/article/310180>.

13 See <http://www.who.int/gender/violence/en/>.

14 See 'Window on the world' in *Development*, Vol. 44, No. 3 ('Violence Against Women and the Culture of Masculinity'), which provides a list of such groups assembled by the Key Women's Health Centre, one of the WHO centres.

15 UNIFEM provides financial and technical assistance to foster women's rights, empowerment and gender equality. Currently it is not a separate agency but reports to the UNDP with 15 sub-regional and two national offices. A visit to the UNIFEM website gives a sense of the campaigns UNIFEM are heading up with women's organizations and donors. They range from a successful national strategy in Morocco – changing the penal code to ensure stronger provisions on domestic violence – to supporting Kenyan women's attempts to counter sexual crimes in the post-election conflicts and training Rwanda Defence forces to prevent and respond to sexual and gender-based violence, among others. See <www.unifem.org>.

16 See <http://www.unifem.org/resources/item_detail.php?ProductID=7>.

17 See <www.unifem.org/resources/audiovideo/detail.php?VideoID=1>.

18 See <www.unifem.org/resources/audiovideo/detail.php?VideoID=2>.

19 See < http://millionwomenrise.com/millionwomenrise>.

20 In May 2008, 63,164 people had signed up, not quite making the US$100,000 target (that would be given by the UN Foundation).

21 Considerable concern was expressed by women's groups who did not take up the funding made available to work with men as they feared that funding and focus would move on to rehabilitating men and away from supporting women. See Win 2001.

22 See <http://www.menengage.org/>.

23 See Kaufman's moving article on his personal vision for setting up the campaign, working with groups around the world, in *Development*, Vol. 43, No. 3.

24 The work of the Australian R. W. Connell (who has changed her gender and her name from Bob to Raewyn) has made a considerable contribution to work on gender, masculinities and gender identities (Connell 2002 and 2005).

25 This was brought home to me in 2005 at the Geneva Centre for Security Policy, one of four training colleges for high-level military and diplomats in Switzerland. After I gave a talk on gender and security, in which I spoke about rape in war and the struggle to make it recognized as a war crime, a bristling red-faced military officer marched up to me at the end of the talk. Bending down to my height he informed me that rape was just a fact of war; there was nothing new in this, and I should focus on human rights which people understood rather than gender relations, which had nothing to do with security policy.

26 Reports in February 2002 of sexual exploitation and abuse committed against women in West Africa by humanitarian aid workers and peacekeepers led to a Task Force on Protection from Sexual Abuse and Exploitation in Humanitarian Crises. Six core principles for a code of conduct on sexual abuse and exploitation were developed. A Secretary-General's Bulletin in October 2003 incorporated these principles into UN Staff Rules and Regulations and set out a code of conduct for all United Nations staff, including those in separately administered organs and programmes, consultants, and implementing partners. It clearly defines sexual exploitation and abuse and prohibits UN staff from engaging in

such acts. See <http://www.unhcr.org/cgi-bin/texis/vtx/excom/opendoc.htm?tbl=EXCOM&id=3f93b2c44>.

27 In Darfur, Sudan, for example, the issue of war babies – the product of rape, not consensual sex – has been raised as a major concern that does not receive enough attention by the women's movement (Watson 2007).

28 See <www.amanitare.org>.

29 The Convention includes 'any exclusion or restriction made on the basis of sex which has an effect or purpose of nullifying the recognition, enjoyment or exercise by women irrespective of their marital status, on the basis of equality of men and women, of human rights and fundamental freedom in political, social, cultural or otherwise or any fields'. See the full text at <http://www.unifem.org.in/CEDAW.pdf>.

30 Traditional customs in many developing countries, especially in Asia and sub-Saharan Africa – a widow may be deprived of home and livelihood, or subjected to social ostracism – lead to dire poverty for widows and their children. Widows' Rights International supports organizations in South and West Asia and Africa working for social justice and human rights for widows, including rights to keep their children, their home and their property; not be forced to marry the dead husband's kin; and to work outside the home. See <http://www.widowsrights.org/aims.htm>.

31 For more details see <http://www.iccwomen.org>.

32 Alongside the National Commission on Reconciliation in Rwanda, traditional *Gacaca* courts at the 'cell' (village) level are another means of expediting the judicial process. Drawing on traditional systems, the *Gacaca* jurisdictions offer a participatory form of justice, bringing together survivors, perpetrators and witnesses to establish the truth of events. The guilty are charged with forms of community service, as a means of making reparations and assisting their reintegration into the community. See <http://www.penalreform.org/english/theme_gacaca.htm> and Naraghi-Anderlini 2005.

33 See the Society for International Development's study on inequality and a series of scenario future studies that predicted the events in December 2007: <www.sidint.org>.

34 Powerful and complex arguments on the issue of Global South women caught between patriarchy and imperialism, tradition and modernization are offered in the post-modernist readings of colonialism and orientalism following Edward Said. See Yegenoglu (1998).

35 These speeches are available on the Internet, see <www. http://www.whitehouse.gov/news/releases/>; on the war on terror in particular, see <http://www.whitehouse.gov/news/releases/2005/06/20050628-7.html>.

36 The 1994 International Conference on Population and Development (ICPD) in Cairo, the 1995 Beijing Conference, the 1999 five-year review of the ICPD (ICPD+5) and the 2000 five-year review of the Beijing Conference (Beijing+5).

37 Vasanthi Raman from the Centre for Women's Development Studies, Delhi, was a member of a five-year research project on women, political conflict and well-being in South Asia. The group met over the five years in different countries in South Asia to discuss the impacts of political disruptions on women's lives, looking at women's abilities to cope with and survive the difficulties that result from such conflicts. The central concern was to explore how women advance their rights and their concerns within the home and community and

at other levels in the wake of conflict. The results of the project, written up in a series of case studies on the different conflicts in the region, are currently being prepared for publication in a book edited by Khawar Mumtaz, *Political Conflict and Women in South Asia*.

38 I have written about the feminist engagement with the WSF (Harcourt 2008).

39 WLUML performs several functions in different localities: advising women on their legal rights, assisting with asylum applications, and directing them to relevant support institutions including psychological support. It also promotes international alerts for collective action, campaigns, networking and information services using a variety of media in French, Arabic and English. See <www.wluml.org>.

40 There are many other groups and individual fighting to stop stoning and other forms of fundamentalism. For example, an Iranian feminist mentioned to me the former Women's Minister Mahnaz Afkhami, who has been involved in women's rights in Iran from afar for 25 years. She has been fighting the issue in exile through her organization Women's Learning Partnership, based in Betheseda, Maryland, which aims to support organizations who continue to work in Iran. A key feature for me of WLUML and the other networks that make up the FDs is an approach to political analysis that is deliberately not elitist and seeks to work in an open and inclusive way, wary of structures that tie them into conforming to patriarchal norms.

41 See <http://www.wwhr.org/sexuality_in_muslim_soc.php>.

42 The following quotes from Eminova are based on the article from her speech at the AWID Conference and published in *Development*, Vol. 49, No. 1, as well as on my email correspondence with her in 2007.

44 In my country of origin, Australia, there is now a much stronger recognition of the need for reconciliation arising from Australia's colonial past. On 13 February 2008 the newly elected Australian Labour Government finally gave an historic apology to indigenous Australians, especially the stolen generation of indigenous Australians who were taken from their parents to be assimilated into white Australia. This official acknowledgement of the exploitation, exclusion and mistreatment of these first peoples of Australia is a step on the road to reconciliation.

Papua New Guinea An estimated 500 women were attacked in 2006-7, suspected of causing AIDS by means of witchcraft.

Malawi An estimated 600,000 women are HIV positive (in a population of 13 million).

New Zealand The only country where women are more promiscuous than men, averaging 20.4 sexual partners.

5

Five

Sexualized Bodies

Sexual anxieties

In November 2005 I sat with over a thousand feminists from around the world watching on an open-air stage a talented transsexual and transgender troupe in Marilyn Monroe pink and pearls performing Helen Reddy's 'I Am Woman', the song of my early Australian feminist days. We were at the celebration dinner of the Association for Women's Rights in Development (AWID) Forum in Bangkok, smiling at each other across a sea of conviviality. As young Thai men in crisp white sailor suits served us cocktails, I started to feel distinctly uncomfortable. What were 'we' – as feminists engaged in the struggle for economic and social justice – doing in these luxurious surroundings? These beautiful singers from Malaysia, 'The Primadonna', looking like real live Barbie dolls, symbols of what many of us professedly did not want women to be – were they celebrating or making fun of 'our' feminism? We wanted to be strong and invincible, as the song said, and we had denounced the high heels, the pink and the pearls in order not to be defined by patriarchies of popular culture. Was it okay for 'others' to perform this kind of fetishized female body, these throwbacks to 1950s repressive attitudes to the female body? Who was choosing what? Who was pleasuring whom? How different were 'we' from the Western men who came to watch similar sexy shows? Was this an orientalizing, an exoticizing of a most sophisticated sort? What did it mean as a transnational feminist experience? What did transgender, transsexuality, pleasure, identities and difference mean to AWID, one of the largest professional gender and development organizations, and now a feminist gathering of (global and local) activists?

Friends from international development agencies and academe told me how they felt after the meeting: that their political and research issues around gender mainstreaming and globalization, economics and trade had been marginalized and displaced by issues that they saw as outside the development policy canon. The organizers, on the other hand, responded by saying that the conference had been based on a call for participation, and issues such as sexuality, mobilization, disability and identity were what feminist movements from around the world proposed. Significantly most of the participants were from the Global South, young activists rather than 'development' professionals or experts.[1] Within that audience sex, sexuality and sexual identity were core issues of 'women's movements'. In this context sexuality was a cross-cutting issue that lies at the heart of the disempowerment of women. If women are to be empowered, work on sexuality is essential (Jolly 2006).

Mad, bad and dangerous to know

Sexuality, however, is rarely directly addressed in gender and development, even if transnational sexual exchanges are avidly discussed in the popular public domain. Newspapers are full of discussions of global sex tourism, for example. We can read reports of married couples in Malindi splitting for the high tourist season to pick up rich white lovers and then coming back and pooling the gains made in order to pay for children's schooling and health in the low season.[2] The migrants who come to rich cities in Europe to sell sex of all types are part of modern cosmopolitan life. Gay rights parades in Delhi are on the front page in newspapers around the world.[3] Western papers report that schools in north-east Thailand are installing transvestite toilets for students who identify as transgender.[4] But in gender and development none of this sexual behaviour appears; instead there is the assumption that, if we discuss sex at all, only heterosexual behaviour is the norm. Even these discussions are usually about inequality, discrimination and coercion within the context of reproductive health and rights. Though ground is shifting,[5] gender and development emphasizes heteronormative sexual behaviour, sidestepping issues of sexual pleasure and sexual identity, unless addressed in terms of deviance (Jolly 2007: 13).

It continues to be very hard to break the taboos around speaking of sexuality because there are so many competing views which frame the debates. Sexuality, even though often at the core of women's movements' work, causes frictions, frissons and even rifts within the women's movements. The chapter looks at some of these competing views in in order to show how, despite the coyness, sexuality is a critical part of human behaviour, embodiment and identity, and therefore of gender and development.

Four debates on sexuality

Here I look first at multicultural feminism or global feminism and inter-sectionality. These largely US-based feminist theorists look at the intersections of race, sex, sexuality, gender, class and ethnicity. They examine the dichotomies between the Global North and South in relation to debates around sexuality, identity politics, and anti-colonial or post-colonial critiques of globalization (Jayawardena 1995; Spivak 1999; Shohat 2000). The work is multidisciplinary, highly creative and visual, often deploying images which work against stereotyped gendered sexual behaviours. The authors unlayer the racialized and sexualized meanings of bodies and desire that inform gender and development discourse. Cynthia Enloe's discussions of sexuality, militarism and development are part of this 'global feminism' that examines race, class, sexuality and gender in colonial, imperial and post-colonial discourse.[6] I look at how this theorizing on sexuality could usefully be taken into account in gender and development.[7]

A second debate is the heated division among feminists on prostitution, sex work and trafficking, a division which infiltrates gender and development. These arguments go to the heart of how different feminisms theorize gender and power relations. On one side are those who see prostitutes as victims, oppressed and exploited by men and patriarchal structures, and on the other are those who speak of sex work or selling sex as a livelihood choice through which children, women and transgender have agency.

Another, somewhat newer debate which seeks to engage with gender and development was started by the sexual rights activists who since the Beijing Conference have challenged the ambivalence around pleasure and sexual choice in gender and development. Their argument is that development discourse focuses on sexual violence and abuse rather than sexual pleasure. The focus on violence and abuse obscures the fact that the pursuit of sexual pleasures is pivotal to social and cultural arrangements and behaviours. The HIV and AIDS pandemic has opened up discussions on sexuality, desire and behaviour. The mobilizing of resources to respond to HIV and AIDS has given the space for once marginalized identity groups identifying as a coalition of 'Lesbian, Gay, Bisexual, Transsexual, Transgender, Queer, Intersexual' (LGBTQI) to speak about their lifestyles and sexual choices.

The last debate is the call for erotic justice that builds on sexual rights activism but shifts from identity politics to political advocacy work to counter the injustices built into social, legal and economic systems controlling and policing sexuality, culture, gender and sexual minorities. Abortion rights is perhaps the best-known struggle, but there are many more – and these groups argue that struggles for sexual rights implicate all of us, whatever our identities and choices. I focus on the work of Sexual Policy Watch, as one of the most vocal groups of feminists and sexual rights advocates on the frontline of 'sex politics'.

The globalized sexualized 'other'

Our first entry point – global feminism – deliberately places itself outside gender and development discourse. It sees gender and development as muddied by the failure of Western white elite European/US women academics and policy makers to see the racist and iconic uses of women's sexualized bodies in development (Yegenoglu 1998; Ahmed 2000; Shohat 2000). These feminists argue that 'gender and development' continues a historical colonial gaze that seeks to rescue sexually oppressed women of other cultures through development projects. Such a position assumes that white European/US women are sexually free subjects and it constructs the object of development as the 'other', the non-white poor woman of the Global South. They argue that the colonized, eroticized female body underlies the subtext of the modernizing project of development. As Anne McClintock puts it, 'sex is the other of civilization and the Global South continues to be the porno tropics for the European imagination' (McClintock 1995: 22).

The essays and artwork found in *Talking Visions* edited by Ella Shohat (2000), for example, reclaims women originating or living in the Global South as subjects and creators of their own sexualities. The authors sharply point out how the sexualized 'other' is bound up in globalized modern (consumer) culture, in which gender and development is ultimately embedded.

For example, The Body Shop, the multinational soap and shampoo company founded by (the late) UK entrepreneur Dame Anita Roddick presents an interesting example of our globalizing modern culture in relation to body politics. Roddick was a feisty woman who showed great flair and commitment to conducting business 'as unusual' (Roddick 2000). She spoke out on many issues, and mounted a frontline attack on the World Trade Organization in the 1999 'Battle of Seattle'; she campaigned against animal testing and for action on AIDS and saving the Amazon; she supported Greenpeace, indigenous peoples' rights and fair trade. Roddick took on the beauty industry and its unspoken goal to 'make women unhappy with what they look like'. She saw the industry as playing 'on insecurities and self-doubts about image and ageing by projecting impossible ideals of youth and beauty' (Roddick 2000: 97). In an interview with Huw Spanner in 1996 she explained that 'The transnational corporations promote a very Caucasian, very young view of perfection . . . it's about creating fashions and needs – now' (Spanner 1996).

The Body Shop is a fascinating experiment in doing 'beauty' and 'business' differently. In the end, though, many people felt she sold out. When you look at the website today, even if the stated values and passion are there, it now seems like a very well-worked marketing ploy interlaced with very familiar gender and development statements and strategies, even if the trick is to promote women as strong rather than passively needing support. To take one example from the UK Body Shop website, Community Trade Babassu Oil is advertised as luxurious; its appeal is enhanced by the fact that buying a 'traditional' product will support the brave women of north-eastern Brazil.[8]

Such narratives position The Body Shop as doing public good with a sense of responsibility to women in faraway places. The Body Shop exoticizes with a twist – it is the strength and beauty of women rather than their passivity that is promoted. Taking products from around the world, The Body Shop finds beauty secrets to pass on to mostly Western women, who can in addition feel better by buying the soap (recommended by UNICEF) to do their bit to stop violence against children.

In her critical reading of The Body Shop and Western commodity fetishism, Sarah Ahmed pushes us deeper to examine how this consumer product mediates encounters between women in different parts of the world, reinforcing colonial histories of racialized economic and social inequalities (Ahmed 2000: 168). These narratives repeat the traditional gender and development approach: the product and the company are presented as helping poor but brave women and violated children, and presenting opportunities for Western women to be more responsible, more ethical as consumers – and more beautiful, if just a little indulgent. Buying Body Shop products, the message goes, makes Western women more sensitive to their own bodies by using traditional exotic products (though these are refined and modernized in Europe). In addition, by using the beauty products of other cultures they show their acceptance of the 'other'. So in the process of buying and beautifying themselves they are also supporting 'other' cultures and women while, by the by, producing profit for The Body Shop (Ahmed 2000: 169–70).

We have not always engaged creatively with our intersecting contradictions around such issues as gender, class, race, sexuality, religion, immigration and globalization. To forge alliances we must face up to disparate sensibilities and contested histories, if only to chart the terrain of shared struggles more effectively. In the era of globalization, the old imperial hegemonies have become 'dispersed'. How do we negotiate these dispersed hegemonies while also acknowledging that the historical thread of (Global North) domination remains a powerful presence? And what are the links between such hegemonies and the national and transnational regulation of the gendered and sexualized body (Shohat 2000: 32–3, 48)?

Questioning my own hegemonic gaze

Ahmed and Shohat forced me to look more closely at some of the assumptions I have held around women's sexualized bodies because they highlighted the importance of confronting the silences around racialized sexualized bodies within modernizing development discourses. They made me think about how people experience sexuality and race within different national and class contexts. To take myself as an example: I am an educated, white, sexual rights advocate from mixed European background (Jewish and Scottish) who lived my formative years in Australia. Australia's history and contemporary reality are riddled with often unspoken histories of racial violence and oppression. I have always felt highly uncomfortable with the silences of Australian history and society, with its embedded racism. I feel compromised by them and unsure of what position or role I should take when attempting to break them.[9] My own voice lacks authenticity. This same unease I have felt with the silences about racism in gender and development.

Sexual narratives promoted by global media cultures are based on the mythical 'Western' ideals, which are profoundly racist. For example, rich women and girls in US, European and Latin cultures have 'elective cosmetic surgery' – such as silicon breast implants, face lifts, vaginal piercings and tucking – to look and feel sexy, while 'traditional' practices in Africa of dry sex and female genital mutilation are depicted as degrading violations of women's rights. I would condone none of the practices but there is an implicit racialized and classist reading of white and Latina women being able to choose risky and life-threatening surgery, often with very little awareness of the full implications, and African women and girls and cultures needing to be rescued and re-educated about such practices (Chambers 2008).

Every culture interprets sexual desire and actions differently. Unquestioned gender systems hold in place particular understandings of the body and create silences or focus on specific aspects of sexual desire and practice (Lewis and Gordon 2008; Tamale 2006; Chambers 2008). Men, women and transgender people are locked into a biological discourse about their body rights. There are many taboos about opening up these discussions, with tremendous pressure from conservative religious forces to be silent about sexuality, and certainly the sexual satisfaction of women is shrouded in complexities.

The thriving informal sex industry for the services of young men and women around the world and commercialized transnational sex on the Internet creates possibilities where all manner of fantasies, including the colonial racialized dreams, can be played out by different people. These global interactions take us beyond simple dichotomies of exploited victims and exploiting clients or what is risky and dangerous and bad versus what is safe and secure and good. In these transnational sex adventures racialized bodies are promoted as natural resources like the natural landscape of sea and palm trees, with travel associations selling erotic, exotic 'porno tropics' (Alexander 2000: 283).[10]

Questions of desire, of how to engage with the 'other', and of agency in an asymmetrical world are not easy to mediate through complex global media and marketing images of sexualized bodies. I would argue that these fantasies form a backdrop also to many international development meetings. Stories abound of romantic liaisons and also sexual harassment along the corridors. I and many others I know are too often confronted by men acting on the sexual stereotype of how Western women should behave when unchaperoned and therefore 'free' – not welcome confrontations, as 'the fragile edges of pride, anxiety, humiliation and rejection that haunt traditional masculinities bear sad fruit' (Lewis and Gordon 2006: 113).

Sarah Bartmann: from victim to nation builder

But exploitative transcultural sexual exchange is not new. One history that is addressed in feminist writing though rarely in gender and development discussions is the infamous story of Sarah Bartmann, the so-called 'Hottentot Venus' of the early 1800s. Her body was exhibited in London and Paris when she was alive and then in a Paris museum after she died. It was returned with great ceremony to South Africa as part of the making of the nation in 2002.

I first came across the story of Sarah Bartmann more than twenty years ago in Sander Gilman's 1985 essay 'White bodies, black bodies: towards an iconography of female sexuality in late nineteenth century art, medicine and literature'. The essay was part of a new and important contribution to feminist histories of the body at a time when black feminists were challenging elite white feminism. Coming back to the subject over 20 years later I found that the story had moved from academic pages and feminist debates around sexuality onto the political stage. Sarah Bartmann had become a subject of many different histories, with numerous articles, books, two televised documentaries, poetry collections and plays: in this reclaiming, she had become a national icon for the newly emerging post-apartheid nation of South Africa.[11]

Bartmann was a slave owned by Dutch farmers near Cape Town who was taken to London in 1810, where she was exhibited principally for her large buttocks: visitors were permitted to touch them for extra payment. As the 'Hottentot Venus', she was paraded in the streets of London.[12] Her exhibition in London, a few years after the Slave Trade Act of 1807 (which abolished slavery), created a scandal. There were many cartoons, articles and verses about Bartmann, and the abolitionist African Association petitioned for her release. In a celebrated court case, Bartmann in fluent Dutch informed the court that she took part in these spectacles under her own volition, and the case was dismissed. Four years later in 1814 she was sold to an animal trainer in Paris. French anatomist Georges Cuvier and French naturalists visited her with particular interest in her buttocks and elongated labia, both common in Khoisan women. Bartmann did not allow herself to be examined but she was the subject of several scientific paintings.

Upon her death in 1815 an autopsy was conducted, and the findings were published by French anatomists. Her skeleton, preserved genitals and brain were placed on display in Paris's Musée de l'Homme until 1974, when they were removed from public view. In the 1980s, calls for the return of her remains began.[13] When Nelson Mandela became President of South Africa in 1994, he formally requested that France return the remains. They were returned to the Gamtoos Valley, east of Cape Town, on 6 May 2002. In August, women's organizations 'enrobed' her remains in a sacred rite which drew on ceremonial rituals from Khoisan, African and Muslim cultures. The funeral took place on the banks of the Gamtoos River. It was televised and attended by a high-profile government delegation. President Thabo Mbeki in his speech referred to a 'historic mission of restoring the human dignity of Sarah Bartmann' and thereby 'transforming ourselves into a truly non-racial, non-sexist and prosperous country, providing a better life for all our people' (Mbeki 2002).

Brigitte Mabandla, Deputy Minister of Arts, Culture, Science and Technology, found

> something hugely significant in the national and international action and cooperation that took place in ensuring that Sarah Bartmann's remains travelled back to her land. In taking this step, there is an implicit acknowledgement that earlier world-views no longer have a place in our world. . . . Sarah Bartmann's return is profoundly significant, as her experience symbolizes the interrelationship of gender oppression, colonialism and racial exploitation. Consequently, the restoration of Sarah Bartmann's dignity through this enrobement ceremony and through a proper burial is a powerful statement about the need to restore and safeguard the dignity of all the women of Africa and the world. In this, the African Millennium, let us not forget the need for a strong Nation to be built on values of dignity, human rights and freedom for all. (Mabandla 2002)

In the ceremony and the statements, Bartmann is presented as a tragic victim rescued and recovered by the nation. National independence is conceptualized as healing and recovering the body, and the land raped and violated under colonialism. In such a discourse Bartmann's body itself provided the rationalization for the violence done both to it and to the land from which it emerged. Ironically in adopting the discourse of the raped body/land the advocates of the 'return' also essentialized Bartmann's body.

The use of Bartmann's body as the icon of colonized, sexualized, and racialized violation – subject to the colonial patriarchal gaze, her body displayed, tricked and stripped of dignity in life and death – is a deeply disturbing one. It raises enormous issues of colonialism, enslavement, and scientific sexualized racism clearly not easily resolved by national ceremonies. As one feminist analyst pointed out, the official memorial and recognition of Bartmann 'fails to grapple with the violence encountered by women in the present . . . moreover by spinning a narrative of the female victim saved by political leaders, it eludes women's agency and resistance and forecloses ways of imagining women in the nation beyond the binaries of sexualized savage and domestic mother' (Samuelson 2007: 100–1).[14]

It is important to understand how feminist demands and struggles for gender equality can through a complex process become captured and subsumed in larger narratives that can unsettle the original purpose and aim of the struggle. The sexualized interest in the women, either as victims, saviours or betrayers of the nation, can enter through an iconic playing out of women as representative of tradition. Women like Bartmann are held up as symbols of tradition in the face of the modernizing project. Such stories are part of what determines what is possible and what is tabooed in gender and development.

Commercial sex and the 'trafficking' debate

Moving from global feminism on intersectionalities to sex work, we enter into even more contested ground. In the chapter about caring productive bodies, I deliberately chose not to discuss sex work or commercial sex. I wanted to place it squarely within the discussion on sexualities. Some feminists would object, saying that I was falsely dividing paid sex work from paid caring work, or domestic work. In many cases a thin line divides care or sex work among the services migrant women are expected to provide or perform. I place it in this chapter because I want to discuss sex work in the context of the ongoing controversy about sex work among feminists, women's movements and in gender and development.

Essentially there are two lines of thought, one that sex work is work like any other and that the rights of women, men and transgender people who engage in it need to be respected and legislated for in ways that do not penalize them. The other line is that any form of sex for money is prostitution and criminal. In this line patriarchal power is all-pervasive and even if women think they freely choose sex work over other forms of labour they are deceived in that choice. In this argument, selling sex for money is one of the worst forms of violence against women and children and a product of deep gender inequalities and human rights violations. Therefore women, girls or boys – there is seldom any mention of transgender – are victims who are trafficked into prostitution. They are only deluded into thinking they have chosen this work and need to be protected and rescued, while the consumers – who are usually men – need to be punished.

In Europe this debate has focused on the Swedish law that in 1999 criminalized the purchase of sexual services. The law against procurement criminalizes the client and makes the following acts illegal: selling sex indoors, profiting from the sexual labour of others, and advertising. The law has received much attention internationally. While the Swedish government claims the law is successful and that the rate of prostitution is now lower, sex workers say it has just made sex work far more risky and dangerous, and that as a result forms of hidden and precarious prostitution have increased. Sex workers on the Internet, and in street protests, conferences and workshops, argue that the law has reinforced stigma and social shame around the sale of sexual services. Sex workers are now hunted on the streets by the police, social workers, and the media, and sometimes even by anti-prostitution activists. The clients are more stressed and scared, negotiation outdoors must be done rapidly, and the likelihood of ending up with a dangerous client is therefore greater.[15]

The European Women's Lobby (EWL) the largest European women's network focusing on women's rights, funded by the European Commission,[16] has been one of the advocates for this law. In the EWL Charter of Principles on Violence Against Women, prostitution is defined as violence against women, and EWL states clearly that the structural constraints of gender inequality mean prostitutes cannot exercise free choice. For EWL, 'prostitution and trafficking in women constitute a fundamental violation of women's human rights' and 'should not be associated with the terms "forced" or "free". . . . It should be recognized that "free choice" is a relative factor, situated at the intersection of economic, social, cultural and political options of women in a given society. Inequality severely restricts freedom of choice' (EWL Charter of Principles on Violence Against Women).[17]

These principles are translated by EWL and its allies into the UN arena around the United Nations Global Initiative to Fight Human Trafficking (UNGIFT). EWL has lobbied hard with other women's NGOs such as the

Coalition against Trafficking in Women (CATW) to push for 110 countries to sign the UN Protocol to Prevent, Suppress and Punish Trafficking in Persons. The debates around and since the United Nations 2000 Protocol on Trafficking reveal the differences between two distinct viewpoints about 'trafficking in persons'. CATW was the first international non-governmental organization to focus on human trafficking, especially sex trafficking of women and girls. It argues that trafficking includes all forms of prostitution, regardless of consent,[18] while others who formed the Human Rights Caucus (HRC) supported the view that prostitution is work and that force was the important factor in defining trafficking.

The anti-prostitution viewpoint questions the wider socio-economic and cultural context within which such 'choices' are being made and warns of systematic reinforcement of male dominance and oppression against women if gender disparities of rights and status are ignored. CATW states that 'prostitution victimizes all women, justifies the sale of any woman and reduces all women to sex'. They stress that the international call for an economic recognition of the sex industry will further widen gender inequality, compromising the status of women. Dismissing reasoning that options for women might be limited and prostitution often a survival tactic, CATW questions all forms of prostitution and the difficulty of resisting a lucrative sex industry that flourishes at the cost of disadvantaged women:

> Commercial sexual exploitation of women and girls of all ages, including prostitution, pornography, the Internet bride industry, and sex tourism, is one of the most devastating, and escalating, practices of gender-based violence assaulting the human rights and dignity of women and girls. No society that purports to uphold gender equality should tolerate and accept the sexual commodification of women and girls.[19]

They demand the criminalizing of the commercial sex industry. They state categorically that criminalizing the demand for prostitution, as in Sweden, South Korea and Nepal, is the most effective way to address the problem of sex trafficking.

The pro-prostitution viewpoint includes groups like the Global Alliance Against Trafficking in Women (GAATW) and Network of Sex Workers Project (NSWP).[20] These groups defend the rights to self-determination, to work, and to self-expression, believing that women can make informed choices about engaging in consensual commercial sex. The NSWP is a global network of organizations and individuals. They share the vision of a world in which sex workers are free from discrimination, persecution and violence; where sex work is considered to be a legitimate and even honourable occupation; and where sex workers' health and human rights are held to be as important as anyone else's. In the UN arena they have collaborated with GAATW's rights-based approach to trafficking, which respects sex workers' right to self-determination.[21]

GAATW is a coalition which includes migrants' rights organizations; anti-trafficking organizations; self-organized groups of migrant workers, domestic workers, survivors of trafficking and sex workers; human rights and women's rights organizations; and direct service providers. GAATW works for changes in the political, economic, social and legal systems and structures which contribute to the persistence of trafficking in persons and other human rights violations in the context of migratory movements for diverse purposes, including security of labour and livelihood. They look at core aspects of trafficking in persons: forced labour and services in all sectors of the formal and informal economy, as well as the public and private organization of work. They advocate for non-discrimination on any grounds, including ethnic descent, age, sexual orientation or preference, religion, gender, age, nationality and occupation (including work in the informal sectors such as domestic work and sex work).

Trafficking across borders of poor women and children, and within borders from rural to urban centres, is indicative of inequalities and desperate survival needs in situations marked by economic and political violence. Such exploitation is managed by the criminal underclass that needs to be legislated and policed against. The problem, though, is the harm done by such policing and legislation. Some of the violence, ill health and harm suffered by trafficked women and girls is due to the situation created by the laws and policing. The trafficked women and children are not in a position to defend their rights; even if their pain and fear and exploitation are recognized, their agency is not. GAATW recognizes women's agency by seeing sex work alongside other forms of human trafficking as intrinsically embedded in global inequality and global migration.

It is important to recognize that in some cultures there is routine monetarization of sex that does involve agency by the parties involved but could from an outsider point of view be construed as 'prostitution'. To take an example mentioned above, when couples in Mali pool resources separately earned from their high-season sex tourist work, this arrangement may not be condemned, but seen as one way for them to gain their living in the face of few alternatives. In the situation of trafficking it is also important to consider the agency of women differently from the capacity of children. Too often it is assumed that both women and children are incapable of expressing agency.

Leaving home for sex

Laura Agustín, who identifies and writes as a lifelong migrant and sometime worker in both non-governmental and academic projects about sex, travel and work, has some interesting insights into migrant sex work (2007a, 2007b) which have helped me understand the argument around sex work and how it impacts on gender and development.[22] She argues that women's groups that attempt to rehabilitate prostitutes continue the nineteenth-century historical practice (and social construction) of rescuing fallen women as part of the moral policing and disciplining of the unruly poor's sexual conduct.[23] The gender and development discourse has translated into a post-colonial context the concept of rescuing with 'missions to rescue non-European poor women' (Agustín 2007a). Agustín underlines the 'othering' of this 'maternalistic' approach based on how to prevent men from buying sex, and women from selling it. In other words, how to get 'others' who are depicted as the disadvantaged, unruly, victimized, unhappy, offensive and addicted to behave differently. Her point is to question not the exploitation and injustices surrounding commercial sex but the maternalistic all-knowing certainty on how others should behave.

Laura Agustín situates herself on the edge of research and advocacy debates among sex workers, women NGOs and migrant workers. Her book, based on her research in Spain, is an unashamedly controversial attack on the moralizing about and stereotyping of sex workers. As a researcher/activist Latin American living in Europe, she provides an important standpoint for viewing the issue of sex work and the women-centred NGO industry spawning around it.

Agustín shows how sex for money is provided in numerous ways in various places, from cyberspace to backs of cars to high-class luxury hotels. Some of the women, transsexuals and men she spoke with see selling sex as temporary work, a good way to earn money and see the world. Others feel trapped and exploited. It may be for some just a job like any other, but unlike any other it is subject to policing, moral scrutiny and control in ways that do little to provide the security that would enable sex workers to negotiate preferable working conditions and terms. Agustín exposes the layers of morality of many no-doubt well-meaning rescuers, as she contrasts the shrill condemnation of prostitution as victimization with the far more understanding and respectful help provided by Catholic nuns. She also draws a telling comparison between women's NGOs and brothel owners who provide organized and secure conditions for their workers. Agustín asks why so many European men (and women) buy sex, and why the people who provide these services are so castigated (either as victims, as illegal, or as carriers of HIV and AIDS).

Agustín is, quite frankly, courageous in taking on the European anti-prostitute campaigners. If women's groups and others in the NGO world concerned with trafficking are to make a real difference in the lives of sex workers, they must stop blaming others – the law, institutional bodies, the communications media and violent men – and look at their own practices and prejudices: in short, they must leave aside their own certainties. She concludes that 'government employees, political appointees, feminists, NGO spokespersons and other social agents' should 'dispense with neo-colonialism, admit that agency can be expressed in a variety of ways, acknowledge their own desires and accept that modernity's dynamic, changing, risky diversity is here to stay' (Agustín 2007a: 43).

It is important to move on from the myth of a clear boundary between commercial sex and normalized sexual activities. The experience of university students selling sex in high-class massage parlours in Europe is not the same as young uneducated girls from rural Vietnam being sent to seedy brothels in cities, even with their family's consent. What is important is to support sex workers' struggles to defend themselves against unjust laws, social stigma and hypocrisy, to raise alarm at the policing and security measures often taken without full respect for sex workers' rights. We need also to be more honest about sexuality and sexual rights, and how sexuality permeates all our lives.

Sex work in Bangladesh

Agustín addressed migrant sex workers in Europe somewhat on the margins of gender and development. Her position – engaging with sexuality while leaving aside moral attitudes and concepts of victims needing to be rescued –

is shared by feminists working in the Global South. Shireen Huq, an activist in the women's movement and a trainer on gender, rights and development in Bangladesh, speaks of the lessons learnt by the Bangladeshi women's movement in their campaign to support the rights of sex workers. Her NGO network Naripokkho began to engage with sexuality as they shared with sex workers stories centred on the painful reality of women's bodies exposed to ill treatment, denial and deprivation at the hands of family and community members, strangers and public institutions. Their stories told of cultural pressures that determined what women should do or not do with their bodies, how to carry themselves under the gaze of others, with whom they could have sexual relations, and if they could have sexual pleasure. Huq underlines how difficult it was to put issues of sexual freedom onto the women's rights agenda:

> we were surrounded by conservative social mores . . . the usually progressive political discourses around us reflected a similar conservatism with respect to sexuality and imposed a sense of propriety totally out of sync with their otherwise radical political stance . . . we were ostracized for taking things too far . . . our discussion on equality did not stop at wages and franchise but went on to talk about the right to love and pleasure . . . to raise the question of sexual freedom was definitely stepping beyond the boundaries of a legitimate rights discourse. (Huq 2006: 134)

In Bangladesh, the attempt to make *Shorir amaar shidhanto* (my body, my decision) the celebratory slogan for International Women's Day in 1994 was met with huge resistance. Huq describes how working with sex workers helped members of Naripokkho work out 'the knotty politics around sexuality' (Huq 2006: 135). In a campaign with sex workers over illegal eviction which received high media visibility, the issue of women's rights in sex work became a focus. Huq describes how renaming prostitutes as sex workers enabled them to gain rights as workers, leading to a landmark ruling that recognized sex work within brothels as legal. The struggle for sex workers' rights overturned conventional frameworks within which many women's NGOs were working. It challenged traditional views and attitudes around 'rehabilitation' and 'rescue' and shifted to a focus on 'accepting sex workers in our midst – in our movements, in our workplaces and in our homes'. Meeting and working with sex workers including the *hijras* (transsexual and intersexual persons of the NGO Bondhon) enabled women-focused NGOs to challenge their own stereotyping of fixed gender categories.

Huq's narrative shows how the Bangladeshi women's movement broke down the 'maternalistic' approach that Agustín identified as typifying many NGO and women's movement engagements with sex workers. What both Agustín and Huq show is that sex is an activity that is part of social and cultural realities. Feminists subject sex to scrutiny whether it is sold as a service or practised among consenting partners. Sexuality can carry ambivalent attitudes and practices that embody gender prejudices and inequalities. Some sex can lead to ill health, injury, injustice and death. But the answer is not to deny agency. It is important to look at how to prevent abusive and life-endangering sex. But it is not enough to leave it there.

As sexual rights activists Jill Lewis and Gill Gordon state:

> Sexual relations are always within social realities that pressure them one way or another but are emergent from conditions, possibilities, securities, fears, incentives, needs and hopes that frame where people are living and what they are aspiring to. (Lewis and Gordon 2006: 115)

Body politics and HIV and AIDS

Brazilian sexual rights activist Sonia Corrêa argues that the onset of the HIV and AIDS pandemic forced the need to rethink the links between sexuality and development (Corrêa 2006: 18). The struggles for sexual rights have become more intense and interconnected as the AIDS pandemic has meant that sexuality can no longer be ignored. 'People have become more willing to talk about sex and have found new ways to explore questions of desire, power and pleasure' (Corrêa 2006: 29).

Sexual rights embrace human rights and they include the right of all persons to sexual fulfilment and to freedom from coercion, discrimination and violence to do with sexuality, whatever their sexual orientation or sexual identity.[24] Sexual rights advocates challenge the idea of sexuality as bad and suspect; nor do they see sexual rights as confined to the rights of a minority, but as including people who conform to the norms around heterosexuality and gender. Their advocacy goes beyond sexuality as a health issue and includes positive rights and pleasure: 'Celebrating or opening possibilities for pleasure can be empowering and affirming, especially for those who are discouraged from enjoying their sexuality, particularly many women, people living with HIV and AIDS, people with disabilities, LGBTQI people' (Ilkkaracan and Jolly 2007: 25). It also recognizes that many people do not fit neatly into categories of male and female – such as the *hijras* in South Asia, the *travesti* in Latin America,[25] the *tommy boys* and *lesbian men* in Africa, the *ladyboys* in Thailand, the *third spirit* among indigenous Americans and globalized identities of queer, transsexual and intersexual people with bodies that genetically and physiologically combine male and female (Jolly and Ilkkaracan 2007: 25, 31–2).

The recognition of all these forms of sexual identity and gender pluralities challenges the accusation that sexual rights is a Western issue. The HIV and AIDS pandemic revealed that African men and women engage in non-heterosexual sex and multiple-partner sex. The money that went to counter HIV and AIDS helped to create spaces that can break the traditional silence around same-sex encounters and queer sex, and has shaped the cultures and politics of gay movements globally. African activists have mobilized continent-wide support and advocacy for gays, lesbians, bisexuals, and transgendered/transsexual peoples through the 2004 All Africa Rights Initiative, linked to Human Rights Watch (Gosine 2004: 21). HIV and AIDS brought attention to people engaged in non-heterosexual sex and made visible existing struggles and the needs of various communities – not only the families of men who have sex with men, drug addicts and sex workers, but also communities where the cultural norm includes homosocial and homoaffectionate support (Gosine 2004: 22).[26]

HIV and AIDS and George W. Bush

The regulation of sex, as I showed in Chapter 2, is a strong component of development policies controlling reproductive sex. The management of sexuality, parenting and morality is at the heart of 'population programmes' that provide contraception, family planning and sexual health advice. As the pandemic hit it became clear that 'risky' sex was not confined to obscure, dark, illegal places but was threaded through many social relationships. HIV and AIDS was not limited to one group in society; it was infecting the whole society. The sheer numbers involved forced issues of desire and sexualities onto the development agenda. HIV and AIDS had to be recast as no longer a sexual minority issue, but a broader social and health issue. The concern with containment and control of sex through family planning moved one step further: from stopping the poor having children to stopping the poor having sex at all. The 'faith' and 'abstinence' policies of the fundamentalist Christian right were aggressively pursued by the George W. Bush administration (Lusti-Narasimhan, Cottingham and Berer 2007).

As one young Namibian woman living with AIDS put it:

> Wanted sex, good sex and right to enjoy sex are not something that is covered in many intervention programmes. All I can say is that sexual reproductive health activities concentrate on ABC [abstinence programmes] and family planning, in other words, more of the shock tactics type of education. How can you expect young women to understand the importance of consensual sex and negotiating skills if education is only limited to prevention of pregnancy, STIs and sex being a no go area in many societies? (Quoted in Ilkkaracan and Jolly 2007)

The political struggle for sexual rights is part and parcel of the struggle to find funds, appropriate treatment and resources for people living with HIV and AIDs.[27] Sexual rights groups such as women living with HIV positivity, men who have sex with men, and sex workers are often the ones providing services for those living with AIDS: helping the dying and reaching out to prisoners, young people, drug addicts and others who are marginalized.[28]

The ongoing struggle of communities coping with HIV and AIDS to provide services and change prejudice and discrimination has been aggravated by the Bush administration's policy on sexual abstinence and faith-based organizations. The imposition and management of US administration conditionalities on HIV and AIDS[29] funding has had a painful impact on many organizations. In the UN arena many struggles are waged between the US, the Vatican and Catholic and Islamic religious states who continue a moralistic and condemnatory stance towards sexuality and development.

For example, in a conference on HIV and sexual and reproductive health held in 2007[30] a strong concern was raised about the promotion of sexual abstinence for young and unmarried people. Young people continue to have unprotected sex and high-risk sex is the dominant mode of transmission among youth. In the USA, for example, oral gonorrhea is higher among youth who have been taught abstinence (Bell et al. 2007: 70). HIV youth are often abandoned by parents, schools and church, but with the change in treatment such HIV children/adolescents live into their twenties and thirties. Most HIV-positive youth are girls or men who have sex with men; they are from racial and ethnic minority groups and economically deprived areas, and face a hostile and discriminatory environment.

HIV and AIDS and new approaches to sexual rights in development

With so many millions of people living with HIV,[31] the need to develop policies and programmes to support the sexual and reproductive health and human rights of people living with HIV has forced a new approach to sexual health and rights (Gruskin, Ferguson and O'Malley 2007; Shapiro and Ray 2007: 3, 67). HIV-positive and AIDS communities have undergone a major shift in how sexuality is articulated. In countries like South Africa, for example, 5 million people live with HIV and AIDS and girls between the ages of 15 and 24 who have unprotected sex with older men have the highest risk of infection. It is therefore critical to speak about the rights of young people to know about sexuality and to take their emotions and fears seriously. The issue is not just one of protection but of recognizing that young people living in the HIV and AIDS era are neither ignorant nor innocent.[32]

There are unresolved problems of insufficient human resources and the economic and social realities faced by many people living with HIV in poverty-stricken communities (Kim et al. 2000). Despite the highly publicized millions given to HIV and AIDS research by the Bill and Melinda Gates Foundation there are still not enough funds to care for HIV and AIDS orphans or to provide home-based care kits, antiretroviral treatment and community and home care support for chronic illness.

A gender lens is surprisingly often missing in HIV and AIDS discussions. The lack of a gender perspective prevents a more realistic assessment of why HIV and AIDS spreads. Safe sex in economically stricken communities is difficult. In particular within married couples practising safe sex[33] is not easy, when blame, shame and violence can accompany a disclosure that a partner is HIV positive. The issue is how to treat HIV-positive people and promote safer sex in a gender-aware and sex-positive way. In this context it is important to look at how to promote breastfeeding, sensitivity to HIV-positive mothers, treatment for sex workers, the need for family planning for men and women, better female condoms and the integration of condoms into sex play in culturally sensitive ways.

There are, however, important efforts being made to highlight the gender dimension. The young Namibian woman quoted above is a member of the International Community of Women Living with HIV/AIDS (ICW). ICW is the only international advocacy network run for and by HIV-positive women. ICW was founded in 1992 in response to the lack of support, information and services available to women living with HIV worldwide, and to the need for these women to have influence and input on policy development. As a network of women living with HIV throughout the world, ICW is based on the mutual respect, honesty and integrity of its members, as well as on the assurance of confidentiality. ICW emphasizes the transformative power of women living self-determined lives, dealing as they do with huge numbers of women at the heart of the epidemic. They have over 6,000 members living in 128 countries around the world. They see their greatest achievement as being able to 'reach isolated women living with HIV/AIDS and, through support, education and training, empower them to be involved in areas of service monitoring and policy development that affect their lives and the lives of their children and family'. ICW is the co-convening agency (with WHO) for the treatment and care arm of the Global Coalition on Women and AIDS, which focuses on preventing new HIV infections among women and girls, promoting equal access to HIV care and treatment, accelerating research on microbicides, protecting women's property and inheritance rights, and reducing violence against women.[34]

The Pleasure Project

Another example of new approaches to sexuality and development is The Pleasure Project, based in the UK and coordinated by Wendy Kerr and Anne Philipott. The Pleasure Project is a transnational education project that aims to 'build bridges between the pleasure sex industry and the safer sex world by avoiding negativity and by ensuring that erotic material includes examples of safer sex'.[35] The Pleasure Project aims to make sex safer by addressing one of the major reasons people have sex – the pursuit of pleasure – instead of concentrating on negative and disease-focused programmes.

One major challenge the project took on is the female condom, which is rarely used in the UK or Europe despite highly expensive media and advertising campaigns in the early 1990s. Its usage in the UK is so low that it registers as 0 per cent.[36] The Pleasure Project has helped to promote the female condom in 80 countries where WHO sells it at a discount to HIV and AIDS sex education programmes for women in countries like Senegal, India, Zimbabwe and Sri Lanka. Philpott reports a major uptake for women who have little say over whether men wear a condom. In Colombo, female sex workers introduced it to their clients as a sex toy, allowing the client to insert it and thus breaking a huge taboo in Sri Lanka about touching the vagina. In Senegal, the condoms are sold with noisy *bine bine* beads, an erotic accessory that women wear around their hips. The rustle of the polyurethane during sex is now associated with the clicking of the beads and is a turn-on. Senegalese women have also shrewdly suggested that the large size of the condom reflects the size of their partner's penis. In Zimbabwe, where 930,000 of the 1,600,000 adults infected with HIV are women, a new word – *kaytec-yenza* – has entered the vernacular to describe the pleasurable 'tickle' created by the inner ring rubbing against the penis. The aim of The Pleasure Project is to raise the quantity of female condoms sold from 10 million to around 200 million – not large compared to the 9 billion male condoms distributed last year in the developing world.[37]

The Pleasure Project raises interesting issues around cultural transference of sexual choice and pleasure, and how best to go about ensuring honest and safe sex. By acknowledging that the search for pleasure is dominant in most sexual interactions, the project sees sex work as a choice for both service provider and client. Sexual pleasure requires knowledge and skills that can be learnt and improved as well as celebrated throughout life. Good sex provides a place where sacred and profane can meet in a joyous way when practised safely, in trust and without fear. This is a positive challenge for any sexual relationship within or outside socially normalized spaces.

Sex is after all a potential source of pleasure, paid or unpaid, and offers well-being, pleasure, happiness, justice, respect, affirmation and the exploration of mutual desire. We need to put sexual pleasure within the context of everyday life in order to work

> constructively and compassionately with the disjuncture between sexual expectations and the contextual realities of real relations, real bodies in real life situations of survival and children to maximize the possibility of pleasure being a real and sustainable

possibility within human relationships. (Lewis and Gordon 2006: 113–14)

Sex, politics and erotic justice

Taking up this challenge to confront such disjunctures, we come to the last debate: on erotic justice. Erotic justice moves sexuality out of the private, individual and biological fields into politics. Advocates of erotic justice challenge injustices built into legal systems defining sexuality, culture, gender and sexual minorities.

One important advocate of erotic justice is Sexuality Policy Watch. SPW calls on 'everyone whose rights to bodily integrity are under attack' to 'come together in strong alliances and with strong resolve to defend social, gender and erotic justice'.

Sexuality Policy Watch (SPW), founded in 2002, is a global forum that contributes to sexuality-related global policy debates through policy-oriented research.[38] The aim of their work is to protect sexual diversity and freedom, to understand sexuality and the body through the lens of political economy, and to build transnational and multisectoral alliances. SPW takes sex as inherently political and points to dangerous times for 'sexual and gender outlaws' in the twenty-first century, in the face of religious extremisms of all kinds, backlashes against women's and LGBTQI movements, the 'war on terror', and its rationalization of unrelenting militarism and torture. They speak especially of the danger for women and girls 'caught in the crossfire of armed and ethnic conflict situations, subjected to rape and assault in refugee camps or to HIV infection by predatory or heedless men'. SPW works to eliminate discrimination and stigma and reduce inequalities, as well as to widen the domain of social and personal rights and access to resources for those who have been excluded. Their work is positioned at the research and global policy level, such as the United Nations institutions.[39]

Their most recent publication *Sexuality, Health and Human Rights* (Corrêa, Parker and Petchesky 2008) places sexual politics in the larger geopolitical context: in the shadow of both religious resurgence and political conservatism; on new research agendas in the face of biomedical discourses and HIV/ AIDS; and from within international LGBTQI and feminist human rights activism.

Other activist research and political work is described by Ratna Kapur, director of the Centre for Feminist Legal Research in New Delhi, in her book

Erotic Justice: Law and the New Politics of Postcolonialism (2005). She argues that colonial discourses, cultural essentialism, and victim rhetoric are reproduced in universal liberal projects such as human rights and international law, as well as in the legal regulation of sexuality and culture in a post-colonial context. Kapur rewrites the scripts that trap ordinary women's lives in a colonized and racialized gender and development 'project', as she unpacks and challenges authoritative gender and development positions. She argues, for example, that anti-trafficking strategies and laws have meant women from the Global South are increasingly limited in their freedom to move, are under greater surveillance, and are ever more constrained by regressive views on sexual integrity and women's central place in the home.

Sylvia Tamale (2006), in her writing on cultural/sexual initiation among the Baganda people of Uganda – the Kiganda institution of the *Ssenga* – seeks to reverse and challenge the colonialist constructions of African women's sexuality as something that needs to be rescued from 'traditional' cultures. In *Ssenga*, traditionally the paternal aunt tutors young women in a range of sexual matters (on erotics and reproduction) pre-menarche, pre-marriage and as a reference during marriage. It is their role to ensure nieces are subservient good wives and give husbands sexual pleasure, and in the process they also teach the women about sexual pleasure itself. Tamale rewrites body politics, seeing African women as empowered subjects through their resistance, negotiation, identity, pleasure and silence. Her narrative shows that, despite modern public health institutions, and colonial and post-colonial attempts to stamp out 'traditions' and replace them with the 'civilized' ways of the white ruling elite, the *Ssenga* survived – partially because the colonial administration dealt with male tribal chiefs and thus 'missed' the importance of the practice. In modern Uganda there are now commercialized *Ssenga* services, booklets, and radio call-in programmes that have transformed the institution through a modernization and urbanization process, taking it from the private to the public domain. In so doing the *Ssenga* are opening up discussions around sexuality and challenging gender inequalities. Tamale also sees the emergence of commercial *Ssengas* as one of the creative ways in which women, particularly those of poor urban families, have responded to the economic and political hardships experienced in Uganda since the 1970s (Tamale 2006: 91).

Tamale argues that, though the *Ssenga* has as its main theme subservience to husbands, there are also subtexts of defiance, manipulation and gender transgression. Women's sensuality and eroticism are recognized in Uganda and their sexuality is greatly feared, indicating a strong degree of power, even if it is officially silenced in public. In the emergence of *Ssenga* in modern Uganda the traditional scripts on sexuality when decoded carry emancipatory messages of how young women can enjoy sexual pleasures and take strength from their skilful love making. Tamale suggests the husky-voiced *Ssengas* on the radio, responding to questions from young men and women about sexual pleasure and rights, engage in a highly radical move, one that could be seen as a countervailing power to Uganda's charismatic evangelical pastors.

In terms of body politics Tamale directly counters the discourse on female genital mutilation by reframing the practice of elongating the labia minora, and critiques the blanket classification of the practice by WHO as FGM type IV under a broad negative rubric viewing the practice as harmful to children's rights and health. Between the ages of 9 and 12, young girls are instructed by the *Ssenga* on how to prepare their genitals for future sex. They 'visit the bush' in this period and are shown how to elongate the labia minora, which is then the mark of identity of a Muganda woman, used in mutual masturbation among partners, and fondled and admired by men during love making. The WHO categorization extracts *Ssenga* from the 'lived experience' of the Baganda and their sexual pleasure, which, according to Tamale, is not always marked by the 'incompleteness, anxiety and depression' the WHO associates with this practice (Tamale 2006: 94–5).[40]

Recasting desire

Erotic justice recasts sexual pleasure as a source of physical, psychological, intellectual and spiritual well-being. It also acknowledges that many people's embodied experience of desire can change throughout their lives.

The concept of erotic justice, instead of 'othering' 'traditional practices' or 'sexual minorities', conceptualizes everyone as having a potential for a diversity in sexual desire, including same-sex desire. Erotic justice breaks down the assumption that heterosexuality is the only reality: a reality jealously guarded by religion and conservative governments, and policed in various controlling and normalizing ways. Instead, the construction and experience of sexuality is seen as a positive, intensely personal and intimate, spiritual realm. Such a conception of erotic justice is very important where there is a continuing resistance and shame associated with sex work, sex between men, lesbianism and transgender sex, preventing safe commercial sexual transactions as well as safe and mutually pleasurable sex among cohabiting married partners. The fear of stigma and relentless assertion of hetero-normativity make sex work and same-sex sex clandestine, and lead to cultures of violence. Sex that is understood in terms of violence, submission and domination carries little scope for safe sex. The challenge is to end the normalizing of rape, the tearing and abuse of women by men, men by men, transgender by men, and children by adults as a 'natural' part of sexual inter-action (Gosine 2004). It is crucial that discussions on sexuality continue to be brought out of the realm of the private and into the public in ways that respect and promote diverse sexuality in trusting, non-moralistic and safe environ-ments. 'The question for erotic justice is how to enable "ordinary women" to feel empowered enough to say that you can be a gay Muslim woman, that is your (my) right' (Feminist Dialogues 2007).

Personal is political

High social costs can be involved in activism that pushes for sexual rights and erotic justice. Within the transnational feminist movement, the dialogue between those advocating for economic and social rights, and those pushing for sexual rights and erotic justice, is not an easy one. The personal dimension of sexuality leads to divisions, suspicions and silences. The issue of sexuality and racism is considered too difficult and radical for core gender and development debate. The tendency is therefore to separate out 'strategies' for women's economic rights from sexual and reproductive health and rights. Sexuality is often seen as a side issue and too personal to mention within serious development debate. It can be viewed as less vital than economic concerns, reflecting neatly the economic bias of development, and also a stereotypically male bias that fails to acknowledge how sexual issues impact on economic and social lives.

Noelene Nabulivou, in her plenary presentation at the Bangkok AWID Conference where the Primadonna troupe performed, spoke of what it meant to come out as a lesbian in Fiji. Fiji, a small island in the Pacific, is a country where sexual orientation and gender identity are heavily and openly contested and politicized by the 'state' and traditionalist political processes (*Vanua*), and where the Methodist Church, the Muslim League and other denominations call for the criminalizing of homosexuality. Nabulivou spoke of the baiting of her organization because it took up issues of gender and sexuality. People in her neighbourhood joke and pass comments as they go by, and her extended family no longer acknowledge her.

Importantly, her testimony is not of victimization but of empowerment and change through support by various women's rights activists and human rights defenders living and working in the Pacific. She saw herself as nurtured by women who live their lives by the personal principles of feminism. With such mentoring and support, and the spaces created by the feminist movement, she was able, 'after a lifetime of fear and pain and confusion and craziness . . . to come out as a lesbian'. She now funnels her energy into her work with younger people to support their self-realization and end the same pain she had felt as a younger woman (Nabulivou 2006).

Even though in this chapter I have tried to emphasize positive approaches to sexuality and sexual rights, there is a lot of pain and misunderstanding bound up in the conversations, silences, struggles and questions that deeply ingrained sexual injustice brings out. My primary point is that the issue of sexual rights is deeply embedded in any discussion around gender equality and is something that impacts on all of us, whatever our lifestyles, histories, desires, hopes or fears. It is a conversation gender and development cannot ignore. Indeed some would argue it is not a question of ignoring. Canada-based researcher Andil Gosine argues that in constructing sex as a problem in development an important rationale is provided for development interventions to control sexualities of peoples of the Global South. He writes:

> Development schemes have imposed heterosexuality, marginalized sexual minorities, and ignored the impact of sexuality-based discrimination, as well as the significance of sexual pleasure to the well-being of people of the Global South. We need to pay more critical attention to how the articulation of sex as problematic not only works to validate and legitimate intensified regulation of bodies and sexual practices, but also harnesses these anxieties about sex to further extend and advance imperialist ambitions. (Gosine 2009)

The challenge is how to build sexual rights as discourse and advocacy, transform ideals such as erotic justice and sexual freedom into realities, identify agents and important decision makers, and create shifting spaces for different voices to be heard. Erotic justice that seeks to counter the myriad injustices built into social, legal and economic systems controlling and policing sexuality, culture, gender and sexual minorities provides an important critical perspective from which to challenge gender and development.

Notes

1 See *Development* Vol. 49, No. 1 (Women's Rights and Development) which published many of the papers as a report on the AWID Conference.

2 See <http://www.eastandard.net/mag/InsidePage.php?id=1143990594&cid=349&>. Thanks to Arthur Muliro for this reference.

3 See *The Guardian* article at <http://www.guardian.co.uk/world/2008/jun/30/india.gayrights>.

4 See 'Thai school introduces toilets for transvestite students', *The Guardian*, 18 June 2008, <http://www.guardian.co.uk/world/2008/jun/18/thailand.gender?gusrc=rss&feed=networkfront>.

5 For example, consider first the Beijing statement on sexuality:

> The human rights of women include their right to have control over and decide freely and responsibly on matters related to their sexuality, including sexual and reproductive health, free of coercion, discrimination and violence. Equal relationships between women and men in matters of sexual relations and reproduction, including full respect for the integrity of the person, require mutual respect, consent and shared responsibility for sexual behaviour and its consequences. (Fourth UN Conference on Women, Beijing Platform for Action, Paragraph 96, 1995, <http://www.un.org/womenwatch/daw/beijing/platform/health.htm>)

Compare with this the World Health Organization official working definition of sexuality which emerged from an expert consultation in 2004:

> Sexuality is a central aspect of being human throughout life and encompasses sex, gender identities and roles, sexual orientation, eroticism, pleasure, intimacy and reproduction. Sexuality is experienced and expressed in thoughts, fantasies, desires, beliefs, attitudes, values, behaviours, practices, roles and relationships. While sexuality can include all of these dimensions, not all of them are always experienced or expressed. Sexuality is influenced by the interaction of biological, psychological, social, economic, political, cultural, ethical, legal, historical, religious and spiritual factors. (World Health Organization, Working Definitions, 2004 <www.who.int/reproductive-health/gender/sexual_health.html#2>)

6 See also McClintock (1997).

7 Another important theorist on sexuality and masculinity is R. W. Connell (2005).

8 Browsing the home page of The Body Shop, <www.bodyshop.com>, I randomly selected three of their products advertised in March 2008. The text runs: 'We're incredibly proud to use Community Trade Babassu Oil in our luxurious fragrance body products . . . it comes to us as a result of a brave struggle by the women of North Eastern Brazil' . . . 'New Neroli Jasmin . . . in the mysterious world of magic, neroli is used as an aphrodisiac . . . enchant admirers . . . . Wear it and embrace your feminine powers.' . . . 'Buy a Stop Violence in the Home Daisy Soap and make a difference to a child's life.' . . . 'Our 2006

Stop Violence in the Home campaign (in partnership with UNICEF) aims to make a difference by raising awareness of the problem and the impact it has on children, and raising funds to help provide better services for those children.'

9   I have written a very personal account about racism in Australia as a white woman for a US academic journal on racism and gender, *Meridians*. See Harcourt (2001).

10 Alexander documents the gay and lesbian niche marketing for sex holidays, looking at the promotional material in the late 1990s of the International Gay Travel Association, linking 1,200 gay and gay-supportive businesses.

11 There is also a Sarah Bartmann Centre for Women and Children volunteer programme and a Sarah Bartmann Cultural Council.

12 See bell hook's essay 'Selling hot pussy' (Weiz 1998) which looks at black female sexuality in the cultural market place. There is also an important longer discussion on the treatment of Sarah Bartmann in Schiebinger (1993) and Samuelson (2007).

13 It is interesting that it was her brains and genitals that were displayed, suggesting the era's racist and colonial primal fears of sexuality, which linked the concept of primitive brains and exaggerated sexual parts, the subject of recent feminist scholarship.

14 As in other cases of appropriation of women's stories and the retelling of them as victims or heroines as part of the national narrative – for example, the foundational myths of the origin of the Mexican nation as a land of *mestizaje*, and the story of La Malinche (the main translator of Cortés, the Spanish conqueror of the Aztec Empire), who betrayed her people (Belausteguigoitia 2004).

15 See the statements at <http://www.bayswan.org/swed/swed_index.html>.

16 The European Women's Lobby (EWL) is the largest umbrella organization of women's associations in the European Union (EU). The EWL Secretariat is based in Brussels and EWL has member organizations in 25 member states of the EU. The EWL works mainly with the institutions of the European Union: the European Parliament, the European Commission and the EU Council of Ministers. See <www.womenlobby.org>.

17 Taken from <http://www.womenlobby.org>.

18 See <www.catwinternational.org>.

19 UN Commission on the Status of Women, oral statement on eradicating commercial sexual exploitation, February 2008, <http://www.catwinternational.org>.

20 See <http://www.thai.net/gaatw> and <www.nswp.org>.

21 See <http://www.brandeis.edu/projects/fse/index.html>.

22 See <http://www.nodo50.org/Laura_Agustin>.

23 These ideas were promoted by the French sociologist Jacques Donzelot in *The Policing of Families* (1979).

24 See varied definitions of sexual rights in the Sexual Rights Charter of the Women's Health Project South Africa, the IPPF Charter on Sexual and Reproductive Rights, Health, Empowerment and Accountability (HERA), and the World Association of Sexology, as listed in Esplen (2007: 5–8).

25 The *hijras* may be born intersexual or male, portray themselves as feminine, and live in kinship groups of other *hijras*; usually, but not necessarily, they have male lovers; some have surgery. *Travesti* in Latin America are generally born with male bodies and grow up to dress

and act feminine; they see their own gender identity as male or *travesti*, and often invest in surgery to increase the voluptuousness of their bodies (Campuzano 2006).

26 In 1995 the journal *Development* featured stories of how gay activists together with women's groups in Africa were dealing with HIV AIDS. The strong message in that journal issue was the importance of organizing and community support (Hyde 1995: 3–5).

27 For example, this strong statement from Latin American human rights activists:
'It is indispensable and urgent that we stop governing ourselves by the absurd notion that only two possible body types exist, male and female, with only two genders inextricably linked to them, man and woman. We make trans and intersex issues our priority because their presence, activism and theoretical contributions show us the path to a new paradigm that will allow as many bodies, sexualities, and identities to exist as those living in this world might wish to have, with each one of them respected, desired, celebrated' (International Gay and Lesbian Human Rights Commission, Latin American Office, 2005, quoted in Campuzano 2007). For a strong feminist statement from Latin America, see Vargas 2006.

28 These groups have now formed into sex rights activists such as Sonagachi Project, Poz and Proud, TASO (Uganda young HIV-positive mothers). See also the charter drawn up in Swaziland on HIV-positive young women's sexual and reproductive rights: <charter www.icw.org/node/106>.

29 The conditionalities are (Corrêa 2006: 21):
• ABC strategies (abstinence, be faithful, use condoms);
• A shift in control of condom funding and distribution;
• A loyalty oath condemning prostitution;
• Global gag rule (organizations providing abortion services or even providing information about abortion services cannot receive funding);
• Rejection of harm reduction strategy for drug users.

30 The conference was organized and hosted by UNFPA, WHO, Engenderhealth, GNP+ and IPPF.

31 The official UNAIDS figure for 2007 is 33.2 million, with 2.8 million losing their lives to HIV AIDS in 2005.

32 According to UNAIDS, the number of children living with HIV in 2007 was 2.1 million (between 1.9 and 2.4 million); the number of children who died of AIDS in 2007 was 290,000 (between 270,000 and 320,000).

33 Safe sex is defined as sexual activities that avoid or reduce exchange of body fluids (semen, blood and vaginal fluids), the avoidance of genital to genital contact; to have non-penetrative sex and to practise mutual monogamy or polygamy where there is no other partner outside the couple or circle. For those unable to practise safe sex condoms are central to prevention (male or female condoms for vaginal, anal and oral sex) with lubricants to prevent condom breakage or vaginal dryness for older women, and for sex workers who have many partners.

34 See <http://www.icw.org/about-ICW>.

35 The Pleasure Project (<www.thepleasureproject.org>) mapped out 30 organizations, programmes, services, events and resources that creatively use sexual pleasure as a primary

motivation for practising safer sex. For example:
The Vida Positiva (Mozambique)
Sex in Queer Places (Australia)
Teaching the Kama Sutra (IISD, Kolkata, West Bengal)
Pleasure Helpline (TARSHI, Delhi)
Inside out Training for Social Change (Namibia)
Eroticizing Female Condoms (Sri Lanka)
Marketing Lube for Pleasure Population Services (Cambodia)
Sexual Healing for Positive Women (ICW).

36 An interview with Anne Philipott reports that the 1992 launch of female condoms had generated 94 articles in the national press and 56 TV and radio features. There was a £1 million advertising campaign, which included a two-week neon-lit display on the famous Spectacolor board at Piccadilly Circus, and people queued outside the stores of the chemist chain Boots to buy it. *The Guardian*, 23 August 2005.

37 Reported in *The Guardian*, 23 August 2005.

38 See <http://www.sxpolitics.org>.

39 Their collective research can be viewed in the e-book *SexPolitics – Reports from the Front Lines*, which looks at the dynamics of sexual politics in Brazil, Egypt, India, Peru, Poland, South Africa, Turkey and Vietnam – and in relation to two global institutions, the United Nations and the World Bank. The full text can be downloaded at <http://www.sxpolitics.org/mambo452/index.php?option=com_content&task=blogcategory&id=5&Itemid=9)>.

40 For another discussion of deconstructing female genital mutilation as a 'traditional practice', see Gunning (2000).

Thailand Prostitution accounts for a third of the Thai economy, which supports **2.8m** female prostitutes.

Colombia From January 2002 to June 2006 **one woman** a day on average died as a result of political violence.

Democratic Republic of Congo More than **3**,500 reported rape cases in the first six months of 2008.

6

Source: 'The state they're in - how women are faring in the rest of the world'
http://www.guardian.co.uk/lifeandstyle/2008/dec/07/women-equality-rights-feminism-sexism-worldwide

Six

Techno-Bodies

Bodies in the cyberworld

In trying to come to grips with this chapter I found myself sliding in and out of all types of cyber spaces. A surfeit of websites kept me clicking further and further, following endless links on issues not imagined five years ago. Blogs twisted in and out of fact, fiction, and opinion, pushing me to refer to yet more blogs. Weekly e-magazines led me to communities of scholars or advocacy 'watchdogs'. Short compelling videos took me inside human bodies, human cells, test tubes and interiors of laboratories. I read articles from feminist, social science, biology and medical journals. I viewed advertisements for surrogacy or pharma products, and wondered at eBay auctions for human organs and human eggs. I sifted through endless newspaper articles heralding or criticizing biotechnologies, nanotechnologies, or the human genome project. I tried to make sense on the screen of strings of gene sequences translated into computer terms. I skimmed pages of UN documents on human rights and biomedicine, declarations on biosecurity and donations of body tissues, umbilical blood banks and national gene data banks. I found witty cartoons on genomics, eugenics and techoscience; I diverted myself with YouTube videos of popular songs about boys in bubbles by Peter Gabriel and 'big science' by Laurie Anderson. I made all these visits while sitting at my desk courtesy of Internet access to the World Wide Web and the curiosity to go looking. This chapter reflects what I found, guided by the conversations I have had with people who have convinced me of the critical importance of understanding technology, science and biotechnology for gender and development.

Because this all seems very new, is very specialized, and is moving very fast, it seems important to find the right questions to make sense of all the information that pours out on human biotechnologies, on nanotechnologies,[1] genomes and artificial reproductive technologies. I know instinctively these technologies have huge implications for global body politics in gender and development, but it is difficult to know exactly how to think about them. The fact that I am connected so easily with all that cyber information is both fascinating and troubling. In what way does my knowledge and research in the flesh overlap with the realities I visit in the cyberworld? How do I know what is science? What is fiction? What is reliable knowledge? Where do I situate myself as a feminist concerned with embodiment, gender equality, women's rights, and ecological and social justice in this world of high tech, high investment and high costs to people's lives? Are the fears raised by civil society advocacy groups about the food I eat, the medicine I buy, the ethical uses of stell cems, foetal research and the invasion of our bodies valid? How does all of this relate to core concerns about gender and development, living standards, livelihoods, health, well-being, environmental security and the rights of men, women and children living in the world's poorest communities?

I have taken as my guide into the world of the new biotechnogies the work of Donna Haraway. Haraway, a professor at the University of California, Santa Cruz, is a creative and brilliant writer who inspires many feminists across the fields of biology, life science, human biotechnologies, social justice and feminist activism. Her books are full of intelligence, humour and honesty.[2] Haraway encourages us to think about many things in her uniquely alluring style as she positions what she calls 'technoscience' politically and ethically. This debate frames the chapter's conversations on: the politics of human biotechnology, synthetic biology, assisted reproductive technologies, stem cell research, new techno eugenics and, finally, technoscience solutions for development.

Haraway on technoscience

As the chapter's opening description of my cyberworld explorations suggests, we are dealing with topics that are very new and seem far from bodily realities. The images tip us into fantasies and fictions in ways that confuse our notions of what is science, what is technology, what is fact, what is fiction. Haraway defines these images as part of technoscience, which assembles 'objects like foetus, chip/computer, gene, race, ecosystem, brain, data base, and bomb' as 'stem cells of the technoscientific body' (Haraway 1997: 129). She explains that these objects are constructs forged in many different practices of technoscience:

> Out of each of these nodes or stem cells, sticky threads lead to every nook and cranny of the world . . . each of these stem cells is a knot of knowledge-making practices, industry and commerce, popular culture, social struggles, psychoanalytic formations, bodily histories, human and non-human actions, local and global flows, inherited narratives, new stories, syncretic technical, cultural processes, and more. (Haraway 1997a)

In modern Western technoscience biology and genetics construct the modern concept of nature through an instrumentalization of life via different cultural practices. Haraway deconstructs our common (Western) under-standing of science and technologies so that we do not see them as 'above' politics, economics and gender relations but rather part of them. For example, the seed and the gene are constructions of meaning within which there is a history of practices. Specific economic, social and cultural practices are represented within the seed and gene, and these meanings spread out and infiltrate throughout the 'tissue of the planet including the flesh of our personal bodies' (Haraway 1997a: 134). Biology and genomics are knowledges created through elite and specialized language and institutions that make the 'facts of life'. The integration of informatics and biology are connecting bodies (ours and other bodies) which leads to reworkings of nature, race, species, family, nation, gender, individual corporealization as well as genetics, biotechnology and biodiversity (Haraway 1997a: 141).

Corporealization

The term corporealization is a key concept here. Corporealization is about the interactions of humans and non-humans in the work processes of technoscience, which involve not only laboratories and computers but also scientific and government institutions, types of technical practices, legal structures, different forms of labour, and economic and political narratives. Cells, organisms and genes are not 'discovered' but are integrated into technoscience in the process of corporealization. The gene signifies an important node of action where many actors meet. Technical, political and economic spheres are all engaged in technoscience, as is evident in the disputes over genetic intellectual property rights or in contests over biodiversity. The sharp separation of the boundaries between science and other kinds of cultural practice is part of what she calls corporeal or, in the case of today's new biotechnologies, gene fetishism (as in the Marxist sense of commodity fetishism of capitalism) (Haraway 1997: 142–3). As Haraway describes it, 'gene fetishism' involves 'forgetting' that the gene and gene maps are ways of enclosing the commons of the body. Gene fetishism 'denies the natural-social relations among researchers, farmers, factory workers, patients, policy makers, molecules, model organisms, machines, forests, seeds, financial instruments, computers and much else'. The focus on the realm of exchange hides the realm of production – the extracting, the publishing, the patenting, the funding and the close links to industry. The gene seems to become itself a thing of value masking all the work that creates that value (Haraway 1997a: 148).

The floating foetus and the blue Earth

This understanding of gene fetishism is fundamental when looking at the work done on the Human Genome Project.[3] Haraway puts it distinctively: the Human Genome Project is presented as biology's equivalent to 'putting a man on the moon'. In a telling piece of analysis she describes an advertisement by New England Biolabs for DNA-restriction enzymes (Haraway 1997a: 164–6). In the advertisement a beautiful indigenous woman is wrapped around a map of the globe so that her body appears to be the mapped terrain of the Earth and her soft contours shape the Earth. Significantly, the map is dotted by clippers of Europe's great age of exploration and the title is 'Mapping the human genome'. The image of Europe discovering the native is suggested in modern technoscience mapping the body genome with the help of New England Biolab's restriction enzymes. The globalized history of race and gender, and of processes of naturalization, are evoked and integrated into this advertisement for DNA code-analysing restriction enzymes.

As the visual metaphors in the advertisement indicate, practices in the laboratory are still about the colonizing project, commercializing future life forms and ways of life for humans and non-humans. Technoscience is about life as:

> a system to be managed, a field of operations constituted by scientists, artists, cartoonists, community activists, mothers, anthropologists, fathers, publishers, engineers, legislators, ethicists, industrialists, bankers, doctors, genetic counsellors, judges, insurers, priests and all their relatives. (Haraway 1997a)

Haraway links the image of the foetus with the planet Earth as representing the two 'seed worlds in technoscience' (Haraway 1997a: 174). Other writers such as Wolfgang Sachs have pointed to the iconic power of the NASA photos of the blue, cloud-swathed sphere of the Earth as representing the modern-day natural/technical object of the environment.[4] Haraway links those images of Earth with the ubiquitous images of free, floating human foetuses.

These two images represent the technoscientific object of knowledge, life itself. The foetus and the round Earth represent the elixir of life as a complex system with each image as the origin of life in a post-modern world. They signify the natural and embodied over and against the constructed and the disembodied; we feel we can touch the wet blue earth, the soft fleshy child.

These innocent and reassuring images contain, however, a charged field of opposing meanings. The first celebrated visible foetuses were the photographs taken by Lennart Nilsson and featured on the April 1965 cover of *Life* magazine. These were in reality pictures of aborted foetuses, though not presented as such. Nilsson's photographs were high art, scientific illustration, research, research tools and mass popular culture. He went on to develop books, CDs and video presentations of the image, which is offered as a picture of life itself in just the same way that DNA has been. The pictures of the foetus dislodged from women's bodies, floating like the Earth, representing life, are in fact images of death (Haraway 1997a: 181).

Feminism and technoscience

Reproduction is at the centre of scientific, technological, political, personal, religious, gender, familial, class, race, and national and international 'webs of contestation'. Both feminists and political leaders are focused on foetal genetic diagnosis and with foetal/embryo experiments. For feminists it is important to examine the focus of technoscience in order to ask questions that could promote shared commitments and serve as a basis for solidarity and coalition among feminists (Haraway 1997a: 191).

Feminists are asking many questions of technoscience. What is meant by choice, agency, life and creativity? What is at stake here, and for whom? Who and what are human and non-human centres of action? Whose story is this? Who cares? What are the conditions of effective reproductive freedom?

In *Our Bodies, Ourselves* (Haraway 1997a,: 192–3), Haraway gives a humorous description of feminists in the US in the 1970s ritually opening up their bodies with hand-held speculums and mirrors to see their own vaginas and cervixes and reclaim the feminist self. Parallel to these home-grown sisterly support groups, technoscience was developing and funding biomedicine and the sonogram, leading to the vast economic and scientific world of human biotechnologies, which did not share the feminist engagement with body politics. I agree with Haraway's comment that 'We had to wonder early if we had seized the right tools' (Haraway 1997a: 194).

What kinds of reproductive freedoms does technoscience offer? It is a major issue in relation to the body politics of development. There are huge inequalities built into technoscience: whereas millions are spent in the Global North on artificial reproduction technologies, literally hundreds of millions of children experience serious deprivation, including millions of poor children in the US. For example, in the favelas of Rio de Janeiro in Brazil many children were dying in the first year of life because they were given powdered milk instead of breast milk. This was not due to neglect or lack of care by the mother or parents, but the direct outcome of transnational market-led development practice in the Global South.[5] A study reports there were several choices of feeding formula on the shelves, even where very little other food was available.

Layered onto this Brazilian story, repeated in other parts of the world, is race: the 'fracturing trauma in the body politic, race kills liberally and unequally and race privileges unspeakably and abundantly. . . . An inherently dubious notion, race like sex is about the purity of lineage, the legitimacy of passage and the drama of inheritance of bodies, property and stories' (Haraway 1997a: 214).

Race and biology cannot be understood as culture-free universal discourses. Biology is part of the conceptualizing of nation, family type, civility, species, sex, humanity, nature and race. Biology is a complex cultural practice with specific meanings that are located in the practice of the life sciences, where human nature is now embodied in a genetic database and where the gene equals information. Emily Martin (1991) illustrates in a well-known article ('The egg and the sperm: how science has constructed a romance based on stereotypical male-female roles') that the construction of what it is to be 'male' or 'female' shows how science represents the 'gender' of cells and projects a gender narrative onto cellular processes. In this scientific fairy tale the sperm heroically pursues the egg, surviving the hostile environment of the vagina and defeating its rivals. The large and passive egg, by contrast, drifts along the fallopian tube until captured by the valiant sperm.

We cannot afford to ignore how race also informs technoscience – for example in the human genome diversity project labelled the 'vampire project' because it collected the blood of indigenous peoples – and remains deeply embedded in global mass culture.[6] How to find knowledge, freedom and justice in a world of consequential facts drawn up by technoscience requires that we understand in what ways science overlaps with the technical and the political. We need to 'interrogate critical silences' and try to understand the reasons why questions seem ridiculous in the face of what seems neutral and rational (Haraway 1997a: 269).

Technoscience in our lives and bodies

With this feminist framing of 'technoscience' as a backdrop, let us now turn to the emerging fields of human biotechnologies, synthetic biology, genomics and nanotechnologies. We can begin to examine the appearance of neutrality and rationality by asking how life is constructed within technoscience. We need to look at the fetishes, the commercial interests, the implicit gender inequalities and broad inequities informing the social and political regimes that determine how technoscience is operating.

Today's technoscience, pulling together informatics, life science, government and business, is deeply embedded in modern society, economics and politics. On our televisions, radios, computer screens and newspapers, along with the stories of elections, wars, rising crime, financial crises and climate change, we have the stories of reproductive cloning, new fertility treatments, cancer cures, technologies to save the Earth and human ills. Images of the rising temperatures of a denuded, ravaged Earth, the computerized depiction of the human genome, the building of life itself from the cloned cells of the embryo are becoming part of our changing vision of nature, the environment, and the knowledge of our own bodies.

As we are all aware, these knowledges are highly specialized and changing rapidly. I focus on some of the troubling questions about technoscience raised by civil society groups, along with some scientists and social scientists. They have sounded the alarm over technoscientific procedures – in terms of the money poured into the research, the ways decisions are made, and how the uses of resulting technologies are coming to determine many areas of our lives. These processes, making up what we see as the 'facts of life', determine how we view our bodies, the food we eat, the medicine we take, our reproductive lives, our overall health and our biosecurity. Yet these scientific regimes, with their close links to business and the state, are evolving in ways that are hard to understand or regulate. There is too little knowledge or time for discussion among the public, even those with the time and education to follow what all these highly technical discussions are about.

Often, as one enters into these discussions with concerns and questions, one faces the accusation of being 'Luddite'.[7] People point out that technoscience brings new possibilities to deal with infertility, malaria and cancer, and ways to deal with other naturally occurring threats to humanity. The point, however, is that technoscience is not happening in some objective, politically free vacuum. It is a powerful part of modernity and of what 'economic progress' is expected to deliver, helping to determine what we perceive as possible, informing the ways in which we understand our bodies and the environment around us. Nor is 'big science'[8] confined to the laboratories of the United States, though much of the money and many of the sites of the entrepreneurial laboratories are situated there. The interconnections between national government interests in the US, Europe, Canada, India, Korea, Singapore, South Africa, Brazil, Australia and the global scientific and business community make it a truly transnational endeavour.

The Human Genome Project

Civil society watchdogs are concerned that the human genome as the common heritage of humankind is endangered along with the forests, atmosphere, oceans and fresh water. Their concern is that the genetic commons is to be lost to technoscience, driven by profit and the logic of privatization rather than public good. The sequencing of the human genome will change the way we understand ourselves and reinforce the view that we are little more than our genes. Yet they are only part of the puzzle. We have yet to learn about how development and environment are layered on our DNA or genes.

Eventually, using the information of the genome, we could eradicate many diseases, ensure longevity and replicate organs as well as design human beings. Being able to make such choices increases the problem of discrimination on the grounds of genetic information and the potential of preventing what would be seen as an underclass of genetically imperfect humans from living. Confidentiality of personal genome information is a serious problem, especially in the areas of health care and insurance. Although scientists take measures to prevent a person's name being linked to particular genetic information, there is continuous discussion in the scientific community about such possible misuse (Katz Rothman 1998).

David King of Human Genetics Alert warns that the DNA revolution brings a new ethics, both for human–nature and human–human relationships.[9] What King calls the power of the molecular biological gaze reconceptualizes nature as a vast Lego kit,[10] to be endlessly and limitlessly re-programmed through genetic engineering. As technoscience can 'tinker' with the biological mechanisms of nature and the human body, the seed and the cell, to make them more 'efficient', this increasing power to re-edit nature leads to shifts in both what is seen as normal and what is seen as pathological. Not surprisingly, the area of intellectual property rights is one of the most contested fields in the realm of technoscience. Over the last decades, legal praxis has been established that enables the patenting of things that were unthinkable earlier (Sexton 1999). For example, in the agro-industry giant Monsanto's literature the manipulation of genes is viewed as 'smart technology', a way of 'working with nature', in contrast to the former, less efficient, industrial techniques of domination of nature through such crude forces as dams or pesticides.[11]

In the new regime technoscience does not dominate nature, but becomes its intellectual originator, allowing and legitimizing scientists and companies to claim human cells and tissues as intellectual property (IP).[12] The IP system was originally set up for mechanical inventions and is very poorly equipped to deal with matters of life. Gene patenting enables commercial enterprises to obtain patents on genetic material when discovered and removed from the body, or on manipulations of genetic material. Not all human cells and tissues can have an IP attached to them, but if something considered new is created from the cells and tissues by the work of scientists and the corporations who fund them, they can lay claim to an IP. They can then charge anyone wishing to use that discovery in the process of medical research or drug development. The commercial companies say that this patenting is essential to cover the costs of research. Such patenting maximizes profits rather than making treatments available, though most of the money is made from full drug sales rather than from the steps that are the patents. Often patents are the procedures to make the drug/additive, not the additive itself. Drug companies are therefore not as interested in making drugs for diseases of the poor, as there is little money in it and they would not recoup their costs.[13] At the core of the debate is the issue of commodification and control – who 'owns' life? Can everything be privatized? What is common heritage and what should be off-limits to either commercial or scientific interests seeking exclusive control?

The Human Genome Project (HGP), the showcase 'man on the moon' project of technoscience, states on its home page that it is driven by a 'longstanding dedication to the transfer of technology to the private sector'. A major aim is to license technologies to private companies and to award grants for innovative research, in order to catalyse the multi-billion-dollar US biotechnology industry and foster the development of new medical applications. The website declares that technology and resources generated by the Human Genome Project and other genomics research are already having a major impact on research across the life sciences. The potential for commercial development of genomics research presents US industry with a wealth of opportunities, and sales of DNA-based products and technologies in the biotechnology industry are projected to exceed $US45 billion by 2009. Their listing of current and potential applications of genome research includes molecular medicine, bio-archaeology, anthropology, DNA forensics (identification), and agriculture, livestock breeding and bioprocessing.[14] This rapid take-up need not incline us to oppose such research, but should lead us to question why it is being paid for by companies and not governments.

In 2005 private companies held 63 per cent of the patents for 4,270 human genes, 18 per cent of the entire genome. A major area of concern is economic control, since unscrupulous firms could use patents to charge high fees for diagnostics (this has already occurred with breast cancer diagnostics). Medical ethicist Donna Dickenson raises the concern that gene fetishism – the 'genes are us' mentality – makes it appear that genetics is the true source of human identity, so that our identity is reduced to the level of a commodified object through patenting.

The famous example of Iceland's genetic heritage being sold to genomics company Decode, which then sold the human data to Hoffman LaRoche Switzerland for US $200 million, illustrates both these points. The deal marked the shift of genomics research to a mainstream commercial venture (Delahanty 2000). As the ethical implications of a company having a monopoly to sell medical and genetic data were questioned, the decision was overturned and Icelanders (who had been given only six months to agree) were given the right to refuse to participate, though not to reclaim the data already sold. There have also been changes involving the issue of consent in the cases of national biobanks in Australia, Estonia and the UK. Biobanks continue to be brokers. In the USA alone, before 1999 when consent was not yet required, 307 million stored tissue samples from 179 million people were registered in various scientific and hospital research data banks. That number was increasing by 20 million tissue samples a year (Dickenson 2007: 126).

Beth Burrows,[15] in her analysis of the Human Genome Diversity Project (HDGP), argues that biotechnologies are burdened by persistent ethical dilemmas, including the problem of how to access resources and engage people in the research endeavour without coopting their rights or harming them or their communities (Burrows 2006). In relation to intellectual property and control of genetic material, she is concerned with 'biopiracy', which she defines as the access to or acquisition of biological material and/or traditional knowledge related to its use, without the prior informed consent of those whose biological material or traditional knowledge has been 'accessed' or 'acquired'. She profoundly questions both industry and academy in their pursuit of plants, microbes and traditional knowledge, whether for potential commercial use or in the name of science (or medicine). The point is: in whose interest and with whose money is it conducted?

Synthetic biology

The newest forms of genetic engineering, however, go beyond the established mapping of genomes and the manipulation of genes in the biology labs. The splicing techniques used in recombinant DNA are now 30 years old and relied on scientists combining pieces of DNA between already existing species. Today, the new field of 'synthetic biology' or 'synbio' sites itself at the level of convergence of nanoscale biology, computing and engineering. It is about the creation and redesign of life forms from the bottom up. Graduating from the clunky old-fashioned 'mainframe' reading of genes, the field has now progressed to the biological equivalent of efficient word processors. They are moving from reading the genetic code to writing the code. Using gene synthesizers they write the 'sentences' of the DNA code one letter at a time. They can add new letters that do not exist in nature and rearrange them into new configurations. Instead of deciphering genetic sequencing in order to identify and understand the role of genes found in nature, the current focus is increasingly on how to produce 'made to order' life forms. Synthetic biology is at the frontiers of what some call 'extreme genetic engineering'.[16] At the core of synthetic biology is the conviction that all parts of life can be made synthetically. Using engineering concepts from electronics and computing, synthetic biologists are 'reprogramming' DNA as if it were a computer code waiting to be hacked, cleaned and fixed in order to assemble new genetic systems (ETC Group 2007: 3).

The field is highly creative and dynamic, full of opportunities to explore and potential to exploit that extend way beyond the walls of the lab. Synthetic biology is a complex web of venture capital companies, computer companies, agribusiness, scientists and patent lawyers, as well as the institutions and mechanisms that determine government funding with little visible regulation. Many scientists are as much business entrepreneurs as they are scientists; the most arrogant among them come across as self-styled gods playing with nature. The more sympathetic and concerned jean-clad young men (fewer women) speak about engineering biology, building life from scratch with 'Lego bricks' of gene sequences. As with the dot.com era, such talk is as much about setting up companies, venture capital and patenting as about the actual discoveries. Indeed there is a fascinating overlap, with the Bill and Melinda Gates Foundation, Google and Virgin being major investors in the field, along with agribusiness and venture capital (ETC Group 2007; Hällström 2008).

Synthetic biology scientists and the companies they start, or which fund their research (backed by government and venture capital), aim to commercialize new biological parts, devices and systems that do not exist in the natural world. Advocates see synthetic biology as the key to cheap bio-fuels, a cure for malaria and the solution to climate change – while choosing not to highlight the risks involved.

One of the more colourful examples of scientific entrepreneurial spirit, J. Craig Venter's company Synthetic Genomics Inc., stated the following on their homepage in May 2008:

> Imagine a future where clean, environmentally friendly micro-organisms produce the bulk of industrial material that today are

made from petrochemicals, where specifically tailored organisms harness the sun to create clean energy, when researchers can use a modular software-like product to design new microbial genomes which are manufactured on an industrial scale. . . . At Synthetic Genomics Inc., we are developing novel genomic-driven strategies to address global energy and environmental challenges. Recent advances in the field of synthetic genomics present seemingly limitless applications that could revolutionize production of energy, chemicals and pharmaceuticals and enable carbon sequestration and environmental remediation.[17]

Venter is the scientist who through his private company beat the public Human Genome Project in the race to sequence the entire human genome in the 1990s. More recently he has made a round-the-world expedition to sample and patent newly discovered life forms collected in international waters, and is now one of the leading figures in the field of synthetic biology (ETC Group 2007: 15).

In 2007 Synthetic Genomics was involved in synbio's most visible and well-funded project to build an artificial chromosome (receiving half its funding from the agribusiness giant Savia)[18] – even filing a patent claim for the exclusive right of creating new life forms. Venter believes in his ability to solve some of the world's most pressing problems through major techno-fixes, and is careful to consolidate control over crucial IP that is likely to render him immensely wealthy.

The brilliant young MIT professor Drew Endy[19] is a more likeable character – full of the excitement of research but also alarmed by the potential risks for society that he is part of unleashing. Endy is aiming to build new biological systems combining computer engineering skills with bio-technology. He has created several hundred discrete DNA modules or biobricks (inspired by Lego), codes for different traits and functions to be used in the design of new life forms. They behave like electronic components that turn genes on and off. The civil society organization the ETC Group describe the community of young graduates that are linked up with Endy in what they call a 'garage' bio-hacking community which attracts considerable interest from venture capitalists. Endy raised US$13 million to found a synthetic biology start-up called Codon Devices that builds DNA to order and sends it back to the customer as a living cell culture, providing a short-cut for genetic engineers (ETC Group 2007: 17). Another start-up company, Amyris Biotechnologies led by Jay Keasling at the University of California, is engineering genetic pathways of cells to produce valuable drugs and industrial chemicals. It is focusing on a powerful anti-malarial compound known as artemisinin, developed with a grant of US$42.5 million dollars from the Bill and Melinda Gates Foundation. Keasling and colleagues funded the synbio start-up to produce cheaper drugs. They claim that their microbially derived chemicals could be used for remediation of radioactive materials and to neutralize dangerous toxins such as sarin; they would boost rubber production and other biomaterial such as Sorona, a spandex-like fibre that DuPont, who funded the Genencor company that produced this new material, hopes will be as big as nylon (ETC Group 2007: 20).

These examples show that right at the heart of the scientific interest in new knowledge frontiers is the closely linked interest in contributing (and gaining from) industry through inventing new plastics, rubbers, fragrances, biofuels, food crops and medicines. Human genetic research is an economic enterprise and the major economic players are venture capitalists, pharmaceutical companies, government departments (health, trade and industry), insurance companies and biotech companies. Venture capital has bankrolled the commercial biotech boom in the US and large pharmaceutical companies have developed a range of relationships with biotech firms. Some have bought up biotech companies, or have entered into some kind of agreement or alliance or strategic partnership with them, such as being granted first rights to any discoveries or products, in return for funding (Sexton 2005).

Biosecurity?

These symbiotic relationships between science and commercialization provoke many questions: are the economic and technical determinants of such research clear? Should the building blocks of life be privatized through patents and owned by companies? And most of all, is this safe? This new field of synthetic biology raises considerable concern about biosecurity. If synthesized microbes can exchange genetic material with soil and gut bacteria, they could at some time in the future cause genetic pollution and alter the functioning and behaviour of natural microbial ecosystems in unforeseen and unpredictable ways (ETC Group 2007: 44). Furthermore, the new technologies have opened up possibilities to create dangerous new bioweapons. For example, scientists have succeeded in recreating the Spanish influenza, which had been declared extinct. For scientists such as Drew Endy, the destructive potential of bioweapons in the 'wrong' hands is a serious threat to humanity.[20]

Biomedical reproductive technologies and the commercialization of women's bodies

While new areas such as synthetic biology open up whole new unforeseen landscapes of concern, a number of existing technologies are already at the centre of feminist debate and struggle. Clearly, women's bodies are deeply implicated in molecular biology and genetic technologies, with assisted reproductive technologies (ARTs) raising new legal, ethical and policy issues around reproduction.[21] ART has enabled millions of people to have biological children. More than three million babies were born using ART world-wide in the last 30 years (Galpern 2007). Some of the questions up for debate by reproductive justice advocates[22] include: do ARTs increase or decrease reproductive choices and control of individuals? Who do they benefit?[23] Do they devalue people with disabilities? Do they exploit young women and economically vulnerable women? Do they increase the com-modification of women's reproductive capacity and reproductive tissues? Is it possible to draw the line between the medical rather than economic purposes of reproductive technologies? Is it possible to ensure industrial accountability?

ART[24] is a multi-billion-dollar industry in the US and elsewhere, as Deborah Spar outlines in her book *The Baby Business: How Money, Science, and Politics Drive the Commerce of Conception* (2006). Spar details the amount com-mercial fertility clinics earn; the premiums paid for sperm and eggs from genetically desirable donors; and the exploitation of poor, non-white and surrogate mothers from the Global South. Most *in vitro* fertilization (IVF) treatment is private and the individual pays: a surrogacy can cost from $40,000 to $100,000 in the US and there is a rapidly growing market. The trade in human eggs is 38 million eggs a year. In the US 75 per cent of egg donors are college students who are paid from $10,000 to $100,000 (Galpern 2007: 16). Sperm donors are paid from 75 to 200 US dollars. In the UK where a culture of donating eggs and sperm for science and research is more common, the amount paid ranges from £15 to up to £1,000 (Sexton 2005).

What is often not emphasized is that IVF techniques expose women to high risks from fertility drugs and egg retrieval, due to ovarian hyperstimulation syndrome as well as risks from multiple gestation (50 per cent of IVF treatments result in multiple births).[25] The process of harvesting eggs can lead to cysts, fluid build-up in the body, in the abdomen, lung and other tissues, clotting disorders, kidney damage and ovarian twisting, and even respiratory or cardiac arrest.[26] There is no real research on the long-term impact of the retrieval process, and the consent forms can fail to mention the real dangers.[27]

ARTs also have international social justice implications, not least those arising from a growing reproductive tourism. US citizens go to India, Thailand and China to find surrogate mothers. British citizens go to Crete, Bulgaria, Romania and Spain to buy eggs, for which economically poor women are paid almost twice their average monthly salary. Such women are typically paid US$200–300 per cycle, whereas clients are charged around US$15,000 (Dickenson 2007). South Africa is another IVF tourist destination, as well as an organ trade hub (Sexton 2005).

With the new biotechnologies of which ART is just a part, things that were formerly thought uncommodifiable are now being turned into private property owned by companies under a new property regime. With the 'enclosure of the body' – of human tissue and human genetic material containing elements of both person and 'things' – our concepts of humanity and of the relationship between the body and the person are changing:

> Biotechnology has made the entire notion of the body much more fluid. On the one hand bodily functions can be replicated or enhanced by objects originally extraneous to the subject . . . on the other hand human biomaterials extracted from the body enter into research and commerce as objects. (Dickenson 2007: 4)

The closure of the body commons

The enclosure of genetic commons and forms of human tissue makes a distinction between the natural and the artificial body harder to pin down. This threatens to extend the objectification and commodification of the bodies of both sexes, but it is women's bodies which continue to be most objectified in this process. Dickenson points out that genetic patenting and biobanking have led to the most public debate because in those cases the bodies of both sexes are owned (Dickenson 2007: 8). It is presented as more 'normal' for female bodies to be objectified, harvested and commodified in new and disturbing ways, unsurprisingly so as in this ART regime the female body proves more valuable.

These new enclosures reverse the struggles for women to gain control over their bodies. Women's bodies are seen as being more manipulable and accessible, and women themselves are also more economically vulnerable. IVF and stem cell technologies have brought the most intimate biological functions of women to the market place. Women's position and contributions as the embodied subject of these technologies has been displaced as the focus goes onto what is taken from their bodies and commodified – rather than on the question whether women are being exploited. Public discussions focus on the embryo rather than the women from whom the ova are removed.

In the framework of technoscience, these debates are integrally linked to issues of power, commercialization and business. Another major research and commercial interest is in the possibilities of regenerative medicine. Techniques focus on how to transform the stem cell into a certain type of body cell that could be inserted into people whose body cells are malfunctioning. In India stem cell research is a thriving area of scientific research, closely following the success of the country's software revolution. Stem cells are provided from its 250 busy IVF clinics to public and private research laboratories in the country (Sexton 2005: 6).

The burgeoning trade in ova for stem cell research has risks, as with IVF. But these risks increase as more eggs are 'harvested': as the number of eggs needed increases, the temptation is to overstimulate the ovaries – and this can be dangerous for the women selling or donating their eggs.[28] There is a lot of hope raised around stem cell research, for example in the search for a cure for diabetes, but the technology is still in its infancy. UK-based researcher and reproductive rights activist Sarah Sexton estimates that huge numbers of eggs would be required as a therapeutic medicine for diabetes. Something like 2.8 million women in the UK would need to donate eggs to treat the 1.4 million people with diabetes. In the US, the world's premier pharmaceutical market, on which all drug research has its eye, there are 17 million people with diabetes, so 34 million women would be required to sell or donate. Scientists are considering other techniques such as harvesting ovaries from female foetuses aborted at a late stage. (A female foetus has 7 million eggs, a new-born girl 1 to 2 million, a teenage girl fewer. An adult woman releases 400 in her lifetime.) Another possibility is to genetically engineer foetuses so that girls are born with 7 million eggs that can then be 'donated'.

Another worrying practice impacting on women's bodies is umbilical cord blood banking. Dickenson sees this technique as feeding into the myth of the infinitely regenerative body. The companies who are collecting blood from the umbilical cord such as Cryo Care or the private cord-blood bank Eurocord claim the procedure is perfectly safe. However medical reviews are concerned that taking the blood during the third stage of labour (before the placenta is delivered) unduly puts the woman and baby at risk. At a very minimum it is adding a medical technique at a very critical moment in delivery, when the mother and child should be resting waiting for the placenta to be delivered. Doctors are concerned that it increases the risk of haemorraging, particularly in low-birthweight babies and anaemic mothers, and advise against the procedure when in doubt. Another concern is that there is little or no evidence that cord-blood cells are actually useful in several conditions, as claimed by the companies. And most cures are from other cord-blood donations (not the child's own cord blood, as featured in the self-regenerative, 'cells for life' promotional narrative). The worry is that the hype surrounding the collection process could lead to a further, risky medicalizing procedure against the interests of the mother (Dickenson 2007: 92).

In this context there are broad social, political and economic issues as well as ethical issues to be considered. How can the public interest be ensured, including the gender equity and justice issues raised by women's health movements, given it is the commercial context that determines the research agenda? The direction of research in molecular biology genetics, reproduction and embryo research is determined by funds from wealthy individuals, universities, corporate foundations, governments, large corporations and venture capitalists. Ova harvesting represents a radical change in the political economy of human tissue. What has not changed radically is the unbalanced power relationship between donors and institutions which take/buy/use the eggs. The British government spends £80 million a year on genomics and biotechnology to help boost industry and commerce and to create wealth (not health) (Sexton 2005). Most research is tied up with commercial interests and there are fewer and fewer independent scientists. And, ultimately, the benefits of the research are for the individuals who can afford them rather than the wider society.

New techno-eugenics

While the reproductive technologies obviously impact on women's lives, the next steps pose even more challenges – going beyond reproduction to fundamental issues about redesigning and 'improving' humans as such. Terms like transhumanism and designer babies seem to take us into a realm of futuristic science fiction far removed from our earlier discussions on global body politics in gender and development (King 2002). This is the realm of science-fiction imaginaries: markets for genetically modified children, 'designer babies' and 'enhanced' and perfected humans. Cloning technology that created Dolly the sheep in July 1996[29] continues in various parts of the world, the leaders being Britain, the US, South Korea, China and Singapore (Sexton 2003). In the view of Richard Hayes, executive director of the Center for Genetics and Society,[30] the era of genetically modified humans is not as far away as we might want to believe (Hayes 2003).

The World Transhumanist Association has nearly 5,000 members and chapters in over 20 countries. The Association's website states that they advocate 'the ethical use of technology to expand human capacities. We support the development of and access to new technologies that enable everyone to enjoy better minds, better bodies and better lives. In other words, we want people to be better than well.'[31] This means the breeding of 'genetically enriched' forms of 'post-human' beings. Princeton University professor Lee Silver predicts that by the end of this century, 'All aspects of the economy, the media, the entertainment industry, and the knowledge industry [will be] controlled by members of the GenRich class. . . . Naturals [will] work as low-paid service providers or as laborers.' The bioethicist Gregory Pence, of the University of Alabama, states:

> [M]any people love their retrievers and their sunny dispositions around children and adults. Could people be chosen in the same way? Would it be so terrible to allow parents to at least aim for a certain type, in the same way that great breeders . . . try to match a breed of dog to the needs of a family? (Quoted in Hayes 2003)

As Harry Laughlin, one of the leaders of the US eugenics movement in the 1920s and 1930s stated, 'Eugenics is simply the application of big business methods to human reproduction.' Prenatal screening, germ-line therapy and cloning are ushering in a new techo-eugenics.[32]

Commentators such as Tom Athanasiou, executive director of EcoEquity,[33] and Marcy Darnovsky (Center for Genetics and Society) fear that in the same way economic development pushed aside the precautionary principle with nuclear power plants, large dams and green revolutions, so a new eugenics based on high-tech reproduction, consumer preferences and market dynamics is being steered around and over all opposition by powerful political and economic interests.[34]

Contemporary biomedicine holds the potential to both screen out 'imperfect' bodies and to enable people with significant disabilities to survive and flourish. The 'genome revolution' holds out promises of designer babies and personalized genetic medicine and other life-extending biotechnologies. This is what colours the feature articles such as those found in *The Economist, The Times* and *Newsweek*, and the hype about genetic futures in the *Financial Times* and *Wall Street Journal*.[35]

Burrows (2003) warns that this technoscience gaze is justifying inequitable social arrangements, racializing and medicalizing various 'others'. She queries the ethics of the new eugenic technologies to create a 'clean gene pool and a narrow range of normalcy in which almost all of us can partake'. It takes us beyond the nature/nurture debate to an obsession with perfection. But what and whose idea of perfection will be the yardstick for unwanted traits?

Disability rights

The new techno-eugenics flies in the face of broader social acceptance of disability. Today's biomedical reproductive technologies include prenatal diagnosis as an increasingly routine part of pregnancy care. A range of tests are taken in order to identify foetal disabilities: sonograms, amniocentesis, and blood screen tests. The very existence of prenatal tests assumes that parents will want to select.

Disability rights activists challenge exclusive visions of 'perfection'. They raise questions about the growing use of prenatal screening to prevent the birth of disabled children. Such concerns fall within the same continuum as ongoing efforts by disability activists to facilitate the presence of people with disabilities in everyday life – rather than to 'get fixed' through any available technological means.

There are tensions around the place of genetic knowledge in society. Women and their families come to decisions regarding amniocentesis in complex ways. What counts as a disability that determines an abortion for one pregnant woman could be an acceptable condition to another. Some conditions that are now diagnosable prenatally – such as Down's syndrome or spina bifida – are feared by families on the basis of very little knowledge about what such conditions entail. A range of economic as well as social factors play a strong role in attitudes towards disability. In most cities in the Global North women are increasingly in the workforce for longer stretches of their lives and less able to take significant time off to care for infants and young children. They tend to live at a distance from the support systems of extended family. With disability activism and medical care, many more young people with chronic conditions are surviving and are raised at home with their families. The caretaking still falls on families, and disproportionately on women. The real or imagined responsibilities of caring for a child with disabilities can weigh heavily on the choice of whether or not to terminate a pregnancy. People with disabilities have become activists to challenge the new techno-eugenics as well as lobbying for radical improvements in home-based health care and personal assistance that would enable people with disabilities to set the research agendas that intimately affect their community and its future.

The emerging field of enhancement medicine 'improves' the body through surgery, pharmaceuticals and implants, and is leading to a convergence of nanotechnology, information technology and biotechnology in the rapid development of neuroscience.[36] Genetic prenatal screening, designer babies and improved genetic engineering are all part of a logic that discriminates against people living with disabilities. Canadian professor and disability activist Gregor Wolbring (2006)[37] sees the new techno-eugenics model as a transhuman version of what he calls ableism. Ableism is a network of beliefs, processes and practices that produce a particular kind of self, body and abilities which are projected as perfect, while at the same time labelling deviations from such a perfect self, body and abilities as diminished (Wolbring 2008).

Wolbring is concerned that advances in technoscience are leading to modifications in the appearance and functioning of the human body beyond existing norms. The direction and governance of science and technology are interrelated with the concept of ability. Those deemed healthy by most people today, but who cannot afford or do not want the technological enhancements, will become in the future the new class of 'techno-poor disabled'. In the new techno-eugenics model of transhumanism all bodies, however conventionally healthy, are defined as limited and defective, in need of constant improvement made possible by new technologies appearing on the horizon (a little bit like the constant software upgrades of our computers). The disability movement's message to all of us who think of ourselves as 'normal' is that we may soon be considered as disabled and as in need of enhancement as the 'disabled' of today. Thus we are all served by trying to learn from and understand their current struggles.

Giampiero Griffo, chair of Disabled Peoples' International/Europe, an international NGO working to protect the human rights of disabled people in 125 countries, outlines some of the challenges:

> one of the biggest threats to the rights of disabled people this Millennium lies within the field of bioethics – the ethics of advances in biological medicine and science . . . we want to see research directed at improving the quality of our lives not denying us the opportunity to live. . . . Human genetics poses a threat to us because while cures and palliatives are promised, what is actually being offered are genetic tests for characteristics perceived as undesirable. This is not about treating illness or impairment but about eliminating or manipulating foetuses. These technologies are, therefore, opening the door to a new eugenics which directly threatens our human rights. . . . We want to live as active, equal and productive members of society, but our perceived value and role as well as our human rights are continually diminished by the questionable medical ideas and discriminatory attitudes spawned by the new genetics. (Griffo 2001)

In the future we may all be confronted by similar quandaries. To fix oneself or not? Stay 'natural', but less competitive? Claim the right to be different or adjust to society's norm? While looking ahead, we cannot afford to lose sight of the present realities. The experience of living with disability in India (70 million people out of 1 billion) underscores such concerns when 'the lives of people with disabilities remain mired in inhumane patterns of helpless cynicism, political inertia, and resistance to social innovation' (Ghai 2002: 51).

In countries marked by widespread poverty, disability merges into conditions of general ill health and is rarely marked out as a cause of greater vulnerability. Now that people living with disabilities are organizing they provide ample evidence that in all countries disabled people, particularly women, have to contend with cultural constructions marked by negativity and stigmatization. In India, for example, disability compounds the already marginal status of women; it adds to the stigma of simply being a woman. Anita Ghai, an Indian woman living with disabilities, describes the discomfort of being doubly pinned by the dominant male gaze coupled with the gaze of a culture that constructs them as objects to be stared at: 'In a culture where being a daughter is considered a curse, being a disabled daughter is a fate worse than death' (Ghai 2002).[38]

In the first decade of the twenty-first century the Indian government has enthusiastically adopted the technoscience model which focuses on the clinical dimensions of impairment, where physical disabilities are perceived as 'genetic and biological' and 'future research must focus on the causes of such disabilities' (Indian Human Development Report, quoted in Ghai 2002). The challenge is how to move away from the persistent assumption that disability is a self-evident condition of physical inadequacy and private misfortune, whose politics concerns only a minority. In India the resolution of any issues concerning disability has to be found in the context of the family and community. A recognition of disability within the technoscience paradigm does not assure an adequate representation of the context of disabled people, and possibilities for their agency and rights.

Technoscience solutions for development

Understanding what it is like to live with disabilities in India takes us back to what these new technosciences mean for global body politics in relation to gender and development.[39] The underlying, often unchallenged assumption is that if the money and skills are available, high-tech solutions are the best option. Even if low-tech or no-tech solutions are available, they are rarely seen as being as effective – or worth the investment. In the technoscience development scenario, the biotech/nanotech industry is set to feed the world and eradicate poverty, despite the fact that many nano products have not even been tested – whether in relation to health or the environment. The potential of modern 'nano' biomedical and engineering capabilities to cure, fix or provide technological assistance for poor countries in the Global South is a dominant refrain. Mohamed Hassan, President of the Third World Academy of Sciences, and Gordon Conway, the UK Government's Chief Scientific Adviser on International Development, see enormous possibilities for nanotech to improve the conditions of poor people in the 'developing world'.[40]

Such an approach sidesteps the whole range of societal, political, cultural and ethical issues within which technologies are framed. Health and social justice advocates are deeply concerned that this modern development project benefits corporate owners and their control of vital biological resources impacting on livelihoods, food security and health. The new nanopatents go below the level of life, claiming ownership and control of the molecular processes and elements of nature. Critics like Vandana Shiva and Pat Mooney of the ETC Group[41] raise alarms about the promotion of biotechnology for society and how life science companies are appropriating and manipulating genes for food and medical purposes, without enough public debate and consensus (Hällström 2008).

Technoscience in agriculture

Current agricultural and biotech research is rapidly moving towards technological convergence at the nano scale, with profound implications for farmers (and fisher people and pastoralists), for food sovereignty worldwide, and for millions of poor women's livelihoods. Major agribusiness firms such as Syngenta, BASF, Bayer and Monsanto are reformulating their pesticides at the nano scale to make them more biologically active and to win new monopoly patents. It is estimated that over the next two decades the impacts of nano scale convergence on farmers and food will exceed those of farm mechanization or the Green Revolution (ETC Group 2004).

It is the small farmers and agricultural workers, the majority of them women, who are set to be the most affected by these technological trends. Particularly at risk are farm communities in the Global South that depend on primary export commodities such as rubber and cotton – products that could be displaced by new nanotech materials (ETC Group 2004).[42]

Technoscience and manufacture

Commodity-dependent nations, often the poorest, face the greatest disruptions from the new technologies. Currently, nanotech innovations and intellectual property are being driven by North America, Japan and Europe. The ETC Group quotes a study conducted by the University of Arizona and the United States National Science Foundation which found that 8,630 nanotech-related patents were issued by the United States Patent & Trademark

Office (US PTO) in 2003 alone, an increase of 50 per cent between 2000 and 2003 (as compared to about 4 per cent for patents across all technology fields). The top five countries represented were: the United States (5,228 patents), Japan (926), Germany (684), Canada (244) and France (183) (Thomas 2006).

As core commodities are replaced by the new technological improvements to cloth and other products, commodity obsolescence or a drop in prices will impact heavily on women and men workers in the Global South who do not have the economic flexibility to respond to sudden demands for new skills or different raw materials.

Given the amount of investment[43] taking place, it is possible to imagine a completely re-ordered economic world if manufacturing becomes nano-sized. Manufacturing jobs would become high-tech jobs that could be done from anywhere –with dire consequences for women workers in the Global South. Hassan believes that 'developing countries have no choice but to embrace nanoscience and nanotechnology if they hope to build successful economies in the long term' (Hassan 2005: 66).

Technomedicine

There is a close link between the debate on genetic engineering in agriculture and manufacture and global distribution of the benefits of human bio-technology and biomedicine, led by the interests of pharmaceutical companies. According to the World Health Organization (WHO), since 2002, 80 per cent of the world drug market has been concentrated in North America, Europe and Japan, a geographic area where only 19 per cent of the world population live. In contrast, 90 per cent of the burden of disease is located in poor countries, where patients do not have the purchasing capacity to buy medicine. According to the Forbes list of top companies,[44] the world's ten best-selling drugs in 2005 were all for rich patients (to treat high cholesterol, heartburn, high blood pressure, schizophrenia and depression). By requiring a highly technical individualizing treatment for the consumer, nanomedicine will further widen the gap between haves and have-nots, and distribution will continue to be concentrated in rich countries.

In situations of poverty with precarious sanitary conditions and no service infrastructure, recovery from one illness is rapidly followed by succumbing to another. For most poor women and their families, new medical benefits, such as nanomedicine,[45] are destined to stay out of reach and out of view. The greater likelihood is that poor men and women will continue to be the testing ground for First World drug companies, which use specialist brokers to arrange clinical trials in the cheaper countries of the Global South. Health rights activists raise concerns that women are already becoming egg suppliers for somatic cell nuclear transfer stem cell technologies (Sexton 2005; Dickenson 2007).

In relation to genetic patenting and pharmacogenetics, peoples with unusual degrees of genetic homogeneity, real or imagined, could be targeted increasingly by European and North American companies wanting to mine genetic databases or test new drugs. In November 2000, for example, the Australian company Antogen made an agreement with the Tongan Ministry of Labour to take tissue samples for genomic research into the cause of diabetes (14 per cent of Tongans have diabetes). The offer was to do both pharmacogenomic and pharmacogenetic research: the Tongan government would receive royalties, and any resulting drugs would be free for all Tongans. Tongan civil society activists blocked the offer because they said it did not respect Tongan life principles of the *tapu*, the Tongan belief that the life spirit of the person and community continues to reside in any living tissue. But also, more shrewdly, Tongan activists saw that the immediate beneficiaries would be the research company. They recognized that such an agreement would attract venture capital, but there were no guarantees of any drugs or royalties if the company failed in its research aims (Dickenson 2007: 163–72).

Biopiracy

US professor and activist Marsha Tyson Darling (2006) problematizes this further, arguing that the expropriation and patenting of indigenous people's ideas, plants and human tissue is a legacy from colonialism. She links slavery or the ownership of people's bodies and the exploitation of labour, together with the colonial expropriation of other people's land, mineral and plant resources. This mentality, over time, has evolved into 'biopiracy, the patenting of human genes, and the creation of technologies that intensify economic domination and technological dependency' (Tyson Darling 2006: 21).

Rose Mensah-Kutin from the NGO 'ABANTU for Development'[46] echoes that concern in a paper on gender and genetics in Africa:

There is a huge vacuum in Africa in relation to policies on the new genetics, compounded by the complete absence of a single regulatory agency to monitor progress. We are worried about the processes and application and whether we have the necessary framework and institutions to manage them. We are worried about the 'potential' attitudes towards the new human reproductive genetics in relation to informed choice and valid consent within the context of pre-implantation genetic diagnosis and the eugenic implications for the disadvantaged individuals in Africa. In Africa, would reproductive autonomy become even more of an illusion as we confront the moral crisis of the new human genetics? How much do the policy makers, academics and the general public in Africa know about the new human genetics? How do we formulate policies if the policy makers themselves are ill-equipped with genetic information? (Mensah-Kutin 2003)[47]

Technoscience and ethics

Are any of us equipped with the knowledge that clarifies all we need to ask about genetic information? Do we understand the implications of synthetic biology? What are the ethics that should govern the 'property' of the body? Is there a risk that the border to Fortress North and affluence will be held in place by a new class distinction between those who can afford to be 'enhanced' and the rest? How do we interpret and respond to the complex institutional, ethical, political, scientific, economic and social practices of biotechnologies that make up our understanding of life and nature? To start with, it is important to look more closely at the political, ethical and cultural consequences of biotechnology. For example, how and where does biotechnological research fit into questions of addressing gendered social determinants for health – such as sound nutrition, exercise, healthier work environments and better housing, and the reduction of poverty and violence – which affect the overall well-being of so many women? Are there creative and effective ways to develop critical public awareness of the political, economic and scientific drivers of biotechnology research and its applications? How do we debate the alternatives? What are the responsibilities of companies, scientists, policy makers and the public in the Global North towards poor women and men in the Global South who are bearing the brunt of the unregulated and unethical practices of biotechnological research and industry? How can we craft a transnational analysis on the nexus between new technologies and the global economy, environment and body politics which takes into account a feminist perspective?

Biotechnology covers scientific disciplines, industrial research and production, and in addition it is a social concept with a strong public policy concern – one in which we all need to engage. It is critical to ensure that the conception, development, dissemination and application of biotechnologies meet ethical and democratic standards that ensure gender equality. We have to look at the economic interests at play: the national interests as well as the private interests of medical and pharmaceutical technologies. In addition, we need to be conscious of gender inequalities in how and where biotechnological research is happening. We need to glean more information on the effects of biotechnologies on women's bodies and the environment, as well as take seriously a broader global responsibility to reframe the debate to take up concerns raised by people I have quoted in this chapter such as Dickenson, Ghai, Hällström, Haraway, Sexton and Wolbring.

The new areas of 'human performance enhancement' and 'trans-humanism' point to scenarios of a dramatically different future where traits and human capabilities can be 'improved' and perfected through technology. To hear and see better than 'normal', increase memory and cognitive capacity, reduce the need for sleep, and manipulate such things as nervousness and past traumas can be appealing to many. With aggressive commercialization and an increasingly competitive society, many may feel obliged to 'enhance' themselves. For women, these scenarios are of particular concern given the cultural pressure already for women not to be satisfied with their body shape and size. 'Enhancement' directly relates to body politics and issues around biological reproduction. There will be huge ethical dilemmas: not only around whether to manipulate one's body further through these new technologies, but also whether to allow or force this upon one's children. We can imagine some frightening scenarios for future parents: Should one stay 'natural' and lose out, or join the enhancement trend? Is it 'fair' to prevent one's children from succeeding as well in school as their enhanced friends and schoolmates?

Feminist responses

Feminists are concerned about how the rapid changes brought by modern technoscience are affecting gender equality and women's rights.[48] They ask questions about increasingly invasive genetic technology as well as the underlying racism and eugenics in some of these practices. They question the drive behind the industrial and medical interest in these technologies as well as querying the 'choice mantra' leading to genetic manipulation, designer babies and so forth, as well as the 'virtual holocaust of girls' in Asia, where access to sonograms and amniocentesis has allowed families to carry male foetuses to term and terminate female ones.

There are several areas of technology development with profound implications for women. Already, major concerns are arising on the possible, or even likely, toxicity of nanoparticles and their impact on both health and the environment. Synthetic biology deals with the design and redesign of life forms with a much more sophisticated approach than past biotechnologies. Already patent claims have been filed for the first construction of life forms from scratch. Advocates are hailing the promises of new, constructed photosynthesizing and CO_2-absorbing bacteria as solutions to the climate crisis, while others see incredibly dangerous possibilities for disturbing ecosystems. This new technology will have dramatic implications for women, both directly and indirectly. Women's movements need to begin to grasp the possible implications of these new technologies, and bring feminist perspectives into these very new debates from our viewpoints and visions from different places and different bodies.

The issue is not whether technologies are good or bad, but about how to ensure participation, engagement and political action that will shape technoscience in ways that promote methodologies and applications that do not misuse or negatively impact on women, men or nature.

Notes

1   The term nanotechnology was coined futuristically in the 1950s to describe a way to manufacture something precisely by controlling single atoms and molecules. During the last decade the field has evolved at a revolutionary pace, and a number of scientific and also commercial applications are now commonplace. It is difficult to define 'nanotechnology' in a very precise way, as it is a conglomerate of different science applications and specific technologies with the commonality of dealing with matter at the atomic level, that is, at a

size below 100 nanometres (nm). The convergence of technologies at the nanoscale is producing unprecedented advancement of understanding and capability of manipulating matter and life. In fact, the boundaries between life and matter are increasingly blurred as nanotechnology, genetics, computer science and neural sciences integrate and give rise to whole new sets of applications (Hällström 2008). Many nano-taxonomies exist which show the numerous fields, processes and products covered under the broad concept of nanotechnology today. See <http://www.nsti.org/leadership/scientific/ http://www. codesta.com/knowledge/market/nanotech_part_one_taxonomy/page_02.aspx http://www.nsti.org/Nanotech2006/ICCN2006/>.

2   Haraway's ongoing legacy is found in the engagement of her large network of students, working in various places in the world. For example, there is the work of Giovanna Di Chiro on feminist political ecology and Sarah Franklin on biotechnology. In Haraway's acknowledgements you can see the close working relationship she has with her students (Haraway 1991: ix–x; Haraway 1997a: vii–ix).

3   According to the official website, the Human Genome Project (HGP), completed in 2003, was a 13-year project coordinated by the US Department of Energy and the National Institutes of Health. During the early years of the HGP, the Wellcome Trust (UK) became a major partner; additional contributions came from Japan, France, Germany, China, and others. The HGP concluded there are approximately 25,000 genes (the closest count is at around 25,947, but estimates range from 20,000 to 30,000) in human DNA, determined by the sequences of the 3 billion chemical base pairs that make up human DNA. A genome is all the DNA in an organism, thus including all its genes. Together, the genes carry all the information necessary for making all of the proteins required by the organism. DNA is made up of four similar chemicals (called bases and abbreviated A, T, C, and G) that are repeated millions or billions of times throughout a genome. The human genome, for example, has 3 billion pairs of bases. Analyses of the human genome working draft were published in the February 2001 and April 2003 issues of *Nature* and *Science*. Though the HGP is finished, analyses of the data will continue for many years. See <http://www.ornl.gov/sci/techresources/Human_Genome/project/about.shtml>.

4   For example, alternative development thinkers and environmental activists like Wolfgang Sachs have written eloquently on the imagery of the blue planet Earth (Sachs 1999).

5   See Richter 1996 and, for an interesting reflection on 25 years of social movement organizing and struggles against the breast-feeding industry, see Allains (2006).

6   Haraway refers to Michael Jackson's iconic status in US culture. He morphs together gender, race and class as he lives out a fantasy world marked by his progressively more androgynous, bizarre appearance, unlikely adventures as husband and father, neverland homes and squandered millions. Investigating this further I looked again at *Scream* and *Earthsong*. These prize-winning videos, costing millions, are fascinating statements of modernity: one evoking panicked images of Jackson and his sister caught in a crazed *Space Odyssey 2001*, the other romanticizing peace and environment struggles with Jackson playing out some type of Jesus complex.

7   The Luddites were a social movement of British textile artisans in the early nineteenth century who protested – often by destroying mechanized looms – against the changes produced by the industrial revolution, which they felt threatened their livelihoods.

8   I refer here to bohemian New York artist Laurie Anderson's album *Big Science* (1982), re-released in 2007, and her performances which you can view on YouTube and her official website <http://www.laurieanderson.com>.

9   See their website <http://www.hgalert.org/> where they describe themselves as 'a secular, independent public interest watchdog group, based in London, UK, committed to informing people about human genetics issues, and to putting forward clear policies that serve the public interest'.

10 Lego is the Danish, now world-wide toy sold in 132 countries. It is made up of building blocks in bright primary colours. In terms of sales, it is the world's sixth-largest manufacturer of toys. See <http://www.lego.com/eng/info/default.asp?page=group>.

11 When I visited The Underground Adventure exhibition at the Chicago Field Museum with my family in July 2008, I was interested to see that Monsanto sponsored the exhibition. After transmogrifying (shrinking down) to bug size and meeting giant-sized (plastic) insects under the ground, our experience ended with the promotion of GMO seeds as a way to improve soil and get rid of bugs, thereby improving harvests and ending hunger in poor countries – a sophisticated Disney-style appeal to largely US families visiting the exhibition. See <http://www.fieldmuseum.org/undergroundadventure/critters/index.shtml>.

12 For example, John Moore, a leukemia patient, underwent surgery in 1976 at the University of California for removal of his cancerous spleen. The Council for Responsible Genetics (Cambridge, Massachusetts) noted that 'the University [of California] was later granted a patent for a cell line called "Mo," removed from the spleen, which could be used for producing valuable proteins [cytokines, including ones which mediate antibacterial and cancer-fighting activity]. The long-term commercial value of the cell line was estimated at over $1 billion. Mr Moore demanded the return of the cells and control over his body parts, but the California Supreme Court decided that he was not entitled to any rights to his own cells after they had been removed from his body' (Dickenson 2007).

13 Donna Dickenson and others document how much money is at stake, and how often the promised benefits to the public are by no means guaranteed.

14 See <umkc.eduhttp://www.ornl.gov/sci/techresources/Human_Genome/project/benefits.shtml>.

15 Beth Burrows is Director of the Edmonds Institute, a US public-interest, non-profit organization that was founded in part to examine issues such as those raised by the Human Genome Diversity Project.

16 Much of the material on synthetic biology I have taken from the ETC Group report (2007).

17 See <www.syntheticgenomics.com/index.htm>.

18 Alfonso Romo, a Mexican tycoon, founded Savia, <http://www.savia.com.mx>. For more information on Savia see the article 'Playing God' by Hope Shand, Jim Thomas and Kathy Jo Wette, <http://www.theecologist.org/pages/archive_detail.asp?content_id=967>.

19 See the videoed interview with Drew Endy, along with other scientists concerned about biosecurity, <www.synbiosafe.com>.

20 When visiting the <synbiosafe.com> site and its gallery of commentaries and interviews

with scientists, it was interesting to see how a major concern, even expectation was that these secrets could get into the wrong hands. As one US scientist rather ingenuously said, thank goodness his laboratory was in the US – not China or somewhere else 'untrustworthy'.

21 Regulations differ hugely across nation states and in the case of the USA within the nation (though mostly the US is far less regulated than in Europe), and they are constantly being revised. In Italy, despite a failed referendum in 2005 to liberalize the law passed in December 2004, IVF can only be carried out with severe restrictions. It is available for 'stable' heterosexual couples only, and no donor sperm or eggs can be used. Only three embryos are allowed to be fertilized in the IVF process and all three must be implanted. Research using human embryos is prohibited, as well as embryo freezing, gamete donation, surrogacy and the provision of any fertility treatments for single women or same-sex couples.

22 Reproductive justice, as defined by 'Asian Communities for Reproductive Justice', a founding member organization of SisterSong, is 'the complete physical, mental, spiritual, political, economic, and social well-being of women and girls'. It will be 'achieved when women and girls have the economic, social and political power and resources to make healthy decisions about [their] bodies, sexuality and reproduction', not only for themselves but also their families and communities. See <http://www.sistersong.net/reproductive_justice.html>. Note that the focus of the debate is largely on women's bodies, and the debate is dominated by views coming from the US, Europe and Latin America, particularly in relation to the politics of the religious right that pushes issues around abortion and the moral status of the embryo.

23 In 2004, in nine states of the US 1 per cent of births were through ARTs and 90 per cent of these mothers were white women (Galpern 2007).

24 The umbrella term ART involves a range of techniques including: fertility drugs; alternative insemination; fertility treatment where both eggs and sperm are handled in the laboratory (in vitro fertilization); genetic diagnosis and preimplantation diagnosis; egg retrieval; gametic donation; cryopreservation; ooplasmic transfer; and surrogacy (Galpern 2007: 10–11).

25 The risks for children, beyond surviving multiple births, are not many, although the emotional impact of donor anonymity is similar to that experienced by adopted children. From 2005 sperm and egg donors in the UK have had to reveal their identity when their offspring reach age 18. An interesting study is presently being conducted in Cambridge on the genetics of assisted reproduction and the impact of these technologies on concepts of the family, parenthood and kin relationships, in particular the impact of male donors and the implications of children finding out they have multiple half-siblings.

26 See the websites <www.popdev.hampshire.edu> and <geneticsandsociety.org>.

27 The consent procedure, as many comment, is really about protecting the commercial interests of researchers and funders from later claims from the persons who donated the eggs or tissue.

28 At the centre of a major scandal was the Korean scientist Hwang Woo Suk, who took 2,200 eggs from 129 women, including his assistants, in highly unethical procedures which only came out because he faked results for new cloned blastocysts (Dickenson 2007: 59).

29 See Sarah Franklin's entertaining *Dolly Mixtures* (2007) for an excellent bioethical, cultural and social historical discussion of the full implications of Dolly for technoscience.

30 In a critique of Richard Dawkins, Hayes comments: 'it is indeed necessary that opinion leaders, politicians and the general public become fully aware of the risks posed by the new human genetic technologies, and of the pernicious vision of the human future being promoted – avowedly or disingenuously – by many of those advocating their development and use', <http://www.biopoliticaltimes.org/article.php?id=2037>. For more information about the Center, see <http://www.geneticsandsociety.org/article. php?list=type&type=10>.

31 See <http://www.transhumanism.org/index.php/WTA/index/>.

32 The World Transhumanist website refutes the charge that they are neo-eugenicists and claims that they respect women's reproductive rights, insisting that they extend the right of women to use conceptive, contraceptive, reproductive and germinal choice technologies. They see disabled people as the natural constituency for transhumanism. Probably the most prominent symbol of disabled transhumanist activism these days is Christopher Reeve, the former Superman actor, who was a tireless campaigner for biomedical research after a horse-riding accident left him quadriplegic. Reeve has been especially important in defending the use of cloned embryos in stem cell research, and in his advocacy of cures for spinal injuries. See <http://www.transhumanism.org/ index.php/WTA/communities/physicallydisabled>.

33 See <www.ecoequity.org>.

34 See also Silver 1998.

35 See Bionet, a website that lists these articles and is devoted to trying to play down the hype around designer babies, <http://www.bionetonline.org/english/content/db_cont1 .htm>.

36 See the NBIC Report (2003) on converging technologies, 'Nanotechnology, biotechnology, information technology and cognitive science', at <http://www. wtec.org/ConvergingTechnologies/>.

37 See Wolbring's extenstive writings, including a biweekly column at <http://www. bioethicsanddisability.org/>.

38 Ghai (2002) gives as an example of the double discrimination against women the case of fourteen mentally challenged girls forced to undergo hysterectomies at Sassoon General Hospital in Poona in the state of Maharashtra in 1994. The girls received care in an institution in which they were prevented from wearing pajamas with drawstrings or sanitary napkins with belts because, it was claimed, the girls might use these to commit suicide. To deal with the problem of menstrual hygiene, the hospital decided to go ahead with hysterectomies. Protests stopped any further operations.

39 Several of the issues raised in this section were discussed in the paper I gave at the Women and Biotechnology Conference (WONBIT) (Molfino and Zucco 2008).

40 See <http://www.publications.parliament.uk/pa/cm200405/cmselect/cmsctech/ 487/5032303.htm>.

41 The ETC Group is the civil society organization that perhaps most effectively tracks and advocates on issues around converging technologies. Their website, <www.etcgroup.org>, offers up-to-date analyses of the kinds of issues highlighted in this chapter. I have relied on

several ETC Group publications, including *Green Revolution 2.0 for Africa?* <http://www.etcgroup.org/_page24?pub_id=611>, *News Release: Food Sovereignty or Green Revolution*, <http://www.etcgroup.org/_page24?pub_id=613>, and *Gambling with Gaia*, <http://www.etcgroup.org/_page24?pub_id=608>.

42 For example, the sale of Monsanto GM cotton seeds to farmers has in many cases led not to a miracle but to a disaster. Instances of 60 per cent crop failure due to the failure of Monsanto Bt seeds (through bollworm pest and 'Lalya' or 'reddening', a disease not seen before), compounded by sliding global prices and dumping of cheap subsidized cotton from outside the country, contributed to thousands of suicides by Indian farmers. In the western state of Maharashtra 4,100 farmers committed suicide in 2004 (Mittal 2006).

43 For example, in 2004, industry and governments world-wide invested more than US$10 billion in nanotechnology research and development. The National Science Foundation in the United States estimated in 2001 that the nanotech market would surpass US$1 trillion by 2015, while the market analyst firm Lux Research predicted in 2004 that it would exceed US$2.6 trillion (Thomas 2006; Hällström 2008).

44 Forbes is a publishing and media company which regularly lists the world's richest people and the top 2,000 companies every year. See <www.forbes.com>.

45 *Development* 48.4 features an article on nanomedicine techniques which requires expensive individual care for the patient and individual surveillance techniques. (Foladori and Invernizzi 2006)

46 ABANTU for Development was established in 1991 by African women based in Europe. Its West Africa office, where Rose Mensah-Kutin is regional programme director, is a leading African gender and policy advocacy organization. See <http://www.abanturowa.org/index.html>.

47 From her paper, available on the website <http://www.biopolitics-berlin2003.org/program.asp?id=62>.

48 Some initiatives have already been taken. AWID had a three-year project on new technologies from 2002 to 2005. The Dag Hammarskjöld Foundation convened in January 2008 a one-off 'What Next' working-group meeting for feminist alternatives, exploring the nexus between economic globalization, environment, new technologies and embodiment to feed into the discussion on technology convergence (Harcourt 2008).

Australia 31 % of babies born since 2001 were to unmarried mothers.

India Over the past 20 years, since the introduction of ultrasound devices, 10 million female foetuses have been aborted.

Sierra Leone For every 100,000 births an estimated 2,000 women die in childbirth, the highest rate in the world.

7

Source: 'The state they're in - how women are faring in the rest of the world'
http://www.guardian.co.uk/lifeandstyle/2008/dec/07/women-equality-rights-feminism-sexism-worldwide

Conclusion

Empowering Bodies

In this book I wanted to reflect on twenty years of engagement in body politics in development. The book has criss-crossed the borders of gender and development policy and women's movements activism. It has looked at the debates on population and development; feminization of work; the care economy; sexual and gender-based violence; sexuality and development; and the new bio- and nanotechnologies. I have highlighted some of the conversations that inspired and spurred me on to try to understand better the embodied experiences of gender and development. Most of all, I have tried to understand why body politics is played out on the fringes of mainstream gender and development policy – even if, from my vantage point, it deeply marks gender and development practice.

The book has explored some of the contradictions such a personal, political and theoretical examination of body politics in gender and development pushes to the surface. At the outset I warned I would ask more questions than I could answer. I also promised I would go back to the initial questions I raised in the introduction and see how the different aspects of body politics discussed in the book can throw light on what troubled me in my encounters at the 1988 SID World Conference in India and in the Rome Parliament, fourteen years later.

Body politics and FGM

Going back, then, to my unease in New Delhi and Rome, let me conclude that discussion via two further encounters with female genital mutilation in the public arena.

As it happened, during my time in Cambridge a public lecture was given on FGM by Henrietta Moore, one of the leading British anthropologists on gender. Attending the lecture I found, to my surprise, that she was almost, but not quite, defending FGM as a cultural practice that symbolized the traditional identity of the community. She presented it as a rite of passage that was at the core of that particular African village way of life, a village which Moore had studied decades before. She depicted outside groups, African-based Christian NGOs, moving in to end FGM as disruptive to the culture and livelihoods of the village. She interpreted the new practices of providing youth camps, where young girls took refuge instead of going through FGM as a traditional rite of passage, as an example of how globalization was invading the village. She was very critical of the Christians' programme to encourage young girls to leave their homes to avoid FGM. She presented a short video she had taken of young boys and girls chanting songs and poems they had written about the dangers and evils of FGM – suggesting, it seemed to me, that the camps and their activities were a sort of brainwashing.

I found her analysis of the impact of Christianization on the community and the breakdown of traditional authority compellingly argued, and clearly she found a lot of support among the Cambridge academic audience. I was also impressed that FGM was the topic Moore chose as her public lecture during the selection process for the William Wyse Professor, and indeed I heard later that she landed the job. But I missed the actual body politics of what happened to those young girls in FGM, and why they were afraid of the pain and mutilation and ran away. I found the absence of body in her discourse puzzling. She did not once describe what FGM entailed. I therefore could not agree that the interventions by the NGOs were so damaging. Indeed, I thought working with young girls and boys a positive approach, and I was impressed by the vehemence the children expressed in their songs and poems against the practice. They certainly looked very happy, which suggested that the camps where poems, songs and dancing replaced FGM were positive and life-enhancing cultural changes for them.

I felt that Moore had presented a modern but still colonial gaze that was 'othering' the children of the village. Even if she spoke the language and knew the people, and had a sophisticated reading of globalization, she missed the fact that FGM is about the body as the site of practice, and that practice involves unnecessary pain and harm to girls. And, most of all, she underplayed the fact that it was the girls who were choosing other rituals of singing and dancing in the youth camps to mark a rite of passage. The NGO was giving them the opportunity to be freed from pain and harm. While I appreciated her suspicion of globalization and the Church, it was disappointing to see that she did not take the girls' bodily integrity and rights into perspective.

Also during my time in Cambridge I attended an African film festival and saw the film *Moolaade* (2004) by Senegalese director Ousmane Sembene. The film focused on women from the village fighting the tradition of FGM and providing *moolaade* (the name means sanctuary in Bambara, the language of the community). It was a fascinating film. It showed subtly the gendered political and social tensions within the village, played out in the clash of cultures, religious traditions and colonial histories. It was deeply moving, presenting just how hard it was for women to find the courage to challenge FGM and in the end succeed. Gender tensions were portrayed in various scenes throughout the film, from the pot seller flirting with the women and then being chased out of the village, to women snatching back their radios from a burning pile in defiance of the men, who did not want women listening to progressive broadcasts. The film did not romanticize village life but gave a very dignified picture of how women in the community, and some men, were able to challenge traditional patriarchal customs.

Sembene's film underlines how important it is to have respect for and knowledge of a community, but also how important it is not to be caught in tradition and to look at how to support women's own agency to lead change. Sembene shows how the patriarchal culture of the village bound women in servitude that marked their bodies in many ways. One scene from the film showed the pain a woman experienced during intercourse due to her FGM. As the youngest of three wives she seeks the support of the elder wives to enable her daughter to find *moolaade*. She is shown as strong and beautiful, but damaged; understandably, she does not wish her daughter to suffer such pain all her life. The collective support of the women for her and her daughter, in particular the friendship among the co-wives, is at the core to the changes the film explores. The role of the radio is also important. Radios are presented as a connection to the outside world, one that allows a questioning of religious and traditional givens, though it is an entry point to modernity which the community has to work through. The tough yet joyous message of the film is that outside intervention is important because it kindles change, but it is the solidarity and courage of the community, both women and men, that shape the change in responding to it.

Sembene presents a very useful way to think about and respond to FGM. In contrast to Moore, he was listening and working with the girls and women; while still respecting tradition, he shows how it needed to change. His film, with its strong African voice, is political, gender-aware and inspirational. I suspect he would not see his work as part of gender and development, but it certainly helped me think what needs to change in gender and development and also why it is still important to keep asking questions about such highly difficult and controversial subjects as FGM.

Still asking questions

So how can gender and development change and open up to the experiences and knowledge of women and men engaged in body politics? I continue to have many questions. As we confront the multiple financial, climate and food crises, I cannot help wondering: what has gender and development achieved? These last two decades have seen growing disparities between rich and poor, increasing poverty, failing trade agreements, huge environmental damage and climate change, and increasing gender disparity and violence on a daily basis. Has gender and development been unwittingly part of some major bluff on the part of the Global North that kept up business as usual, despite all the very evident fault lines of the fracturing world order? Did anyone listen to feminists' protests at the loss of state autonomy and ownership, privatized water and health care, feminization of the workforce (without child care), the increase in maternal mortality, huge increases in youth unemployment and migration, rising fundamentalism, and the denigration of local cultures and local knowledge of the environment?

Today's crises show that it is right to raise those questions, and challenge patriarchal injustice, colonialism, skewed development, gender oppression, and military, economic and social power. But these tensions and perversities are not 'somewhere out there', to be addressed by gender and development policy that directs a tiny fraction of Northern wealth via inadequate aid to women in the South. It is vital to go beyond the gender and development heterodoxies, and acknowledge the connections between the Global North lifestyles and consumption patterns and their impact on women in other parts of the world.

Can projects set within gender and development support and strengthen the lives of poor women and men without objectifying them? How do projects challenge the unjust economic system that creates the poverty in the first place? Do they address the inequality, or are they heterosexist, racist, neo-colonial, and culturally blind?

How can people living and working in gender and development in situations of relative social, political and economic power speak out about violent and unfair situations experienced by others in strategic ways oriented towards finding constructive solutions, public support and resources without deepening marginalization and discrimination?

How can such projects deal with deep bodily pain in a manner that attests to concern and commitment, making a positive difference for all involved? How is it possible to conduct dialogues across the borders dividing the Global North and Global South, the global and the local, academe and activism, diverse identities and cultures? How can feminists creatively engage in knowledge and network building and not become caught in institutional power games and bureaucratic routines, lost in jargon and over-theorizing, media hype, scientific confusions, individual narratives and romanticism?

And last, there is the main question by which all the others are framed: how can feminists collectively understand multiple differences and asymmetries of power, use the insights from differences, hear the anger, note the silences, and keep conviction?

Challenges to gender and development

Just to ditch gender and development is not an answer. Our fractured global landscape is visibly and interestingly criss-crossed by connections, forged by ordinary people who do not just await their fate. The election of President Obama has awoken a profound sense of hope for many: that connections among communities can bring change and reshape global society and therefore the development agenda.

It is precisely because there continues to be so much inequality, and so much blindness as to what could be possible, that we have to engage in the debates. Feminists need to acknowledge and speak up about collective responsibilities, knowing that the multiple crises the world faces – financial, food, climate, social – demand multiple solutions from different actors, including those working in development. But it is no longer a case of the rich North bailing out the poor South. Today's financial crisis shows that all too clearly. It is important, following the example of Obama and other leaders, to ensure that the world stops fragmenting along race, class, gender and religious divides.

Feminist voices need to be positioned clearly in those debates. In this book I have referred to a whole range of actors who are engaged in and around gender and development: focusing on body politics; attempting to work across borders and divides; using and creating policy instruments while also reaching out to the personal, embodied realities of the discrimination, violence and pain – as well as the pleasure, the care and the love. No one is engaged in such debates innocently. It is important to question all of our roles in a world marked by a development that has led to climate change, water and food scarcity; to oil crisis and spiralling consumer costs; and to deepening gender inequalities. And those questions are the source of vision, networking and connection with others around the world.

The discussion I have offered on reproductive rights and health, care work, migration, sexual and gender-based violence, sexuality and technoscience shows that body politics from the community to the international level is crucial for gender and development policy direction. Gender and development needs to address much more comprehensively the complex links between health, reproductive life cycles, the caring economy, the market economy, the environment, technologies, 'big science' and globalization which have been put through the development machine. Gender and development policy has to be pulled out of the mire of progressive-sounding orthodoxy that fails to engage with the realities of women's experience and aspirations around the world.

Women cannot continue to pay the price of ecological, financial and distribution failures. It is critical to change social norms, institutions and relationships in order to redress social, economic, climate and gender injustices. Self-congratulatory 'feel good talk' about empowering women – that pretends to put women at the forefront of achieving peace, prosperity, democracy and development – is no longer possible. There are no short-cuts to gender justice, but it is vital that we strive towards it, with honesty and conviction and without pretence.

Therefore, it is important to cut away a tangle of assumptions and stereotypes that have filled the field of gender and development. Starting from the lives of women as they feel and experience political, social, economic and cultural change, we need to bring critical scrutiny to the taken-for-granted assumptions of gender and development. Opening up a feminist debate on development means asking new questions about what politics is. It is not only about getting women and minority groups into power. It is about vision and building on alternatives. It is not about blueprints but about recognition of difference and strategic agreement on how to move forward without being hampered or weighed down by institutions, management plans, jargon and unwinnable power games. We need to define the rules of the game.

This requires the collective work of transnational feminism, fully aware of the intersections of class, caste, race, gender and geographical/post-colonial divisions. Such a gender and development agenda needs to be informed by the passionately held hope that collectively we can find inspirational and creative ways to bring about political change. It remains important to engage with the multilateral gender and development agenda. But, equally important, it is vital for feminists to continue building collective responses to the deep global inequalities – the pain and the passion that inform our world – working in coalitions with progressive social movements under a growing multitude of banners: anti-war, anti-racist, ecologist, peace-seeking, LGBTQI, human rights, HIV and AIDS, youth, and fair trade.

The intertwining economic, political, cultural and social processes that underpin body politics are not easy to address. We are talking about violated bodies, ravished environments and spiralling poverty despite endless working days. The crude figures of increasing inequality reflect obscene wealth spun out of deepening violence and racism. New images, ideas and visions do not come from staid government solutions. But talking of failure just takes us further from, not nearer to, the goal of gender equality. How do you reach an audience already overloaded in a world of text messages, blogs, instant news on websites, Googled facts, Wikipedia, YouTube, Ipod casts, popular science magazines, competing ads for Viagra, health food, networks of never-met contacts, endless spam, and (no doubt) surveillance? How to connect to those people not inter-connected? What justice is there for the nameless people who flash across our screens in images that hoover up our passions and spew them out in a sense of desperation?

Gender and development needs to work as honestly as it can with feminists to challenge and engage with structural inequalities that frustrate their work. It is important to historicize and denaturalize the ideas, beliefs and values that underpin the intergovernmental interactions in the UN, governments and other decision-making spaces. Equally it remains important for feminists, inside and outside gender and development, to continue building collective responses to the deep global inequalities, keenly aware of differences of lived bodily experiences, yet also unafraid to own and explore those differences. It is both the pain and the passion that allows us to question ourselves and to continue to want to shape in what world 'we' belong.

Changing gender and development

Gender and development is about transforming society and achieving social justice and equality. That process needs to avoid building highly bureaucratic technical institutions in order to 'deliver' aid to women and their families or communities in countries labelled 'developing'. Gender and development instead needs to be about ensuring the recognition and value of *all* women's care work, unpaid labour in the home, volunteer work in communities and market work. The complexities of gender inequalities, as they are lived and experienced on the body, need to be upfront in all gender and development analysis. Gender and development would then design and support economic and social policies that respect women's and men's embodied rights and needs. These policies would recognize the centrality of both the production of commodities and reproductive work as well as the embodied complexities of the gender division of labour within the market economy, community and home. Gender and development can make visible women's and men's layered and complex lives and roles, recognizing that all people are valued social and economic subjects embedded in their own cultures. Embodied realities, quality of life, rights and access to resource as well as pleasure, cultural diversity and expression must be factored in, not as additional but as integral to well-being and the development agenda.

With such an agenda, gender and development could transform gender norms in the political arena, workplace, community and family, and at the individual level. Policies would be premised on the need to challenge economic, political and social structures that perpetuate gender inequality. Such policies would challenge discrimination and inequalities – within families, social spaces, public sectors, political arenas and markets – and look for redistribution of resources, economic and social justice. In this way men's and women's embodied realities and intrinsic rights would not be overshadowed by development goals that count numbers, aiming solely for efficiency and economic growth. Such a gender and development policy agenda would work to end inequalities in health systems; guard against neo-

Malthusianism, racism and homophobia; and ensure that discussion on climate change is not premised on racist and gender-blind assumptions. Care work would be rewarded alongside productive work and the search for well-being rather than growth would guide economies. The documents in place – such as Beijing, Cairo, CEDAW and UN Resolution 1325 – would be honoured, and help to bring about the structural changes required.

Too often stuck within its own logic and power games, gender and development needs openly to derive its vision and power from feminists within and outside its institutional structures. These feminists and women's movement activists seek a world where gender is not constraining, where bodies can be enjoyed, where peace, care and pleasure, not profit, are at the heart of a sustained development. Gender and development needs to engage with and celebrate this commitment, hope, vision and energy. Through honest dialogues with feminist and women's movements, gender and development can help to mobilize new forms of politics that bring about not only bodily integrity and gender equality, but also economically and technologically just, secure, ecologically sound and peaceful societies.

There are many places where gender and development is already engaging with women's movements, for example in the AWID Forum in Cape Town[1] on the power of movements. Thousands of women and men came to that forum, held in November 2008, the month when Obama won his historic presidential victory. The vibrancy of that eclectic gathering, the wealth of knowledge, the mix of medias, the range of professions – trade unionists, HIV-positive activists, sex workers, gender and development professionals, researchers, young and not-so-young feminists, diverse ethnicities, sexualities and genders, the majority of the participants coming from the South – pointed to the hopeful possibilities for body politics in the future.

Note

1   The report of the meeting is published in *Development*, 'Power, change movement', Vol. 52, No. 2 (June 2009) and is available on the AWID website, <www.awid.org>.

References

Adebon, L. (1993) *Making Bodies, Making Histories,* University of Nebraska Press, Lincoln, NE and London.

Agustín, L. (2007a) *Sex at the Margins: Migration, Labour Markets and the Rescue Industry,* Zed Books, London.

—— (2007b) 'Introducing sex at the margins', *Development* ('Migration and Development'), Vol. 50, No. 4 (December).

Ahmed, S. (2000) *Strange Encounters: Embodied Others in Post-Coloniality,* Routledge, London and New York, NY.

Akhter, F. (2004) 'Family planning in Bangladesh', *Development* ('The Politics of Health'), Vol. 47, No. 2 (June).

Alexander, J. (2000) 'Imperial desire/sexual utopias: white gay capital and transnational tourism' in E. Shohat (ed.), *Talking Visions: Multicultural Feminism in a Transnational Age,* MIT Press, Cambridge, MA.

Allain, A. (2002) 'Fighting an old battle in a new world', *Development Dialogue,* No. 2 (2002), Dag Hammarskjöld Foundation, Uppsala.

Andermatiz, C., T. Lovell and C. Wolkowitz (eds) (1997) *A Glossary of Feminist Theory,* Arnold, London.

Antrobus, P. (2004) *The Global Women's Movement: Origins, Issues and Strategies,* Zed Books, London.

Bandarage, A. (1997) *Women, Population and Global Crisis: a Political-Economic Analysis,* Zed Books, London.

Barker, G. (2001) '"Cool your head, man": preventing gender-based violence in favelas', *Development* ('Violence against Women and the Culture of Masculinity'), Vol. 44, No. 3 (September).

Barker G., C. Ricardo and M. Nascimento (2007) 'Engaging men and boys in changing gender-based inequity in health: evidence from programming interventions', World Health Organization and Promundo, Geneva.

Barton, C. (2005) 'Women's movements and gender perspectives on the MDGs' in *Civil Society Perspectives on the Millennium Development Goals*, UNDP, New York, NY.

Basu, A. (ed.) (1995) *The Challenge of Local Feminisms: Women's Movements in Global Perspective*, Westview Press, Boulder, CO.

Beasely, C. and C. Bacchi (2000) 'Citizen bodies, embodying citizens', *International Feminist Journal of Politics*, Vol. 2, No. 3 (Autumn).

Belausteguigoitia, M. (2004) 'Naming the Cinderellas of development: violence and women's autonomy in Mexico', *Development* ('The Violence of Development'), Vol. 47, No. 1 (March).

Bell, E., P. Methembu and S. O'Sullivan (on behalf of the International Community of Women living with HIV/AIDS) and K. Moody (on behalf of the Global Network of People Living with HIV/AIDS) (2007) 'Sexual and reproductive health services and HIV testing: perspectives and experiences of women and men living with HIV and AIDS', *Reproductive Health Matters*, Vol. 15, No. 29, Supplement 1 (May).

Beneria, L. (2003) *Gender, Development and Globalization: Economics As If People Matter*, Routledge, New York, NY and London.

Bigo, V. (2004) 'Gender and care: an overview of the "hidden" economy', unpublished paper, University of Cambridge.

Bordo, S. (1993) *Unbearable Weight: Feminism, Western Culture, and the Body*, University of California Press, Berkeley, CA.

Boserup, E. (1970) *Women's Role in Economic Development*, St Martin's Press, New York, NY.

Boston Women's Health Collective (2005) *Our Bodies, Ourselves: a New Edition for a New Era*, New England Free Press, Boston, MA.

Burrows, B. (2003) 'Old and new eugenics: getting rid of other people', paper presented at the 'Working Conference on the Limits of the New Genetics Technologies. Within and Beyond the Limits of Human Nature', Berlin, Germany, October, <http://www.biopolitics-berlin2003.org/docs.asp?id= 190>.

—— (2006) 'Reflections on the human genome', *Development* ('New Technology and Development'), Vol. 49, No. 4 (December).

Butler, J. (1993) *Bodies That Matter*, Routledge, London.

Butler, J. and J. Scott (1992) *Feminists Theorize the Political*, Routledge, London.

Cagatay, N. (2003) 'Engendering macro-economics' in M. Gutierrez (ed.), *Macro-Economics – Making Gender Matter: Concepts, Politics and Institutional Change in Developing Countries*, Zed Books, London.

Çalışkan, S. (2006) 'Women fighting violence in war-torn societies', *Development* ('Women's Rights and Development'), Vol. 49, No. 1 (March).

Campuzano, G. (2006) 'Reclaiming travesti histories', *IDS Bulletin* ('Sexuality Matters'), Vol. 37, No. 5 (October).

—— (2007) 'Are two genders enough? The travesti museum in Peru', *Gender and Development in Brief*, No. 18 (January).

Chambers, C. (2008) *Sex, Culture and Justice: the Limits of Choice*, Pennsylvania State University Press, PN.

Chandler, D. (2008) 'Keeping humanity secure', *The Spiked Review of Books*, <www.spiked-online.com>, 25 January.

Charckiewicz, E. (2004) 'Beyond good and evil: notes on global feminist advocacy', paper presented at the National Council for Research on Women, New York, May.

Chodorow, N. (1999) *The Reproduction of Mothering: Psychoanalysis and the Sociology of Gender* (updated edition), University of California, Berkeley, CA.

Conboy K., N. Medina and S. Stanbury (eds) (1997) *Writing on the Body: Female Embodiment and Feminist Theory*, Columbia University Press, New York, NY.

Connell, R. W. (2002) *Gender*, Polity Press, Cambridge.

—— (2005) *Masculinities* (second edition, revised), Polity Press, Cambridge.

Cornwall A. (ed.) (2006) *Spaces For Change? The Politics of Citizen Participation in New Democratic Arenas*, Zed Books, London.

—— (2007) 'Pathways of women's empowerment', *Open Democracy*, <http://www.opendemocracy.net/trackback/34188>, 30 July.

Cornwall, A., E. Harrison and A. Whitehead (2007) *Gender Myths and Feminist Fables: the Struggle for Interpretive Power in Gender and Development*, Blackwell, Oxford.

Cornwall, A., S. Jolly and S. Corrêa (2008) *Development with a Body: Sexuality, Human Rights and Development*, Zed Books, London.

Corrêa, S. in collaboration with R. Reichmann (1994) *Population and Reproductive Rights: Feminist Perspectives from the South*, Zed Books, London.

Corrêa, S. (2006) 'Realising sexual rights', *IDS Bulletin* ('Sexuality Matters') Vol. 37, No. 5 (October).

Corrêa, S., R. Parker and R. Petchesky (2008) *Sexuality, Health and Human Rights*, Routledge, London.

Dalla Costa, M. (1972) *The Power of Women and the Subversion of the Community*, Falling Wall Press, Bristol.

de Pinho, H. (2005) 'Health sector reforms and rights', *Development* ('Sexual Health and Reproductive Rights'), Vol. 48, No. 4 (December).

Delahanty, J. (2000) 'Gender and the gene giants', <http://www.cwhn.ca/groups/biotech/availdocs/13-delahanty.pdf>.

Delahanty, J. and M. Shefali (1999) 'Improving women's health and labour conditions in the garment sector', *Development* ('Responses to Globalization: Rethinking Equity and Health)', Vol. 42, No. 4 (December).

Development Alternatives with Women for a New Era (DAWN) (1999) *Implementing ICPD: Moving Forward in the Eye of the Storm*, DAWN, Suva, Fiji, <www.dawn.org.fj>.

Dickenson, D. (2007) *Property in the Body: Feminist Perspectives*, Cambridge University

Press, Cambridge.

Dinnerstein, D. (1999) *The Mermaid and the Minotaur: Sexual Arrangements and Human Malaise*, Other Press, New York, NY.

Diprose, R. (1994) *The Bodies of Women: Ethics, Embodiment and Sexual Difference*, Routledge, London.

Donzelot, J. (1979) *The Policing of Families,* Random House, New York, NY.

Ehrlich, P. (1969) *The Population Bomb*, Sierra Club/Ballantine Books, New York, NY.

Eisenstein, Z. (2004) 'Sexual humiliation, gender confusion and the horrors at Abu Ghraib', Znet, <http://www.zmag.org/znet/viewArticle/8326>.

—— (2007) *Sexual Decoys: Gender, Race and War,* Zed Books, London.

Elson, D. (1991) *Male Bias in Macro-economics: the Case of Structural Adjustment*, Manchester University Press, Manchester.

—— (2004) 'Feminist economics challenges mainstream economics' in Agarwal, B. (ed.), special issue of the *Newsletter of the International Association for Feminist Economics*, Vol. 14, No. 3.

Eminova, E. (2006) 'Negotiations: feminism, racism and difference' *Development* ('Women's Rights and Development'), Vol. 49, No.1 (March).

Enloe, C. (2007) 'Feminist readings on Abu Ghraib: introduction', *International Feminist Journal of Politics,* Vol. 9, No. 1 (March).

Escobar, A. (1993) *Encountering Development: the Making and Unmaking of the Third World*, Princeton University Press, Princeton, NJ.

Esplen, E. (2007) 'Gender and sexuality' in 'Supporting Resources Collection', Bridge Cutting Edge Pack, Institute of Development Studies, University of Sussex, January.

ETC Group (2004) 'Down on the farm: the impact of nano-scale technologies on food and agriculture', ETC Group, Ottawa, November, <http://www.etcgroup.org/en/materials/publications.html?pub_id=80>.

—— (2007) 'Extreme genetic engineering: an introduction to synthetic biology', ETC Group, Ottawa, January, <http://www.etcgroup.org/en/materials/publications.html?pub_id=602>.

Fausto-Sterling, A. (2000) *Sexing the Body: Gender Politics and the Construction of Sexuality*, Basic Books, New York, NY.

Feminist Dialogues (2007) 'Transforming democracy: feminist visions and strategies', report on the Third Feminist Dialogues at the Seventh World Social Forum (Nairobi), Isis International Manila, Manila.

Firestone, S. (1979) *The Dialectics of Sex: the Case for Feminist Revolution*, The Women's Press, London.

Flax, J. (1992) *Thinking Fragments: Psychoanalysis, Feminism and Postmodernism,* University of California Press, Berkeley, CA.

Foladori, G. and N. Invernizzi (2006) 'Nanomedicine, poverty and development',

Development ('New Technologies and Development'), Vol. 48, No. 4 (December).

Folbre, N. (1994) *Who Pays for the Kids? Gender and the Structures of Constraint,* Routledge, New York, NY.

—— (2001) *The Invisible Heart: Economics and Family Values,* The New Press, New York, NY.

Foucault, M. (1976) *The History of Sexuality. Volume 1,* Penguin, Harmondsworth.

Fox Keller, E. and H. Longins (eds) (1996) *Feminism and Science,* Oxford University Press, Oxford.

Franklin, S. (2007) *Dolly Mixtures,* Routledge, London.

Fraser, A. and I. Tinker (eds) (2004) *Developing Power: How Women Transformed International Development,* The Feminist Press, New York, NY.

Freedman, L., R. Waldman, H. de Pinho and M. Wirth (2005) *Who's Got the Power? Transforming Health Systems for Women and Children,* Task Force on Child Health and Maternal Health, UN Millennium Project, New York, NY, and Earthscan, London.

Galpern, E. (2007) 'Assisted reproductive technologies: overview and perspective using a reproductive justice framework', paper for Center for Genetics and Society, December, <http://www.geneticsandsociety.org/article.php? list=type &type=181>.

Garcia-Moreno, C. (2001) 'The World Health Organization addressing violence against women' *Development* ('Violence Against Women and the Culture of Masculinity'), Vol. 43, No. 3 (September).

Ghai, A. (2002) 'Disabled women: an excluded agenda of Indian feminism', *Hypatia,* Vol. 17, No. 3 (Summer).

Gibson-Graham, J. K. (1996) *The End of Capitalism (As We Knew It): a Feminist Critique of Political Economy,* Blackwell, Oxford.

—— (2005) 'Building community economies: women and the politics of place' in W. Harcourt and A. Escobar, *Women and the Politics of Place,* Kumarian Press, Bloomfield, CT.

—— (2006) *A PostCapitalist Politics,* University of Minnesota Press, Minneapolis, MN.

Gilman, S. (1985) 'White bodies, black bodies: towards an iconography of female sexuality in late nineteenth-century art, medicine and literature', *Critical Inquiry* Vol. 12, No. 1.

Gosine, A. (2004) 'Sex for pleasure, rights to participation and alternatives to AIDS: placing sexual minorities and/or dissidents in development', Working Paper No. 228, Institute of Development Studies, University of Sussex, Brighton, October.

—— (2009) 'Monster, womb, MSM: the work of sex in international development' *Development* ('Sexuality and Development'), Vol. 52, No. 1 (March).

Grewal I. and C. Kaplan (1994) *Scattered Hegemonies: Postmodernity and Transnational Feminist Practices,* University of Minnesota Press, Minneapolis, MN and London.

Griffo, G. (2001) 'Disabled people speak on the new genetics: DPI Europe position statement on bioethics and human rights', <http://www.mindfully.org/GE/Disabled-People-Speak.htm>.

Grosz, L. (1994) *Volatile Bodies: Towards Corporeal Feminism*, Indiana University Press, Bloomington, CT.

Gruskin, G., L. Ferguson and J. O'Malley (2007) 'Ensuring sexual and reproductive health for people living with HIV: an overview of key human rights policy and health systems issues', *Reproductive Health Matters*, Vol. 15, No. 29, Supplement (May).

Gunning, I. (2000) 'Cutting through obfuscation: female genital surgeries in neoimperial culture' in E. Shohat, *Talking Visions: Multicultural Feminism in a Transnational Age,* MIT Press, Cambridge, MA.

Hällström, N. (2008) 'What next? Climate change, technology and development', *Development* ('Climate Justice and Development'), Vol. 51, No. 3 (September).

Haque, Y. (2001) 'The women-friendly hospital initiative in Bangladesh', *Development* ('Violence Against Women and the Culture of Masculinity'), Vol. 44, No. 3 (September).

Haraway, D. (1991) *Simians, Cyborgs, and Women: the Reinvention of Nature,* Free Association Books, London.

—— (1992) 'A cyborg manifesto: science technology and socialist feminism in the late twentieth century' in J. Butler and J. Scott, *Feminists Theorize the Political*, Routledge, London.

—— (1997a) *Modest_Witness@Second_Millennium: FemaleMan©_Meets_OncoMouseTM*, Routledge, London and New York, NY.

—— (1997b) 'The persistence of vision' in K. Conboy, N. Medina and S. Stanbury (eds), *Writing on the Body: Female Embodiment and Feminist Theory*, Columbia University Press, New York, NY.

Harcourt, W. (1987) 'Medical discourse related to the female body in late nineteenth-century Melbourne', unpublished PhD thesis, Australian National University, Canberra.

—— (ed.) (1999) *Women@Internet: creating cultures in cyberspace,* Zed Books, London.

—— (2001) 'Politics of place and racism in Australia: a personal exploration', *Meridians*, Vol. 1, No. 2.

—— (2006) 'The global women's rights movement: power politics around the United Nations and the World Social Forum', Civil Society and Social Movements Papers, No. 25, UNRISD, Geneva.

—— (2007) 'Heading blithely down the garden path? Some entry points into current debates on women and biotechnologies', paper presented at the WOMBIT Conference, Rome, July, and forthcoming in F. Molfino and F. Zucco (eds), *Women and Biotechnologies*, Springer Academic Books, Berlin.

—— (2008) 'Global women's rights movements: feminists in transformation', *What Next: Volume II*, The Dag Hammarskjöld Foundation, Uppsala.

Harcourt, W. and A. Escobar (eds) (2005) *Women and the Politics of Place*, Kumarian Press, Bloomfield, CT.

Harding, S. (2006) *Science and Social Inequality: Feminist and Postcolonial Issues*, University of Illinois Press, Urbana and Chicago IL.

Hartmann, B. (1995) *Reproductive Rights and Wrongs: the Global Politics of Population Control* (revised edition), South End Press, Massachussets.

—— (ed.) (2005a) *Making Threats: Biofears and Environmental Anxieties*, Rowman and Littlefield, London.

—— (2005b) 'In Dialogue with Betsy Hartmann', *Development* ('Sexual Health and Reproductive Rights'), Vol. 48, No. 4 (December).

Hayes R. (2003) 'The new human genetic technologies: a threshold challenge for humanity', paper presented at the University of California at Berkeley Energy and Resources Colloquium, Center for Genetics and Society, 24 September.

Hendrixson, A. (2004) 'Angry young men, veiled young women: constructing a new population threat', Corner House Briefing No. 34, The Corner House, Dorset, December.

Hermann, A. C. and A. Stewart (eds) (1994) *Theorizing Feminism: Parallel Trends in the Humanities and Social Sciences*, Westview Press, Boulder, CO.

Howson, A. (2005) *Embodying Gender*, Sage, London.

Huq, S. (2006) 'Sex workers' struggles in Bangladesh: learning from the movement', *IDS Bulletin* ('Sexuality Matters'), Vol. 37, No. 5 (October).

Hyde, J. (1995) 'Guest editorial', *Development* ('Fighting Back: HIV-AIDS and Development'), Vol. 38, No. 2 (June).

Ilkkaracan, P. and S. Jolly (2007) 'Gender and sexuality', in 'Overview Report', Bridge Cutting Edge Pack, Institute of Development Studies, Brighton, January.

Jacobus, M., E. Fox Keller and S. Shuttleworh (eds) (1990) *Body/Politics: Women and the Discourses of Science*, Routledge, London and New York, NY.

Jayawardena, K. (1995) *The White Women's Other Burden: Western Women and South Asia during British Colonial Rule*, Routledge, London.

Jolly, S. (2006) 'Not so strange bedfellows: sexuality and international development', *Development* ('Women's Rights and Development'), Vol. 49, No. 1 (January).

—— (2007) 'Why the development industry should get over its obsession with bad sex and to start to think about pleasure', Working Paper No. 283, Institute of Development Studies, University of Sussex, Brighton, May.

Jolly, S. and P. Ilkkaracan (2007) 'Sexuality, gender and development' in 'In Brief', Bridge Cutting Edge Pack on Gender and Sexuality, Institute of Development Studies, University of Sussex, Brighton.

Jones, R. (2005) 'The feminist dialogue: multidimensional identities and internal diversities', *Development* ('Movement of Movements'), Vol. 48, No. 2 (June).

Kabeer, N. (2003) *Reversed Realities: Gender Hierarchies in Development Thought*, Verso, London.

—— (2007) 'Marriage, motherhood and masculinity in the global economy: reconfigurations of personal and economic life', Working Paper No. 290, Institute of Development Studies, University of Sussex, Brighton.

Kapur, R. (2005) *Erotic Justice: Law and the New Politics of Postcolonialism*, Permanent Black, New Delhi.

Katz Rothman, B. (1998) *Genetic Maps and Human Imaginations: the Limits of Science in Understanding Who We Are*, W. W. Norton, New York, NY.

Kaufman, M. (2001) 'Building a movement of men working to end violence against women', *Development* ('Violence Against Women and the Culture of Masculinity'), Vol. 44, No. 3 (September).

Kerr, J., E. Sprenger and A. Symington (2004) *The Future of Women's Rights: Global Visions and Strategies*, Zed Books, London.

Kiai, M. and M. Wanyeki (2008) 'A deal we can live with', *New York Times*, 12 February <http://www.nytimes.com/2008/02/12/opinion/12kiai.html?_r=1&oref=slogin>.

Kim, J., J. Millen, A. Irwin and J. Gershman (2000) *Dying for Growth: Global Inequality and the Health of the Poor*, Courage Press, Maine, NH.

King, D. (2002) 'How to prevent a new eugenics', presentation at Genetics and Law Conference, Commonwealth Institute London, 19 November.

Lan, P. C. (2006) *Global Cinderellas: Migrant Domestics and Newly Rich Employers in Taiwan*, Duke University Press, Durham, NC.

Lassonde, L. (1996) *Coping with Population Challenges*, Earthscan, London.

Leach, M. and J. Fairhead (2000) 'Challenging neo-malthusian deforestation analyses in West Africa,' *Population and Development Review*, Vol. 26, No. 1 (March).

Silver, Lee M. (1998) *Remaking Eden: How Genetic Engineering and Cloning Will Transform the American Family*, Avon Books, New York, NY.

Lewis, J. and G. Gordon (2006) 'Terms of contact and touching change: investigating pleasure in an HIV epidemic', *IDS Bulletin* ('Sexuality Matters'), Volume 37, Number 5 (October).

—— (2008) 'Terms of contact and touching change: investigating pleasure in an HIV epidemic' in A. Cornwall, S. Jolly and S. Corrêa (eds), *Development with a Body*, Zed Books, London.

Lohmann, L. (2003) 'Re-imagining the population debate', Corner House Briefing No. 28, The Corner House, Dorset, March.

Lusti-Narasimhan, M., J. Cottingham and M. Berer (2007) 'Ensuring the sexual and reproductive health of people living with HIV: politics, programmes and health services' *Reproductive Health Matters*, Vol. 15, No. 29, Supplement 1 (May).

Mabandla, B. (2002) 'The message of the Deputy Minister of Arts, Culture, Science and Technology at Cape Town Civic Centre', <http://www.info.gov.za/speeches/2002/02080611461001.htm>, 4 August.

Macleod, C. and K. Durrheim (2002) 'Foucauldian feminism: the implication of governmentality', *Journal for the Theory of Social Behaviour*, Vol. 32, No. 1.

Marchand, M. (2004) 'Neo-liberal disciplining, violence and transnational organizing: the struggle for women's rights in Ciudad Juárez', *Development* ('The Violence of Development'), Vol. 47, No. 1 (March).

Martin, E. (1991) 'The egg and the sperm: how science has constructed a romance based on stereotypical male–female roles', *Signs, Journal of Women in Culture and Society*, Volume 16, No. 3, pp. 485–501.

Maskey, M. (2004) 'Practising politics as medicine writ large in Nepal', *Development* ('The Politics of Health'), Vol. 47, No. 2 (June).

Mbeki, T. (2002) 'The President of South Africa's speech at the funeral of Sarah Bartmann', <http://www.dfa.gov.za/docs/speeches/ 2002/mbek0809.htm>, 9 August.

McClintock, A. (1995) *Imperial Leather: Race, Gender and Sexuality in the Colonial Contest*, Routledge, London.

—— (1997) 'No longer in a future heaven: gender, race and nationalism' in A. McClintock A. Mufti and E. Shohat, *Dangerous Liaisons: Gender, Nation and Post-colonial Perspectives*, University of Minnesota Press, Minneapolis, MN.

Mensah-Kutin, R. (2003) Unpublished speech at the conference on 'The Challenges of the New Genetic Technologies: Within and Beyond the Limits of Human Nature', convened in Berlin by the Heinrich Böll Foundation and the Institut Mensch, Ethik und Wissenschaft, in collaboration with the Center for Genetics and Society , 12–15 October.

Molfino, F. and F. Zucco (2008) (eds) *Women and Biotechnologies*, Springer Academic Books, Berlin.

Nabulivou N. (2006) 'Feminisms, identities, sexualities: a personal journey', *Development* ('Women's Rights and Development'), Vol. 49, No. 1 (March).

Nair, S. and P. Kirbat with S. Sexton (2004) 'A decade after Cairo: women's health in a free market economy', Corner House Briefing No. 31, The Corner House, Dorset, June.

Nakano Glenn, E., G. Change and L. Forcey (1994) (eds) *Mothering, Ideology, Experience and Agency*, Routledge, London.

Naraghi-Anderlini, S. (2005) 'Women and peace through justice', *Development* ('Peacebuilding Through Justice'), Vol. 48, No. 3 (September).

Narayan, D. (with R. Patel, K. Schafft, R. Rademacher. and S. Koch-Schulte) (2000) *Voices of the Poor: Can Anyone Hear Us?*, Oxford University Press, Oxford.

Nast, H. J. and S. Pile (1998) *Places Through the Body*, Routledge, London.

Nowrojee, B. (2005) 'Your justice is too slow: will the ICTR fail Rwanda's rape victims?', UNRISD Working Paper No. 10, UNRISD, Geneva.

Nussbaum, M. (2005)'Women's bodies: violence, security, capabilities', *Journal of Human Development Alternative Economics in Action*, Vol. 6, No. 2 (July).

Ojiambo Ochieng, R. (2003) 'Supporting women and girls' sexual and reproductive health and rights: the Ugandan experience', *Development* ('Globalization, Reproductive Health and Rights'), Vol. 46, No. 2 (June).

Pearson, R. (2008) 'Feminisation of labour in the global economy: challenges and opportunities', talk given at the WIDE Annual Conference, The Hague, October, <www.wide-network.org>.

Petchesky, R. (2001) 'Phantom towers: feminist reflections on the battle between global capitalism and fundamentalist terrorism', presentation at Hunter College Political Science Department teach-in, 25 September, <http://ebf.stanford. edu/FS101/2001/2001lectures/petchesky.html>.

—— (2002) *Global Prescriptions. Gender, Health and Human Rights,* Zed Books in association with UNRISD, London.

—— (2005) 'Rights of the body and perversions of war: sexual rights and wrongs ten years past Beijing', *International Social Science Journal,* Vol. 57, No. 2 (June).

Philipose, L. (2007) 'The politics of pain and the end of empire', *International Feminist Journal of Politics*, Vol. 9, No. 1 (March).

Pitanguay, J. (1999) 'Reproductive rights are human rights', *Development* ('Reproductive Health and Rights: Putting Cairo into Action'), Vol. 42, No. 1 (March).

Porter, E. (2006) *Peace-Building:Women in International Perspectives,* Routledge, London.

Qadeer, I. (2005) 'Maternal mortality in South Asia', *Development* ('Sexual and Reproductive Health and Rights'), Vol. 48, No. 4 (December).

Rademacher, A. and R. Patel (2002) 'Retelling worlds of poverty: reflections on transforming participatory research for a global narrative' in K. Brock and R. McGee (2002) *Knowing Poverty: Critical Reflections on Participatory Research and Policy,* London, Earthscan.

Rai, S. (2008) *The Gender Politics of Development*, Zed Books and Zubaan, London and New Delhi.

Raman, V. (2008) 'Gujarat 2002: political conflict and women in South Asia', unpublished MS, Centre for Women's Studies, New Delhi, India.

Rao, M. (2005) 'India's population politics', *Development* ('Sexual and Reproductive Health and Rights'), Vol. 48, No. 4 (December).

Ravindran, S. and H. de Pinho (2005) *The Right Reforms? Health Sector Reform and Sexual and Reproductive Health*, Women's Health Project, School of Public Health, University of the Witwatersrand, South Africa, Johannesburg.

Razavi, S. (ed.) (2002) *Shifting Burdens: Gender and Agrarian Change under Neoliberalism,* Kumarian Press, Bloomfield, CT.

—— (2007) 'The political and social economy of care in a development context: conceptual issues, research questions and policy issues', Gender and Development Programme Paper No. 3, UNRISD, Geneva, June.

Razavi, S. and C. Miller (1995) 'From WID to GAD – conceptual shifts in the WID discourse', UNRISD Occasional Paper Series for Beijing, No. 1, UNRISD, Geneva.

Riccutelli, L., A. Miles and M. McFadden (2004) *Feminist Politics, Activism and Vision,* Zed Books, London.

Rich, A. (1979) *Of Woman Born: Motherhood as Experience and Institution,* Virago, London.

Richter, J. (1996) *Vaccination Against Pregnancy: Miracle or Menace?,* Zed Books, London.

Richter Montpetit, M. (2007) 'A queer transnational feminist reading of the prisoner abuse in Abu Ghraib and the question of gender equality', *International Feminist Journal of Politics,* Vol. 9, No. 1 (March).

Robinson, F. (2006) 'Beyond labour rights: the ethics of care and women's work in the global economy', *International Journal of Feminist Economics,* Vol. 8, No. 3.

Roddick, A. (2000) *Business as Unusual: the Triumph of Anita Roddick and The Body Shop,* Thorsons, London.

Ross, E. (2000) 'The Malthus factor: poverty, politics and population in capitalist development', Corner House Briefing No. 20, The Corner House, Dorset, July.

Rowbotham, S. and S. Linkkogle (2001) *Women Resist Globalization: Mobilizing for Livelihoods and Rights,* Zed Books, London.

Roy, R. (2001) 'The eyes are silent . . . the heart desires to speak: exploring masculinities in South Asia', *Development* ('Violence Against Women and the Culture of Masculinity'), Vol. 44, No. 3 (September).

Sachs, J. (2005) *Investing in Development: a Practical Plan to Achieve the MDGs,* UN Millennium Project, New York, NY, and Earthscan, London.

Sachs, W. (ed.) (1992) *The Development Dictionary: a Guide to Knowledge as Power,* Zed Books, London.

Sachs, W. (1999) *Planet Dialectics: Explorations in Environment and Development,* Zed Books, London.

Salbi, Z. and L. Becklund (2006) *Between Two Worlds – Escape from Tyranny: Growing Up in the Shadow of Saddam,* Gotham Books, New York, NY.

Samuelson, M. (2007) *Remembering the Nation, Dismembering Women? Stories of the South African Transition,* University of KwaZulu-Natal Press, Scottsville.

Sassen, S. (1998) *Globalization and Its Discontents,* The New Press, New York, NY.

Scarry, E. (1985) *The Body in Pain: the Making and Unmaking of the World,* Oxford University Press, Oxford.

Schiebinger, L. (1993) *Nature's Body.* Harper Collins, London.

Sen, A. (1997) 'Population policy: authoritarianism versus cooperation', *Journal of Population Economics,* Vol. 10, No. 1.

Sen, G. and S. Corrêa (2000) 'Gender justice and economic justice: reflections on the five-year reviews of the UN conferences of the 1990s', report, DAWN, Suva, Fiji.

Sexton, S. (1999) 'If cloning is the answer, what was the question? Power and decision making in the geneticisation of health', Corner House Briefing No. 16, The Corner House, Dorset, October.

—— (2003) 'Ethics or economics? Public health or private wealth?', paper presented at the 'Working Conference on the Limits of the New Genetics Technologies. Within and Beyond the Limits of Human Nature', Berlin, Germany, October, <http://www.biopolitics-berlin2003.org/docs.asp?id=123>.

—— (2005) 'Transforming "waste" into "resource": from women's eggs to economics for women', paper given at the workshop on 'Commodification and Commercialisation of Women's Bodies' at the Femme Globale Conference, The Cornerhouse, Dorset, September, <http://www.thecornerhouse.org.uk/pdf/document/eggs.pdf>.

Shaheed, F. (2006) 'Resistance by victimized women', *Development* ('Women's Rights and Development'), Vol. 49, No. 1 (March).

Shapiro, K. and S. Ray (2007) 'Sexual health for people living with HIV', *Reproductive Health Matters*, Vol. 15, No. 29, Supplement (May).

Shildrick, M. (1997) *Leaky Bodies and Boundaries: Feminism, Postmodernism and (Bio) Ethics*, Routledge, London.

Shildrick, M. and J. Price (eds) (1998) *Vital Signs: Feminist Configurations of the Bio/logical Body*, Edinburgh University Press, Edinburgh.

Shirkat Gah, (2005) 'Report of the Society for International Development South Asia Network and Shirkat Gah Regional Conference on Maternal Health and Well-being in South Asia: strategies for meeting the Millennium Development Goals', Shirkat Gah, Lahore, <www.sidint.org>, 3–5 February.

Shohat, E. (2000) 'Introduction' in E. Shohat (ed.), *Talking Visions: Multicultural Feminism in a Transnational Age,* MIT Press, Cambridge, MA.

Shorter, E. (1982) *A History of Women's Bodies*, Allen Lane, London.

Silliman, J. and Y. King (eds) (1999) *Dangerous Intersections: Feminist Perspectives on Population, Environment and Development*, South End Press, Cambridge, MA.

Silver, Lee M. (1998) *Remaking Eden: How Genetic Engineering and Cloning Will Transform the American Family*, Avon Books, New York, NY.

Singh, J. (1998) *Creating a New Consensus on Population,* Earthscan, London.

Sjoberg, L. (2007) 'Agency: militarized femininity and enemy others: observations from the war in Iraq', *International Feminist Journal of Politics*, Vol. 9, No. 1 (March).

Spanner, H. (1996) 'Body politics', *Third Way*, <http://www.spannermedia.com/interviews/Roddick.htm>.

Spar, D. (2006) *The Baby Business: How Money, Science, and Politics Drive the Commerce of Conception*, Harvard Business School Press, Harvard, MA.

Sparr, P. (ed.) (1994) *Mortgaging Women's Lives: Feminist Critiques of Structural Adjustment*, Zed Books, London.

Spivak, G. (1987) *In Other Worlds: Essays in Cultural Politics*, Methuen, New York, NY.

—— (1999) *A Critique of Postcolonial Reason: Toward a History of the Vanishing Present*, Harvard University Press, Harvard, MA.

Stein, J. (1997) *Empowerment and Women's Health*, Zed Books, London.

Summerfield, G. (2007) 'Transnational migration, gender and human security', *Development* ('Migration and Development'), Vol. 50, No. 4 (December).

Talpade Mohanty, C. (2003) *Feminism Without Borders. Decolonizing Theory, Practicing Solidarity*, Duke University Press, Durham, NC.

Tamale, S. (2006) 'Eroticism, sensuality and women's secrets among the Baganda', *IDS Bulletin* ('Sexuality Matters'), Vol. 37, No. 5 (October).

Thomas, J. (2006) 'An introduction to nanotechnology: the next small big thing', *Development* ('New Technologies and Development'), Vol. 48, No. 4 (December).

Turner, B. (1984) *A History of the Body*, Basil Blackwell, Oxford.

Tyson Darling, M. (2006) 'Reproductive and genetic biotechnologies: taking up the challenge', *Development* ('Women's Rights and Development'), Vol. 49, No. 1 (March).

Underhill-Sem, Y. (2002) 'Embodying post-development: bodies in places, places in bodies', *Development* ('Place, Politics and Justice: Women Negotiating Globalization'), Vol. 45, No. 1 (March).

UN (2005) *Gender Equality – Taking Action: Achieving Gender Equality and Empowering Women*, Earthscan, London.

UNAIDS (2006) *Global Report 2006*, UNAIDS, Geneva, <http://data.unaids.org/pub/GlobalReport/2006/2006_GR_CH02_en.pdf>.

Underhill-Sem, Y. (2005) 'Bodies in places, places in bodies' in W. A. Harcourt and A. Escobar (eds), *Women and the Politics of Place*, Kumarian Press, Bloomfield, CT.

UNIFEM (2000) *Progress of the World's Women*, UNIFEM, New York, NY, <http://www.unifem.org/resources/item_detail.php?ProductID=9>.

UNRISD (2005) *Gender Equality: Striving for Justice in an Unequal World*, UNRISD, Geneva.

Uprety, A. (2005) 'Body politics in Nepal', *Development* ('Peacebuilding Through Justice'), Vol. 48, No. 3 (September).

van Staveren, I. (2001) *The Values of Economics: an Aristotelian Perspective*, Routledge, London.

Vargas, V. (2005) 'Feminisms and the World Social Forum: space for dialogue and confrontation', *Development* ('Movement of Movements'), Vol. 48, No. 2 (June).

—— (2006) 'Second Manifesto of the Campaign for a Convention on Sexual Rights and Reproductive Rights', Cladem, Lima, October.

Walker, S. (2008) 'Ensler continues fighting against violence against women', *Toronto Star*, 8 March 2008, <http://www.thestar.com/article/310180>.

Wanyeki, M. (2008) 'Don't give into a climate of fear', *East African*, 4 February 2008, <http://www.nationmedia.com/eastafrican/04022008/Opinion/op0402085.htm>.

Waring, M. (1989) *If Women Counted*, Macmillan, London.

Watson, A. (2007) 'Children born of wartime rape: rights and representations', *International Feminist Journal of Politics,* Vol. 9, No. 1 (March).

Weiz, R. (1998) *The Politics of Women's Bodies, Sexuality and Appearance*, Oxford University Press, Oxford.

Wichterich, C. (2000) *The Globalized Woman*, Zed Books, London.

—— (2007) 'EU trade and China', WIDE, Brussels.

Win, E. (2001) 'Men are not my project: a view from Zimbabwe', *Development* ('Violence Against Women and the Culture of Masculinity'), Vol. 44, No. 3 (September).

Wolbring, G. (2006) 'Nanotechnology for health and development', *Development* ('New Technologies and Development'), Vol. 49, No. 4 (December).

—— (2008) 'The politics of ableism', *Development* ('Gender and Fisheries'), Vol. 51, No. 2 (December).

Women's Environment and Development Organization (WEDO) (2005) *Beijing Betrayed:Women WorldWide Report that Governments Have Failed to Turn the Platform into Action*, WEDO, New York, NY.

Women's Voices '94 (1993) 'A declaration on population policies', *Population and Development Review*, Vol. 19, No. 3 (September).

World Health Organization (2006) *World Report on Violence and Health*, World Health Organization, Geneva.

Yegenoglu, M. (1998) *Colonial Fantasies: Towards a Feminist Reading of Orientalism*, Cambridge University Press, Cambridge.

Young, K. C. Wolkowitz and T. McCullagh (eds) (1984) *Of Marriage and the Market: Women's Subordination Internationally and Its Lessons*, Routledge, London.

Zarro, A. (2007) 'Sahara there and back: a photo essay', *Development* ('Migration and Development'), Vol. 5., No. 4 (December).

Index

220